CASEBOOKS PUBLISHED

Austen: *Emma* DAVID LODGE
Austen: *'Northanger Abbey' & 'Persuasion'* B. C.
Austen: *'Sense and Sensibility', 'Pride and Prejudice*
Blake: *Songs of Innocence and Experience* MARGARE
Charlotte Brontë: *'Jane Eyre' & 'Villette'* MIRIAM
Emily Brontë: *Wuthering Heights* MIRIAM ALLOTT
Browning: *'Men and Women' & Other Poems* J. R.
Bunyan: *Pilgrim's Progress* ROGER SHARROCK
Byron: *'Childe Harold's Pilgrimage' & 'Don Juan'* JOHN JUMP
Chaucer: *Canterbury Tales* J. J. ANDERSON
Coleridge: *'The Ancient Mariner' & Other Poems* ALUN R. JONES & WILLIAM TYDEMAN
Congreve: *Comedies* PATRICK LYONS
Conrad: *'Heart of Darkness', 'Nostromo' & 'Under Western Eyes'* C. B. COX
Conrad: *The Secret Agent* IAN WATT
Dickens: *Bleak House* A. E. DYSON
Dickens: *'Hard Times', 'Great Expectations' & 'Our Mutual Friend'* NORMAN PAGE
Donne: *Songs and Sonets* JULIAN LOVELOCK
George Eliot: *Middlemarch* PATRICK SWINDEN
George Eliot: *'The Mill on the Floss' & 'Silas Marner'* R. P. DRAPER
T. S. Eliot: *Four Quartets* BERNARD BERGONZI
T. S. Eliot: *'Prufrock', 'Gerontion', 'Ash Wednesday' & Other Shorter Poems* B. C. SOUTHAM
T. S. Eliot: *The Waste Land* C. B. COX & ARNOLD P. HINCHLIFFE
Farquhar: *'The Recruiting Officer' & 'The Beaux' Stratagem'* RAYMOND A. ANSELMENT
Fielding: *Tom Jones* NEIL COMPTON
Forster: *A Passage to India* MALCOLM BRADBURY
Hardy: *The Tragic Novels* R. P. DRAPER
Hardy: *Poems* JAMES GIBSON & TREVOR JOHNSON
Hopkins: *Poems* MARGARET BOTTRALL
James: *'Washington Square' & 'The Portrait of a Lady'* ALAN SHELSTON
Jonson: *'Every Man in his Humour' & 'The Alchemist'* R. V. HOLDSWORTH
Jonson: *Volpone* JONAS A. BARISH
Joyce: *'Dubliners' & 'A Portrait of the Artist as a Young Man'* MORRIS BEJA
Keats: *Narrative Poems* JOHN SPENCER HILL
Keats: *Odes* G. S. FRASER
D. H. Lawrence: *Sons and Lovers* GAMINI SALGADO
D. H. Lawrence: *'The Rainbow' & 'Women in Love'* COLIN CLARKE
Marlowe: *Doctor Faustus* JOHN JUMP
Marlowe: *'Tamburlaine the Great', 'Edward the Second' & 'The Jew of Malta'* JOHN RUSSELL
  BROWN
Marvell: *Poems* ARTHUR POLLARD
Milton: *'Comus' & 'Samson Agonistes'* JULIAN LOVELOCK
Milton: *Paradise Lost* A. E. DYSON & JULIAN LOVELOCK
Osborne: *Look Back in Anger* JOHN RUSSELL TAYLOR
Peacock: *The Satirical Novels* LORNA SAGE
Pope: *The Rape of the Lock* JOHN DIXON HUNT
Shakespeare: *A Midsummer Night's Dream* ANTONY W. PRICE
Shakespeare: *Antony and Cleopatra* JOHN RUSSELL BROWN
Shakespeare: *Coriolanus* B. A. BROCKMAN
Shakespeare: *Hamlet* JOHN JUMP
Shakespeare: *Henry IV Parts I and II* G. K. HUNTER
Shakespeare: *Henry V* MICHAEL QUINN

Shakespeare: *Julius Caesar* PETER URE
Shakespeare: *King Lear* FRANK KERMODE
Shakespeare: *Macbeth* JOHN WAIN
Shakespeare: *Measure for Measure* G. K. STEAD
Shakespeare: *The Merchant of Venice* JOHN WILDERS
Shakespeare: *'Much Ado About Nothing' & 'As You Like It'* JOHN RUSSELL BROWN
Shakespeare: *Othello* JOHN WAIN
Shakespeare: *Richard II* NICHOLAS BROOKE
Shakespeare: *The Sonnets* PETER JONES
Shakespeare: *The Tempest* D. J. PALMER
Shakespeare: *Troilus and Cressida* PRISCILLA MARTIN
Shakespeare: *Twelfth Night* D. J. PALMER
Shakespeare: *The Winter's Tale* KENNETH MUIR
Shelley: *Shorter Poems & Lyrics* PATRICK SWINDEN
Spenser: *The Faerie Queene* PETER BAYLEY
Swift: *Gulliver's Travels* RICHARD GRAVIL
Tennyson: *In Memoriam* JOHN DIXON HUNT
Thackeray: *Vanity Fair* ARTHUR POLLARD
Trollope: *The Barsetshire Novels* T. BAREHAM
Webster: *'The White Devil' & 'The Duchess of Malfi'* R. V. HOLDSWORTH
Wilde: *Comedies* WILLIAM TYDEMAN
Woolf: *To the Lighthouse* MORRIS BEJA
Wordsworth: *Lyrical Ballads* ALUN R. JONES & WILLIAM TYDEMAN
Wordsworth: *The Prelude* W. J. HARVEY & RICHARD GRAVIL
Yeats: *Poems, 1919–35* ELIZABETH CULLINGFORD
Yeats: *Last Poems* JON STALLWORTHY

Medieval English Drama PETER HAPPÉ
Elizabethan Poetry: Lyrical & Narrative GERALD HAMMOND
The Metaphysical Poets GERALD HAMMOND
Poetry of the First World War DOMINIC HIBBERD
Thirties Poets: 'The Auden Group' RONALD CARTER
Comedy: Developments in Criticism D. J. PALMER
Drama Criticism: Developments since Ibsen ARNOLD P. HINCHLIFFE
Tragedy: Developments in Criticism R. P. DRAPER
The English Novel: Developments in Criticism since Henry James STEPHEN HAZELL
The Language of Literature NORMAN PAGE
The Pastoral Mode BRYAN LOUGHREY
The Romantic Imagination JOHN SPENCER HILL

CASEBOOKS IN PREPARATION

Beckett: *'Waiting for Godot' & Other Plays* JOHN RUSSELL BROWN
Defoe: *'Robinson Crusoe' & 'Moll Flanders'* PATRICK LYONS
Dickens: *'Dombey and Son' & 'Little Dorrit'* ALAN SHELSTON
T. S. Eliot: *Plays* ARNOLD P. HINCHLIFFE
O'Casey: *'Juno and the Paycock', 'The Plough and the Stars' & 'The Shadow of a Gunman'* RONALD AYLING
Pinter: *'The Caretaker' & Other Plays* MICHAEL SCOTT
Sheridan: *Comedies* PETER DAVISON

Poetry Criticism: Developments since the Symbolists A. E. DYSON
Post-Fifties Poets: Gunn, Hughes, Larkin & R. S. Thomas A. E. DYSON
Shakespeare: Approaches in Criticism JOHN RUSSELL BROWN
The Gothick Novel VICTOR SAGE

Medieval English Drama

A CASEBOOK

EDITED BY

PETER HAPPÉ

MACMILLAN

First published 1984 by
Higher and Further Education Division
MACMILLAN PUBLISHERS LTD
London and Basingstoke
Companies and representatives
throughout the world

Typeset by
Wessex Typesetters Ltd
Frome, Somerset

Printed in Hong Kong

British Library Cataloguing in Publication Data
Happé, Peter
    Medieval English drama.—(Casebook series)
    1. English drama—to 1500—History and
    criticism
    I. Title   II. Series
    822′.099   PR641
    ISBN 0–333–34082–5
    ISBN 0–333–34083–3 Pbk

CONTENTS

General Editor's Preface   7

List of Abbreviations   8

Note on Early Letters   9

Introduction   10

Part One: *Early Documents*

A Tretise of Miraclis Pleyinge (14th c.), p. 27 – Robert
Mannynge of Brunne (1303), p. 28 – The Mercers' Pageant
Waggon at York (1433), p. 29 – David Rogers (1609), p.
30.

Part Two: *Modern Criticism*

1 Introductory

DAVID MILLS: Approaches to Medieval Drama   (1969)   35

2 The Corpus Christi Plays

V. A. KOLVE: The Drama as Play and Game   (1966)   54
DONNA SMITH VINTER: Didactic Characterisation – The
   Towneley *Abraham*   (1980)   71
ROSEMARY   WOOLF: 'The   Wakefield   Shepherds'
   Plays'   (1972)   89
ELEANOR   PROSSER: The   *Woman   Taken   in   Adultery*
   Plays   (1961)   95

CLIFFORD DAVIDSON: The Realism of the York Realist and the York Passion (1975)   101

STANLEY J. KAHRL: Of History and Time (1974)   117

3 Morality Plays and Interludes

ROBERT A. POTTER: Forgiveness as Theatre (1975)   130

BERNARD SPIVACK: 'The Vice as a Stage Metaphor' (1958)   140

JOANNE SPENCER KANTROWITZ: Allegory (1975)   144

T. W. CRAIK: On *Enough is as good as a Feast* (1958)   152

4 Aspects of Performance

DAVID M. BEVINGTON: 'The Popular Troupe' (1962)   162

MEG TWYCROSS & SARAH CARPENTER: Purposes and Effects of Masking (1981)   171

WILLIAM TYDEMAN: 'Costumes and Actors' (1978)   180

PAULA NEUSS: The Staging of *The Creacion of the World* (1979)   189

SHEILA LINDENBAUM: The York Cycle at Toronto – Staging and Performance Style (1978)   200

Select Bibliography   212

Notes on Contributors   213

Acknowledgements   215

Index   216

GENERAL EDITOR'S PREFACE

The Casebook series, launched in 1968, has become a well-regarded library of critical studies. The central concern of the series remains the 'single-author' volume, but suggestions from the academic community have led to an extension of the original plan, to include occasional volumes on such general themes as literary 'schools' and genres.

Each volume in the central category deals either with one well-known and influential work by an individual author, or with closely related works by one writer. The main section consists of critical readings, mostly modern, collected from books and journals. A selection of reviews and comments by the author's contemporaries is also included, and sometimes comments from the author himself. The Editor's Introduction charts the reputation of the work or works from the first appearance to the present time.

Volumes in the 'general themes' category are variable in structure but follow the basic purpose of the series in presenting an integrated selection of readings, with an Introduction which explores the theme and discusses the literary and critical issues involved.

A single volume can represent no more than a small selection of critical opinion. Some critics are excluded for reasons of space, and it is hoped that readers will pursue the suggestions for further reading in the Select Bibliography. Other contributions are severed from their original context, to which some readers may wish to turn. Indeed, if they take a hint from the critics represented here, they certainly will.

A. E. DYSON

LIST OF ABBREVIATIONS

The following abbreviations are used for works frequently cited in notes to the Introduction and to the critical studies in Part Two.

I PLAYS

Chester, Diemling	*The Chester Plays*, ed. H. Diemling & Dr Matthews, 2 vols, EETS, e.s. 62, 115 (London, 1892, 1916).
Chester, Mills	*The Chester Mystery Cycle*, ed. R. N. Lumiansky & D. Mills, EETS, s.s. 3 (London, 1974).
Corpus Christi Plays	*Two Coventry Corpus Christi Plays*, ed. H. Craig, EETS, e.s. 87, 2nd edn (London, 1957).
Digby	*The Digby Plays*, ed. F. J. Furnivall, EETS, e.s. 70 (London, 1896).
Dodsley	R. Dodsley (ed.), *A Select Collection of Old Plays*, 12 vols (London, 1744).
EETS	*Early English Text Society* (publications)
Macro	*The Macro Plays*, ed. M. Eccles, EETS 262 (London, 1969).
Magnyfycence	John Skelton, *Magnyfycence*, ed. R. L. Ramsay, EETS, e.s. 98 (London, 1908).
Non-Cycle Plays	*Non-Cycle Plays and Fragments*, ed. N. Davis, EETS s.s. 1 (London, 1970).
Towneley	*The Towneley Plays*, ed. G. England & A. W. Pollard, EETS, e.s. 71 (London, 1897).
Wakefield Pageants	*The Wakefield Pageants in the Towneley Cycle*, ed. A. C. Cawley (Manchester, 1958).
York	*The York Plays*, ed. L. T. Smith (Oxford, 1885).

II CRITICISM

Anderson	M. D. Anderson, *Drama and Imagery in English Medieval Churches* (Cambridge, 1963).
Chambers	E. K. Chambers, *The Medieval Stage* (Oxford, 1903), 2 vols.
Coogan	M. P. Coogan, *An Interpretation of the Moral Play 'Mankind'* (Washington, D.C., 1947).
Craig	H. Craig, *English Religious Drama of the Middle Ages* (Oxford, 1955).
Frank	G. Frank, *The Medieval French Drama* (Oxford, 1954).
Hardison	O. B. Hardison, *Christian Rite and Christian Drama in the Middle Ages* (Baltimore, Md. 1965).
Kolve	V. A. Kolve, *The Play Called Corpus Christi* (Stanford, Cal., and London, 1966).
Prosser	E. Prosser, *Drama and Religion in the English Mystery Plays* (Stanford, Cal., 1961).
Salter	F. M. Salter, *Medieval Drama in Chester* (London, 1956).
Southern	R. Southern, *The Medieval Theatre in the Round* (London, 1957).
Wickham	G. Wickham, *Early English Stages, 1300–1660* (London: vol. 1, 1959 [rev. edn, 1980]; vol. 2 Pt 1, 1963; vol. 2 Pt 2, 1972; vol. 3, 1981).
Woolf	R. Woolf, *The English Mystery Plays* (London, 1972).
Young	K. Young, *The Drama of the Medieval Church* (Oxford, 1933), 2 vols.

NOTE ON EARLY LETTERS

Readers not acquainted with Early and Middle English texts may find two letters unfamiliar:

Þ þ ('thorn') stands for the voiced and voiceless sounds now represented by *th*, as in *these* and *think*.

Ȝ ȝ ('yogh') stands for a sound now represented by *y*, as in *year*; and also for a sound now lost in English, (roughly equivalent to that in the German *ich*), which formerly appeared in words like *nyȝt* (night).

INTRODUCTION

The criticism of English medieval drama has not, on the whole, attracted the attention of major writers, or indeed of major critics. Perhaps the main reason for this is that the texts of medieval plays have proved singularly difficult to determine. In order to establish the material upon which the critic has to work, it has been necessary to carry out a complex and prolonged process of definition and reconstruction which appears to be a work appropriate to scholarship rather than to criticism, in so far as these two activities can be separated. The mystery cycles were performed for nearly two centuries from about 1375 with extensive civic support in many towns and cities, but in spite of this there is virtually no contemporary critical comment upon them. On the whole they were treated with some suspicion by the Church, and yet it seems that they were written and revised by the clergy. In the first years of the sixteenth century, until the break with Rome, the cycles had flourished, and indeed were still developing. The Reformation saw a curtailment, particularly in the reign of Edward VI. Under Mary they were again in favour, but by 1575 they were virtually extinct.[1] The decline is apparent to us by events rather than by written analysis, and its objective was ideological rather than aesthetic.

Whilst the disappearance of the mystery plays, though regretted by many, was accomplished in a few years, the morality plays proved capable of further adaptation and development. Though they were performed through roughly the same period – the earliest to survive is the *Pride of Life* (c.1350) – we have very few plays upon which to base conclusions, and this has no doubt inhibited criticism. As the subject matter was at first concerned with religious didacticism and inspired by devotional intent, their dramatic qualities were not perceived. From the moralities there developed in the first half of the sixteenth century the rather shorter and more topical interludes. These plays, which were mostly polemical, allowed greater versatility in subject matter and dramatic technique, but they became an object of scorn to the professionals of the Elizabethan theatre. Shakespeare offered a touch of ridicule in his treatment of the Vice:[2]

CLOWN I am gone, sir, and anon, sir,
      I'll be with you again,

> In a trice, like the old Vice,
>   Your need to sustain;
> Who, with a dagger of lath, in his rage and his wrath,
>   Cries 'Ah, ha!' to the devil:
> Like a mad lad, 'Pare thy nails, dad.
>   Adieu goodman devil!'   [*Twelfth Night* IV ii 125–32]

After the Restoration, we are left with two principal activities by critics: a cultural rejection of medieval plays as inept, not to say barbaric, because they were thought not to match later achievements, especially Shakespeare's; and a historical process of recovery which in itself is motivated by cultural considerations, but which adopts for its methodology an antiquarian or even an encyclopaedic approach. It is perhaps only of recent years, when the reconstruction of performance has been based upon the fruits of scholarship, that we can see the beginnings of a critical theory, and a disposition to appreciate the quality and richness of what has come down to us, fragmentary though it it.

The construction of this collection reflects these considerations. As a preliminary there are four short pieces from medieval and Tudor times. Two of them, the Wycliffite sermon and the translation by Robert Mannynge, are concerned with religious controversy over the enactment of holy subjects. The other two are about the pageant waggons used for the mystery cycles: one from the York Mercers' Documents of 1433 detailing the pageants and their furnishings and some costumes, and the other from the *Breviary* of Archdeacon Robert Rogers (who died in 1595) describing the procession of pageants at Chester, and giving some details of their shape.

The preoccupations of scholars during the next three hundred years are described in the following section of this Introduction, which incorporates some short extracts. The context of the main collection in the period of modern scholarship is reviewed in the concluding section.

Some aspects of the earlier criticism of the medieval plays have but limited interest today because they were so intimately associated with the standards of taste of their own times and were concerned with the development of theatre only as it might be seen to anticipate the greatness of Shakespeare. In a few cases, however, we shall find that some modern preoccupations, like the interest in dramatic records, folk analogues, and civic processions, are foreshadowed.

It is in the former category that we should place Thomas Warton.[3] He was partly concerned to characterise the types of medieval plays, and he helped to establish the terms 'morality' and 'mystery play', neither of which were in general use before the eighteenth century. His criticism, however, was part of the age of enlightenment, and he wrote from an assumption of a superior standard of civilised manners. Whatever the basis for this in general, it is not now clear that Warton had adequate grounds for his claims in respect of drama. The tone of the following passage reveals this air of superiority, and it also shows how comedy was held to degrade religious experience:

... It is certain that these Miracle-Plays were the first of our dramatic exhibitions. But as these pieces frequently required the introduction of allegorical characters, such as Charity, Sin, Death, Hope, Faith, or the like, and as the common poetry of the times, expecially among the French, began to deal much in allegory, at length plays were formed entirely consisting of such personifications. These were called Moralities. The Miracle-Plays, or Mysteries, were totally destitute of invention or plan; they tamely represented stories according to the letter of scripture, or the respective legend. But the Moralities indicate dawnings of the dramatic art: they contain some rudiments of a plot, and even attempt to delineate characters, and to paint manners. From hence the gradual transition to real historical personages was natural and obvious. It may also be observed that many licentious pleasantries were sometimes introduced in these religious representations. This might imperceptibly lead the way to subjects entirely profane, and to comedy, and perhaps earlier than is imagined. ... It is certain that our ancestors intended no sort of impiety by these monstrous and unnatural mixtures. Neither the writers nor the spectators saw the impropriety nor paid a separate attention to the comic and the serious part of these motley scenes; at least they were persuaded that the solemnity of the subject covered or excused all incongruities. They had no just idea of decorum, consequently but little sense of the ridiculous: what appears to us to be the highest burlesque, on them would have made no sort of impression.[4]

The key here seems to be an offence to good taste, stressed by expressions like 'monstrous and unnatural mixtures', 'incongruities' and 'burlesque'. One must also suspect acceptance of Neo-Aristotelian decorum in the expectation of a division between comedy and tragedy.

It is perhaps not surprising to find that a few years earlier Robert Dodsley had offered a firmly critical attitude. In the Introduction to his collection, which became the chief access to these texts for scholar and gentleman alike until the mid-twentieth century, he writes:

This period one might call the dead sleep of the Muses. And when this was over they did not presently awake, but in a kind of Morning Dream produced the Moralities that followed.[5]

He adds later:

I hope the Reader will not imagine I give any of the pieces in the Volume as good: but only as Curiosities to show from what low beginnings our stage has arisen.[6]

He notes with satisfaction 'the Progress and Improvement of our Taste and Language'.[7]

Edmund Malone, to whom much is owed as a collector and preserver of early printed texts, had hardly a better opinion in 1800:

The drama before the time of Shakespeare was so little cultivated or so ill understood that to many it may appear unnecessary to carry out theatrical researches higher than that period.[8]

Later in the nineteenth century the antiquarian interest became stronger, and the cultural attitudes less dismissive. We find among the topics raised themes and material that are still of great interest, particularly in connection with the mystery cycles. William Hone offered lengthy extracts from texts linked by paraphrase, especially from *Ludus Coventriae*.[9] But he was interested in the Apocryphal Gospels and some folk analogues, especially in the case of Joseph and Mary. He derived his historical framework from Warton, but showed a notable disinclination to condemn the plays. On the other hand, he did not positively advocate their virtues. It is of interest, too, that he was curious about public shows and processions, including the Lord Mayor's Show. Thomas Sharp, equally enquiring, turned his attention specifically to the Guilds themselves, and quoted from their records many details of staging and costuming, an activity in which he is an important forerunner of current interest. For the most part he eschews comment on quality, though he does not deny himself a quotation from J. Brand: 'They [the Mystery Plays] are reported to have been many of them very indelicate and obscene.'[10]

J. P. Collier has been seen as one whose scholarship is somewhat unreliable, yet his work was both comprehensive and influential. He followed Warton in the matter of the origin of the Mystery Plays, but proposed a continuous development from miracle plays (he rejected the term 'mysteries') to moralities:

... by the gradual intermixture of allegory with sacred history until Miracle-plays were finally superseded. This view of the subject does not seem to have occurred to anyone who has gone before me.[11]

He recorded methodically the annals of the stage item by item. He did betray some critical interest: the *Wakefield Second Shepherds' Play* is 'singular, novel and humorous', and he quoted extensively from it, but this observation was not developed very far.[12] His judiciousness is well seen on *Mankind* which was

... mixed up with the grossest obscenity, and seems calculated for an audience of lower rank ... The piece contains a good deal that is curious and some characters are introduced that have much individuality about them.[13]

But such comment is rare, and his work is more remarkable for the accumulation of information.

Thomas Wright, an industrious antiquarian, studied early texts and associated documents (including the *Tretise of Miraclis Pleyinge*). His Introduction to the *Chester Plays* reviewed a familiar collection of factual material. Occasionally he struck the lofty tone of his eighteenth-century predecessors, illustrating the divide between him and the playwrights;

Mysteries and Miracle Plays ... possess an interest not only as illustrating the history of the stage in its infancy, but as pictures of the manners and conditions of our forefathers, and also as indicating the quality and peculiar character of the religious knowledge inculcated into the populace in Catholic times.[14]

Nevertheless his scholarly interests led him to accumulate a wide variety of material from non-dramatic literature and from records and related documents.

In accepting the role of critic and historian, A. W. Ward acknowledged debts to Collier and Sharp, and attempted to create a more comprehensive narrative. This need not greatly concern us here save that he discussed the evolution of vernacular drama as against the liturgy,[15] and was concerned with the movement of drama outside the churches, and the establishment of the Feast of Corpus Christi. As a critic he defined his view of drama:

Strictly speaking dramatic literature is that form of literary composition which accommodates itself to the demands of an art whose method is imitation in the way of action.[16]

He firmly curtailed his field to what is purely literary:

The use of words is necessary not to every kind of drama but to every kind of drama which falls within the range of literature.

The point is very much in question today, as there are attempts both through iconography and through performance to explore non-verbal elements in the semiotics of the medieval drama.

Ward's criticism of the Wakefield Shepherds' plays was caustic:

The low humour – and it is very low – of these two plays doubtless constituted their special attraction for their audience.[17]

He accepts an increasingly important historical concept which

depended upon this low view of the plays, and the change which the
Renaissance was to bring:

What seems to us so profane in the readiness of our forefathers to allow the
highest conceptions of religion to be associated with the crudest attempts at
reproducing them in bodily form, was the result of an aesthetic rather than a
religious deficiency; and if the mystics prepared the growth of a more spiritual
age of religious life, the Renascence made impossible the continued
depression of the sublimest subjects to the level of a treatment satisfactory
only to the uncultivated and unrefined.[18]

John Addington Symonds was closely concerned with the canons of
literary or dramatic taste, and with an historical model which saw the
medieval drama as leading up to Shakespeare. This meant that he
tended to measure the success of the medieval plays by qualities
which he conceived to be present in Shakespeare:

The authors of the Moralities had not advanced beyond the point of
personification and dramatic collocation. To take the further step and display
the reciprocal interaction between persons was beyond them.[19]

Though he condemned 'colossal rudeness' and the structural deficiency of unrelated parts, he brought formidable ingenuity to bear in
seeking out virtues which he could demonstrate to extend into
Shakespeare's works. The Miracles he found contained the tragic, the
pathetic, the melodramatic, the idyllic, the comic, the realistic, and
the satiric. He also found them 'emphatically popular and national',[20]
a theme followed up by E. K. Chambers. Though Symonds's critical
judgements do not have wide acceptance today, it appears that he did
to some extent free himself from the purely narrative or antiquarian
approach. Nevertheless, like his predecessors, he was not able to
appreciate the characteristic conventions and, through them, the
qualities of medieval drama, and he tried instead to impose the
conventions of the Shakespearean stage.

The developments of modern critical thinking about the medieval
theatre which are represented in the main part of this collection have
taken place in the last twenty-five years. From the late 1950s it has
become more a matter of looking at the plays in their own right as
exhibiting qualities which reflect skill in the art of play-making. This
has obvious difficulties since it implies a good deal of historical
speculation, but it is clear that although most of the extracts do reflect
historical considerations there is also an attempt to reveal the
aesthetic qualities – whether literary or dramatic – which they
embodied. In view of the pejorative nature of so much earlier

comment, this has required some courage, but the process has been very strongly supported by the growing success and popularity of the performance of the early plays by modern acting companies, amateur and professional, often guided by scholarly opinion.[21] This has enabled the relationship between play and audience to be more deeply felt by means of the actors' interpretative skill.

Between the nineteenth century and this fundamental change in critical appraisal the work of historical scholarship has continued, impressively comprehensive, but in general avoiding comment upon the qualities of the plays. Because of this the work of a number of significant authorities – indispensable in other ways – is not appropriate to the selection. There is no doubt that O. B. Hardison's introductory chapter[22] identified definitively some outstanding trends in the work of E. K. Chambers, Karl Young and Hardin Craig, all of whom assembled and considered a great deal of primary source material. Hardison was especially concerned to show that these scholars followed an evolutionary model in their researches, depending upon the idea of smooth development of drama from simple and crude beginnings to the sophistication of the Shakespearean stage. He directed attention to the weakness of refusing to discuss the meanings of the plays, or to consider what appeal they might have, either in medieval times or since. He also indicated that the concept of drama upon which their work was based – chiefly impersonation, action and dialogue – was too narrow.[23]

Chambers, in dealing with origins, placed a good deal upon the folk analogues of the drama and the widespread popularity of the folk festivals. It is interesting, though, that he did not take individual plays and show in any detail how these elements could be illustrated. He was very critical of religious attitudes, and made little attempt to trace the close integration between the religious and the dramatic.[24] By contrast, Craig was a little more successful in this, stressing the religious, and showing that the absence of realism was not a handicap but a characteristic which made for a more effective presentation of religious ideas:

It might make the matter clearer to say that the pageant stage had no realism, and the absence of any attempt to be realistic on the part of the players and of any expectation on the part of the spectators of seeing the actual thing tended to put stress on action and event, for action and event were the bases of interest. The pageant stage was thus adequate for the purpose it sought to serve.[25]

One might wish to increase the force of 'adequate'.

Hardison's contribution to the development of criticism was of profound importance: his perception that the liturgical drama has a separate existence and history from the mystery cycles has cleared the way both for a more extensive evaluation of the liturgical drama in itself and for a more intensive study of the mystery cycles which is less dependent upon a doubtful historical model. The study of the former has not been made a topic in this selection because of its separateness.[26] As to the mystery cycles, the work of Kolve and of Woolf (see section 2 of Part Two, below) has given keys to a re-interpretation of the medieval theatre, based primarily upon intellectual discipline supported by a consideration of dramatic method. Kolve's discussion of the principles of selection fundamental to an appreciation of the cycles is considered by Mills (section 1, Part Two).

Because Hardison was primarily concerned with the identification of the evolutionary model of earlier critics, followed by a re-examination in detail of the development of the liturgical drama, his work should be seen as an influence on the development of the criticism of medieval theatre. As such it lies outside the scope of this anthology. Other pioneers of comparable importance in pioneering have had to be excluded. Chief among these are Glynne Wickham, Richard Southern and M. D. Anderson: it is perhaps valuable to mention them briefly in order to help define the major topics of the collection.

Wickham must be considered the most comprehensive historian of the medieval English theatre since 1945.[27] He has illuminated it by a detailed treatment of processions and pageants, by attending to practical details of performance, and by looking at the importance of 'device' in centring the attention of the audience upon the theoretical concerns of the plays. Wickham has also attempted a new chronology for the origin of the Chester cycle.[28] These are activities of a primarily scholarly and historical nature: it is only with the recent suggestion that successful medieval plays are essentially tragi-comedy that he has turned to a more critical stance.

The most conspicuous, and at the same time the most controversial, piece of work by Richard Southern has been his performance analysis of *The Castle of Perseverance*. The controversial aspect was his notion of the use of a surrounding mound, but his analysis of the text stanza by stanza, and indeed line by line at times, gives a fine sense of the dramatic qualities of the play – dramatic in an awareness of the way what is enacted may grip the audience:

Now comes what must have been one of the great dramatic monents of the play. With the triumphant Ladies, flushed with victory, aloft round Mankind on the tower; with the six Sins spread in a circle of misery round the Castle-foot, licking their wounds; with Flesh and the Devil fuming, sullen and

despondent; and with the green of the Place littered with the battery of roses –
Covetyse walks slowly out on his own and calls Mankind very softly and
reasonably.[29]

Creative enthusiasm of this kind has been of great importance in
revealing the qualities of the plays.

The work of M. D. Anderson was seminal in the consideration of
the relationship between the drama and other medieval religious art.
Its importance in the process by which the qualities of the drama
came to be appreciated for themselves cannot be overestimated. It
helped to ensure that medieval drama came to be looked upon as an
art form with an aesthetic to be discovered. But now it appears that
her work was insufficiently strict over dating. A passage like the
following leaves one in doubt as to which comes first, the visual art or
the drama – though it must be admitted that the grounds for certainty
are sometimes difficult to find:

If, after seeing a majestic theme such as the Creation, the Flood or the Last
Judgement, presented upon the small stage of a pageant cart, the carver of an
alabaster panel or a roof boss was called upon to depict it within an even more
restricted space, he would naturally have tended to reproduce the tableau
which he remembered. . . . If we accept the probability that medieval
craftsmen were thus inspired by the plays it is certainly likely that what they
show us in their work is some sort of a record of what they had seen on the
stage.[30]

These authors could no doubt be seen as part of the formative
influences upon the writers of the extracts, most of whom are
academic. Like many other literary genres today, the medieval drama
is served by critics who are mostly involved in teaching and research
at university level, aiming largely at an academic readership. We
shall probably not go far wrong in assuming that what is in common
among these authors is broadly the changing critical scene viewed
through academic eyes. Some of the main traits in the selection may
best be seen in relation to four preoccupations of critical thinking in
the last twenty-five years. These are concerned with the modern
theatre, with narrative, with a changing approach to language, and
with metaphor.

There is space here to do little more than hint at lines of
development in the modern theatre which have undoubtedly altered
the approach to and the expectation about dramatic texts. Broadly,
one might say that up to the time of Ibsen the appreciation of drama
in England was largely dominated by an attempt to recover
Shakespearean, or even classical drama, and this is one of the chief
reasons for the poverty of criticism we have observed. The impact of

Ibsen was to bring these expectations into question. Following his lead, and also by introducing other preoccupations, the modernist theatre has widened the breach to the extent that many of the standards by which plays were judged have been altered. Chief among these preoccupations (not necessarily anticipated by Ibsen himself) I would put the abandonment of verisimilitude and with it the disintegration of character. These have led us to respond to drama in a way which recognises it without expecting it to be necessarily like real life, and to respond to persons in plays without expecting them to be complete or even consistent.[31] However long it has taken, we are now capable of seeing drama quite differently and this has facilitated perception of the medieval drama in which both these aspects have a striking similarity with the modern drama – or they can at least be perceived to be so. Instead of the willing suspension of disbelief we are also perhaps aware of the illusion of drama and quite willing that this awareness become part of the dramatic action.[32] It is probable too that the changed modern attitude to theatrical space, and the relationship between this and the audience, has informed the concept of the medieval theatre in the round advocated by Southern and many other practitioners of the stage.[33]

These attitudes to the modern theatre lead us to the extracts by Vinter, Spivack, and Twycross and Carpenter. Vinter sees character-isation in didactic terms and suggests that an anticipation of a Brechtian *gest* is involved in the Towneley *Abraham* where a character and an attitude to that character are implied. The changing concept of character is very clear here. Spivack's work is important in realising the true nature of the Vice of the moralities and interludes as a 'homiletic showman' rather that an in-depth character. Once the controlling nature of his role is grasped, it becomes clear that drawing upon a large group of stage conventions which include language, gesture, movement, and probably costume, he carries the central dramatic experience of many plays in respect of both meaning and performance. With Twycross and Carpenter one is made aware that the function of masks is both to hide and to reveal, and that the presence of masked figures among unmasked ones leads to a fruitful co-existence of both stylised and realistic dramatic modes.

The treatment of narrative has undergone its most vigorous examination in the criticism of the novel. The greater awareness of modes of narration is perhaps cognate with or influential upon the consideration of narrative in medieval drama. In the mystery cycles there may indeed be a concern to tell the story for its own sake, to make out of the stuff of narrative the 'quick books' of the *Tretise of Miraclis Pleyinge*. (See the excerpt in Part One, below.) But even in that case there is perceived a didactic motive behind the narrative. Modern critics have seen in the cosmic narrative from Adam to Doomsday principles of selection and patterning which unquestionably draw attention to typological and redemptive functions. Here we find reasons for the parallels between Adam and Isaac and Christ which illuminate the structure of the cycles and allow cross-references between parts – cross-references which could have been underlined by costume, gesture and action where required. In the morality plays the didactic control of narrative is even more explicit. Perhaps here we can also see similarities with modern polemical theatre in the work of critics like Kantrowitz (section 3, Part Two), who observes the manipulation of narrative through allegorical figures, and in doing so reflects consideration of the politically determined drama of our time.

Changing attitudes to language have encouraged critics to look at the language of plays more in terms of dramatic effectiveness than its lack of Shakespearean 'poetic' qualities. The study of linguistics has led to a view of language as a series of codes having relevance to a social or political milieu, and in plays this accounts for the restriction of individual types of language to specific scenes. The process is one by which the qualities are more closely perceived, and the close attention to 'earnest' and 'game' by Kolve, and to the language of the Vice by Spivack, perhaps reflect it.

Metaphor has been much examined in stage terms. Like the co-existence between narrative and doctrine, stage metaphor embodies significance upon different levels. Its most obvious effect has been in the use of iconographic interpretation, of which Davidson's piece here is a notable representative. It is also true that the figural interpretation of time proposed by Kahrl in his excerpt here has significance in relation to metaphor. Spivack, developing the idea in another way, sees the Vice as a 'dramatised metaphor'. The concept of actions upon the stage having emblematic significance is clearly a fruitful one for the investigation of medieval plays.

In these four ways, then, the extracts reflect some of the central concerns of contemporary criticism, and an awareness of this more general background perhaps enables us to understand why the critics in this volume have come to interpret the plays in the way they do. It is difficult to go far beyond the preoccupation here suggested for, on the whole, there is little ideological criticism as such: most of what has been written so far comes from the standpoint of the committed student of literature whose concern is largely aesthetic. As Mills suggests, there is a possible division between those whose concern is primarily literary and those who seek a more radical grasp of dramatic qualities, but both are still branches of the newly-found aesthetic criticism of the plays. It is perhaps true that Potter's interpretation of the morality drama as drama of forgiveness is theological, but essentially his comments are well-founded in the text (see section 3, Part Two).

Of the remaining contributions one may at least say that they cannot easily be fitted in with the four categories, and in this way they give the lie to too prescriptive an interpretation of the critical disciplines and impulses here presented. They embody in various ways a disciplined approach through scholarship, as befits their academic origins, and in general they do much, it is hoped, to reveal the qualities of the plays. Bevington's work on the size and nature of the acting troupes shows the influence of these on structure and dramatic effects. Tydeman, whose perspective is European, looks carefully at the medieval actors themselves and their possible strengths and weaknesses. Neuss is concerned with the configurations of staging in the Cornish plays and offers comparison with *Castle of Perseverance*. Lindenbaum, speaking from direct experience of a modern production which set out to be as historically accurate as possible, gives an account of some of the problems of performers, and of the staging, particularly in relation to the pageant waggons themselves. Craik and Prosser by detailed analysis of text seek to project a dramatic experience onto the stage of our imaginations, and in doing so illuminate many aspects of structure, contrast and mood.

NOTES

1. H. C. Gardiner, *Mysteries' End* (New Haven, Conn., 1946; repr. 1967).

2. Cf. Ben Jonson's possibly more pointed disgust in *The Divell is An Asse* (1616) [I i 37–85] and *The Staple of News* (1626) [First Intermeane 60–6, and Second Intermeane 5–17].

3. T. Warton, *A History of English Dramatic Poetry*, 3 vols (London, 1774–81).

4. Warton, I, pp. 161–2.

5. R. Dodsley (ed.), *A Select Collection of Old Plays*, 12 vols (London, 1744): I, p. *xiii*.

6. Ibid., p. 2.

7. Ibid., p. *xxxvi*.

8. E. Malone, *A Historical Account of the Rise and Progress of the English Stage* (Basle, 1800), p. 1.

9. W. Hone, *Ancient Mysteries Described* (London, 1823), pp. 90–3, 116–19, 157, 169.

10. T. Sharp, *A Dissertation on the Pageants or Dramatic Mysteries Anciently*

Performed at Coventry (Coventry, 1825), quoting from J. Brand, *A History . . . of Newcastle-upon-Tyne* (London, 1789), vol. 2, p. 379.

11. J. P. Collier, *The History of English Dramatic Poetry to the Time of Shakespeare*, 3 vols (London, 1831; rev. edn 1879), pp. *ix–x* (of rev. edn). This view cannot be sustained today.

12. Ibid., p. 182.

13. Ibid., p. 293.

14. T. Wright (ed.), *The Chester Plays* (The Shakespeare Society, London, 1843), p. *v*.

15. A. W. Ward, *A History of English Dramatic Literature*, 3 vols (London, 1899): I, p. 18.

16. Ibid., p. *viii*.

17. Ibid., p. 38.

18. Ibid., p. 44.

19. J. A. Symonds, *Shakspere's Predecessors in the English Drama* (London, 1883, repr. 1969), p. 132. (The spelling-form is that used by Symonds.)

20. Ibid., pp. 4–5, 95, 81.

21. Reviews of modern performances are regularly published in *Research Opportunities in Renaissance Drama*, and *Medieval English Theatre*. For the view of an actor-director see Carl Heap, 'On Performing *Mankind*', *Medieval English Theatre* 4 (1982), pp. 93–103.

22. O. B. Hardison, Jnr, *Christian Rite and Christian Drama in the Middle Ages* (Baltimore, Md, 1965). Essay I: 'Darwin, Mutations and the Origin of Medieval Drama', pp. 1–34. He writes specifically about E. K. Chambers, *The Medieval Stage*, 2 vols (Oxford, 1903); K. Young, *The Drama of the Medieval Church*, 2 vols (Oxford, 1933); H. Craig, *English Religious Drama* (Oxford, 1955).

23. Hardison, p. 17.

24. In his later work Chambers offers a little more comment upon qualities in the cycles. For example, he writes on the Chester cycle: 'The dramatic action is generally simple and straightforward without much attempt to exploit the psychological possibilities of the themes dealt with.' *English Literature at the Close of the Middle Ages* (Oxford, 1945), p. 27.

25. Craig (note 22, above), pp. 8–9.

26. The most valuable recent contribution is William L. Smoldon, *The Music of the Medieval Church Dramas*, ed. C. Bourgeault (London, 1980).

27. G. Wickham, *Early English Stages, 1300–1660* (London: vol. 1, 1963 – rev. edn 1980; vol. 3, London, 1981).

28. Ibid., 3, pp. 177–218.

29. R. Southern, *The Medieval Theatre in the Round* (London, 1957; rev. edn 1975), p. 199 (of rev. edn), referring to *Castle of Perseverance* (2445ff.).

30. M. D. Anderson, *Drama and Imagery in English Medieval Churches* (Cambridge, 1963), p. 5. See also Otto Pacht, *The Rise of Pictorial Narrative in Twelfth-Century England* (Oxford, 1962).

31. On the disintegration of character and a parallel between medieval plays and modern expressionist drama, see Northrop Frye, *Anatomy of Criticism* (Princeton, N.J., 1957; rev. edn, 1966), pp. 291–3.

32. Changing attitudes to drama and theatre in modern times are discussed in A. P. Hinchcliffe, *Drama Criticism: Developments Since Ibsen* (Casebook Series, London, 1979), pp. 11–21.

33. Cf. Southern, *passim*; and K. Elam, *The Semiotics of Theatre and Drama* (London, 1980), pp. 63–4.

PART ONE

Early Documents

A Tretise of Miraclis Pleyinge (14th century)

[*This Wycliffite tract is an attack upon the mystery plays in which the unknown author seeks to demolish the arguments of their defenders. The tract thus embodies what are presumed to be generally held orthodox views, of which the chief appears to be that if the people are to learn from iconography, they must also be allowed to learn from a physical enactment which would be even more effective.*]

. . . Þanne syþen myraclis of Crist and of hyse seyntis weren þus effectuel, as by oure bileve we ben in certeyn, no man shulde usen in bourde and pleye þe myraclis and werkis þat Crist so ernystfully wrouȝte to oure helpe; for whoevere so doþ, he erriþ in þe byleve, reversiþ Crist and scornyþ God. He erriþ in þe bileve, for in þat he takiþ þe most precious werkis of God in pley and bourde, and so takiþ his name in idil, and so mysusiþ oure byleve. . . .

Siþen it is leveful to han þe myraclis of God peyntid, why is it not as wel leveful to han þe myraclis of God pleyed? syþen men mowen bettre reden þe wille of God and his mervelous werkis in þe pleyinge of hem þan in þe peyntynge, and betere þei ben holden in mennus mynde and oftere rehersid by þe pleyinge of hem þan by þe peyntynge, for þis is a deed bok, þe toþer a qu[i]ck.

SOURCE: extracts from *Here bigynnis a tretise of miraclis pleyinge* (BL MS Additional 24202, fols 14–17v); reprinted in T. Wright, *Reliquae Antiquae* (London, 1845), vol. 2, pp. 42–3, 46.

GLOSSARY

syþen since *bileve, byleve* faith *in certeyn* certainly *bourde* sport *reversiþ* contradicts *in idil* in vain *mysusiþ* abuses *leveful* lawful *mowen* are able to *reden* learn *rehersid* repeated *bok* book *quick* living.

Robert Mannynge of Brunne   (1303)

. . .

Hyt ys forbode hym, yn þe decre
Myracles for to make or se;
For, myracles ȝyf þou bygynne,
Hyt ys a gaderyng, a syght of synne,
He may yn þe cherche þurgh þys resun
Pley þe resurreccyun, –
Þat ys to seye, how God ros,
God and man yn myȝt and los, –
To make men be yn beleve gode
Þat he ros with flesshe and blode;
And he may pleye withoutyn plyght
Howe God was bore yn ȝole nyght,
To make men to beleve stedfastly
Þat he lyght yn the Vyrgyne Mary.
Ȝif þou do hyt yn weyys or grenys,
A syght of synne truly hyt semys.
Seynt Ysodre, y take to wyttnes,
For he hyt seyþ þat soþe hyt es;
Þus hyt seyþ, yn hys boke,
Þey forsake þat þey toke –
God and here crystendam –
Þat make swyche pleyys to any man
As myracles and bourdys,
Or tournamentys of grete prys.

. . .

Source: extract from F. J. Furnivall (ed.), *Robert of Brunne's Handlyng Synne*, EETS, o.s. 119 and 123 (London, 1901, 1903), lines 4637–60.

GLOSSARY

forbode forbidden   *ȝyf* if   *gaderyng* gathering   *gode* good   *plyght* risk
bore born   *ȝole* christmas   *lyght* descended   *grenys* village greens   *y* I
here their   *crystendam* christian way of life   *swyche* such
bourdys amusements   *prys* esteem.

The Mercers' Pageant Waggon at York (1433)

Play XLVIII The Judgement Day

. . . And so all Pagent Maisters to deliver forth þe is endenture to other Pagent Maisters at sall occupy for þe ȝere while þe Pagent gere lastes:

first a Pagent with iiij wheles

helle mouthe

iij garmentes for iij devels

vj develles faces in iij vesernes

array for ij evell saules, þat is to say ij sirkes, ij paire hoses, ij vesenes, and ij chavelers

array for ij gode saules, þat ys to say ij sirkes, ij paire hoses, ij vesernes, and ij chevelers

ij paire aungell wynges with iren in the endes

ij trumpes of white plate and ij redes

iiij aubes for iiij appostels

iij diademes with iij vesernes for iij appostels

iiij diademes with iiij chevelers of ȝalow for iiij apostels

a cloud and ij peces of rainbow of tymber

array for god, þat ys to say a sirke wounded, a diademe with a veserne gilted

a grete coster of rede damaske payntid for the bakke syde of þe pagent

ij other lesse costers for ij sydes of þe pagent

iij other costers of lewent brede for þe sides of þe pagent

a litel coster iiij-squared to hang at þe bakke of god

iiij irens to bere uppe heven

iiij finale coterelles and a iren pynne

a brandreth of iren þat god sall sitte uppon when he sall sty uppe to heven with iiij rapes at iiij corners

a heven of iren with a naffe of tre

ij peces of rede cloudes and sternes of gold langing to heven

ij peces of blu cloudes payntid on bothe sydes

iij peces of rede cloudes with sunne bemes of golde and sternes for þe hiest of heven, with a lang small border of þe same wurke

vij grete aungels halding þe passion of god, ane of þame has a fane of laton and a crosse of iren in his hede giltid

iiij smaller aungels gilted holding þe passion
ix smaler aungels payntid rede to renne aboute in þe heven
a lang small corde to gerre þe aungels renne aboute
ij shorte rolls of tre to putte forthe þe pagent.

SOURCE: extract from Mercers' Pageant Documents, in A. F. Johnston and M. Rogerson (eds.) *York*, Records of Early English Drama (Toronto, 1979), pp. 55–6.

GLOSSARY

be by   *vese(r)ne* mask, vizor   *sirke (wounded)* shirt (bloodied)   *chavelers*, *chevelers* wigs   *aube* alb (white vestment)   *coster* hanging, curtain   *coterelles* bolts   *brandreth* swing   *sty* ascend   *rapes* ropes   *naffe* ? roof   *sternes* stars *fane* flag   *laton* latten (alloy)   *gerre* cause to.

David Rogers   (1609)

. . . And everye companye broughte forthe theire pagiant which was the cariage or place which the[y] played in. And before these playes weare played there was a man which did ride as I take it upon Saint Georges daye throughe the Cittie and there published the tyme and the matter of the playes in breeife. The[y] weare played upon mondaye, tuesedaye and wensedaye in Whitson weeke, and thei firste beganne at the Abbaye gates. And when the firste pagiante was played at the Abbaye gates then it was wheled from thense to Pentice at the Highe Crosse before the maior, and before that was donne the seconde came. And the firste wente into the Watergate Streete and from thense unto the Bridge Streete, and so one after an other tell all the pagiantes weare played appoynted for the firste daye. And so likewise for the seconde and the thirde daye. These pagiantes or carige was a highe place made like a howse with 2 rowmes beinge open on the tope. The lower rowme theie apparrelled and dressed them selves, and the higher rowme(s) theie played. And thei stoode upon vi wheeles.[1]

SOURCE: extract from *A Breviary or some fewe Collectiones of the Cittie of Chester*, Chester Archives copy, 1609 (originally written by Rogers's father, c. 1595).

NOTE

1. [Ed.] The other four copies of the *Breviary* all give four (iv) wheels.

PART TWO

Modern Criticism

1. Introductory
2. The Corpus Christi Plays
3. Morality Plays and Interludes
4. Aspects of Performance

1. INTRODUCTORY

David Mills   Approaches to Medieval Drama   (1969)

Until fairly recently, critics of medieval literature were fairly sure of their criticial ground. Their task was to promote a full understanding of a text by placing it within its appropriate context, which was possibly literary, more probably social and philosophical, and almost certainly linguistic. But in recent years something of a revolution has occurred in the criticism of medieval literature, and critics would probably now reverse this order of evaluative contexts and place the literary evaluation first. At the same time, there is considerable variety in the critical standards adopted, ranging from attempts to treat medieval literature as if it were modern literature to criticisms which propound specifically 'medieval' standards of evaluation.

Medieval drama has not been a central issue in the criticial discussions about medieval literature, mainly because critics of medieval drama have come under the dominating influence of E. K. Chambers's two-volume work, *The Mediaeval Stage*. Published in 1903 and written in a tradition of historical criticism, Chamber's thorough and scholarly work traced the development of theatre from the decline of the classical stage to the beginnings of the Elizabethan stage, and focused attention upon two points in that development, the liturgical plays and the vernacular play-cycles, which are linked by a process called 'secularisation'. Chambers's work has been developed by writers such as Young and Craig,[1] and his convenient framework of historical development has been accepted by many critics of the vernacular cycles.[2] The many interrelated presuppositions behind this historical approach have seldom been seriously questioned.

Now, however, the criticial revolution which has taken place in other fields of medieval literature is reaching the drama. O. B. Hardison has compelled us to reconsider the liturgical drama in its liturgical context and V. A. Kolve has advanced a theory of the construction of the cycles which divorces them to a large degree from the liturgy.[3] The historical approach is being questioned, a development which I welcome for reasons stated below; but critics may now be tempted to react excessively against this approach, rejecting some of its valid conclusions and perhaps over-emphasising doctrinal influences upon the plays. I suggest that any such tendency may be corrected by considering the cycles in relation to the long tradition of English vernacular poetry which precedes them, and by assessing the way in which audiences might respond to performances of the plays.[4]

Before beginning my discussions of the medieval drama, however, I would emphasise a problem of terminology which is connected with the general problem of critical standards. In discussing the range of medieval dramatic activities, from liturgical ritual to communal civic celebrations, it is convenient to employ terms such as *drama* and *play*, *dramatist* and *actor* to describe the text, its author and performers; and to use words such as *setting, dialogue, action, structure, development* and *character* in analysing these works. With the exception of *play*, which could refer to a theatrical performance even in Old English and which had acquired its modern sense of 'a drama' before 1500,[5] this critical terminology is modern, either because the words themselves have entered the English language since 1500 or because they have been applied to drama only since that time.[6] The application of these terms, with all their modern connotations, to medieval dramatic activities may lead critics to dwell upon certain aspects of these activities, to the exclusion of other important features, and may suggest a degree of continuity between medieval and modern play-construction which is unhelpful or even misleading. It is extremely difficult to make clear distinctions between the various forms of dramatic activity in the Middle Ages, to determine the limits of the play, the liturgy, the civic procession, the sermon, the tournament, the dance. It is also uncertain how far the Middle Ages themselves were aware of the drama as a distinct genre. I do not wish to advocate a new critical terminology for medieval drama, but it will be necessary to consider what the familiar terms signify when applied to this drama.

The 'Liturgical' Approach

Perhaps nowhere is it more important to be aware of the significance of traditional terminology than in the discussion of the beginnings of medieval drama. Critics who define drama as the coming-together of distinct elements, such as action, impersonation and dialogue,[7] have argued that the origins of medieval drama lie in the liturgical plays of the Church, themselves developments from earlier liturgical observances, and that the Latin liturgical drama evolves into vernacular drama by the growth of its constituent elements, which are still present in the later play-cycles. Such an idea underlies Chambers's account of secularisation:

The evolution of the liturgic play . . . may be fairly held to have been complete about the middle of the thirteenth century. . . . The following hundred years are a transition period. During their course, the newly shaped drama underwent a process which, within the limits imposed by the fact that its subject-matter remained essentially religious, may be called secularisation. . . . From ecclesiastical the drama had become popular. Out of the hands of the clergy in their naves and choirs, it had passed to those of the laity in their market-places and guild-halls. And to this formal change corresponded a spiritual or literary one, in the reaction of the temper of the folk upon the handling of the plays, the broadening of their human as distinct from their religious aspect. In their origin *officia* for devotion and edification, they came, by an irony familiar to the psychologist, to be primarily *spectacula* for mirth, wonder and delight.[8]

It is clear that secularisation, as here described, involves a number of transitions rather than a single process. The place of performance, the occupation of the actors and the language of composition all change, but it would seem (though this is not stated) that these transitions should be regarded as part of a single process because the basic elements of drama, present in Latin liturgical plays, remain in the vernacular forms. Hence, although it is difficult to point to examples in which the three transitions are taking place simultaneously, Chambers stresses the continuity of development and treats the various transitions as the accidental results of a general expansion. The plays were forced through the west door of the church, the laity had to be co-opted to cope with the continued expansion of the plays, and odd lines of vernacular were slipped in here and there. Hence, the text outstrips the staging-resources of the church building, while at the same time the change in the staging produces changes in the text.

Yet it is improbable that such important changes could take place almost accidentally, and it is certain that they could not take place without fundamentally changing the nature and function of the drama. The liturgical plays of the Church were designed to be performed in Latin by clerics within the church, and their true context was one of the services for the day to which their subject related. The liturgical drama was an ancillary to worship, just like the tropes, lections, processions and symbols which played such an important part in its evolution. Development in this form is a process of expansion and amalgamation whereby one episode can serve as a growth point to which related episodes can be added.[9] Yet the liturgical context is the determining factor in this process, limiting the amount of development possible and providing the wider context in which the plays should be seen and understood. The result is that these plays cannot be considered as independent dramatic units, each with its own central theme and self-contained internal structure. Comparing even the most extensive liturgical dramas with the later play-cycles, it is evident that the later works show a new concept of drama as an independent form, with its own thematic and structural organisation which is not dependent upon a wider setting.

The evolutionary approach to literature necessarily minimises such basic distinctions, but it also sustains its argument by using critical terminology in a special way. It is generally agreed, for example, that the Resurrection play, the *Visitatio Sepulchri*, is the earliest liturgical drama, and it may be used to indicate the general characteristics of the genre. Its setting is the concrete symbolic focal point of the service, the Easter sepulchre, and its action is simple and processional movement towards that focal point. Its dialogue is a development of a chant appropriate to the service of the day. Yet, to apply terms such as *setting*, *action* and *dialogue* to this play is to use these terms with a meaning somewhat different from that which they have in modern dramatic criticism. The setting contributes much to the meaning of the dialogue and action, but its importance is extra-dramatic; its symbolic significance is independent of the action which focuses upon it and belongs to the wider pattern of church symbolism. The action is only minimally significant and hardly underlines the symbolic significance of the play or the humanity of its participants. The dialogue is a simple exchange of information; it does not involve a revelation and interplay of character and emotion. Both action and dialogue are further limited in scope by the liturgical situation since the stylised chant produces an effect very different from that usually suggested by the term *dialogue*, and the instructions concerning the dress and actions of the actors do not suggest impersonation (there is no suggestion of verisimilitude) but mime. We are aware of three clerics whose role as representatives, rather than representations, of the three Maries is established primarily by the day, the service, and their relationship to the symbolic focal point. Moreover, the action and dialogue are not really fused – the exchange of information interrupts the processional movement and it would easily be possible to divide the play into silent procession and static dialogue.

It could be argued that processional action towards a symbolic focal point and independent moments of chanted dialogue are characteristic of this liturgical form. Hence, in the Resurrection sequence we could see processional action in the visit of the Maries to the tomb, the race of Peter and John to the tomb, and – although this episode is not so common – the journey to Emmaus, while the dialogues would include that between the Maries and the angels or between Christ and Mary Magdalene. In the Nativity sequence, processional action would include the journeys of the Magi and of the shepherds, and the dialogues would include those between Herod and the Magi and the angel and the Magi. It would be untrue to claim that all action was unrepresentational and devoid of dialogue, or that all dialogue could be separated from action and conveyed nothing of the humanity of the speaker – witness the presentation of the angry Herod in certain liturgical plays. But the separation of the elements is far more marked in liturgical plays than in modern drama and, in consequence, the final effect is very different. The separation of the elements of drama is part of the general dependence of these plays upon liturgical actions for their staging and liturgical contexts for their meaning.

It is arguable, then, whether terms such as *play* or *drama* should be applied to these rituals which, like the elements from which they sprang, existed as aids to worship – not to draw interest to themselves but to point the meaning of the day and service. This is liturgy at its most dramatic, but hardly drama. Moreover, its characteristic features could not develop into vernacular cyclical drama, for only a limited number of Biblical episodes combine the elements of symbolic focus, processional action and chanted dialogue. Movement towards a symbolic focal point could hardly comprehend the complex actions of many of the Biblical episodes, even if such a focal point was available within the church, and the chanted dialogue would be a barrier to a rapid emotional interchange, as opposed to a mere exchange of information or leisurely lament. It would thus be difficult to treat episodes such as the Temptation and Fall, the Flood, scenes from the ministry of Christ, the Acts of the Apostles and the Last Judgement without changing the character of liturgical drama. Again, the diversity of the full Passion sequence, from Betrayal to Crucifixion, is far removed from the simple progressions and exchanges of information of the liturgical plays.

Yet if the structure of liturgical plays reduces the possibility of dramatic development, the extant vernacular play-cycles stand in marked contrast. These cycles all dramatise the Passion of Christ, each treating it with a particular emphasis.[10] A thematic focal point holds together the various 'plays' within the cycle, as opposed to the liturgical plays where the focus was concrete and symbolic. The cycle-plays which present the three major interventions of God in human history – Creation. Passion, Judgement – have no counterparts in liturgical drama at all. Furthermore, in the cycle-plays both dialogue and action serve a thematic purpose. For example, in the Chester play of Cain and Abel[11] the two characters establish themselves by their speeches and actions. A chain of cause and effect is established, so that the opening dialogue is a preparation for the tithing and God's first judgement, and this in turn leads to Cain's verbal and physical reaction which constitutes the climax of the play. Here one may speak of dialogue and action in relation to theme, structure and plot. The setting, so important for liturgical drama, is not significant here; the play is intelligible without reference to an extra-dramatic context, for it creates its own standards of evaluation, whereby the dramatic contrast of Cain and Abel is a realisation of the contrast of evil and good which is made explicit in God's condemnation of Cain's action. And this incident in turn contributes to the wider structure of the whole cycle.

Consequently, I would welcome a reappraisal of the whole range of medieval drama, for I feel that our critical terminology may lead us to see connexions where none exist. Some historical connexion could certainly exist between the liturgical plays and the later cycles, but I would question whether it is as important as critics have often made it appear. I am far more conscious of the differences between the liturgical plays and the later cycles than of the similarities. The liturgical plays are a by-product of liturgical activity inside the church and are intelligible primarily within a liturgical context. The play-cycles were written to be acted on an open-air stage and can be more readily approached as self-sufficient dramatic forms with their own thematic and structural unity. Each form, cyclical and liturgical, requires its own standards of critical evaluation.

The 'Literary' Approach

V. A. Kolve has already proposed an alternative to the traditional theory of evolution from liturgical to cyclical drama. He takes the celebration of the Feast of Corpus Christi as the *raison d'être* of the cycles, but after examining the episodes dramatised in the extant cycles or listed as dramatised in lost cycles, he concludes that the Old Testament plays pose a problem:

The Christian story begins with the Fall of Man and ends with Doomsday, termini perfectly adequate in themselves to make sense of the Nativity-Passion-Resurrection story. There is no need for filling.[12]

He explains the dramatisation of the Old Testament episodes in terms of two selective principles – the figural significance of events and persons in the episodes, and the importance of the same events and personages in the traditional chronological division of the Ages of the World. Other episodes, apart from these major ones, might be dramatised in particular cycles, but only the major episodes are common to several cycles.

A number of suppositions are involved in this theory, but perhaps the most important is that of the primacy of structure resulting from concentration upon a particular theme:

These two organising ideas are, one might say, the beams in the building, largely hidden under decoration and surface detail, but there all the while and of utmost importance. They hold the building together, they give it its shape; and by its shape, we know it.[13]

Yet although only certain episodes are dramatised in the cycles, it does not follow that the selection was made with a particular thematic and structural concern in mind. To appear in a play-cycle, an episode might have to fulfil a number of conditions. There would have to be a guild capable of performing it and willing to do so. The episode would have to be translated into dramatic terms. And it would then have to be accommodated in the cycle. Since a cycle consists of plays of Biblical events arranged in chronological sequence, it can be studied in chronological and figural terms, but this approach is not neces-sarily the most useful. Rather, it represents an attempt to project a modern concept of structural unity upon a medieval form which can just as readily be approached from a different standpoint.

Critics of medieval drama could learn much from the discussions of similar problems of theme and structure in Old English poetry, for the events dramatised in the cycles are, in many cases, treated at length or in brief allusions in Old English poems. Thus the Old English poem, *Genesis A*, follows the Biblical narrative in Genesis up to Abraham's sacrifice of a ram instead of his son Isaac, while the Fall of the Angels and the Fall of Man are treated in *Genesis B*, a fully developed and lively narrative work inserted into *Genesis A*.

Exodus combines praise of Moses with the narrative of the crossing of the Red Sea and includes 'digressions' on Noah and Abraham. The life of Christ is represented by poetic accounts of the Temptation, the Passion, the Harrowing of Hell and the Last Judgement, and there are other incidental accounts of the Fall and lyric elaborations on Christ's Birth and Passion which stand outside the narrative traditions. *Beowulf* may well be the adaptation of a secular heroic legend to a Christian context, and in that poem there are references to Cain and to the Flood among other Christian allusions. Anglo-Saxon poets, like later cyclical writers, had to select their subjects and often chose the same ones as the dramatists. Indeed, they might also treat events in a dramatic manner, as in the dialogue between Joseph and Mary in *Christ III* concerning Mary's supposed adultery, which has been described as 'the earliest dramatic scene in English literature'.[14]

It is possible to approach such works from a number of directions.

B. F. Huppé emphasises figural selection and in his discussion of *Genesis A* finds an overall plan, in which the inserted *Genesis B* has a thematic function. This plans develops

the related concepts of the Fall and the Redemption, as they are prefigured in Genesis, in order to reinforce the basic theme announced at the beginning of the poem – the praise of God.[15]

Huppé continues:

Genesis A stands at the beginning of the great medieval literature that, with the symbolic meaning of the Bible always at the center of consciousness, was to extend the imagination beyond the structural limitations of biblical commentary in such works of culmination as the *Divine Comedy* and *Piers Plowman*.[16]

Such a development would clearly comprehend the play cycles.

Huppé reaches his valuation in figural terms, while recognising that the poet 'is thinking in English terms, making full use of, "re-employing", the language of his pagan ancestors for Christian purposes with flexibility and subtlety of connotation'.[17] Other critics would see the influence of the Old English poetic tradition which, in concept and diction, was well equipped to treat of themes of heroic martial and social import, as a major factor in the elaboration of scenes of action in terms of traditional battle-description, and of social situations in terms of Germanic social organisation. Thus S. B. Greenfield, commenting on Huppé's approach, states:

The thematic pattern perceived in *Genesis A* seems quite a lucid account of that poem's coherence, but also . . . many of the 'spiritual' meanings need no specific exegetical knowledge to fathom, but are rather naturally inherent in the narrative material.[18]

On the other hand, the influence of the vernacular tradition could be minimal. R. B. Burlin, in a recent study of the *Advent Lyrics*, which are outside the narrative tradition, has pointed out that

though the *Advent* poet's immediate inspiration was liturgical, it would be more accurate to define his metaphoric domain as scriptural. What God expressed at the Incarnation, in terms of actual event, shed light on all other human happenings before and since, on the entire process of history from Creation to Judgement.[19]

Somewhere in between stands a poem such as the *Exodus*. Its editor, E. B. Irving, agrees that its poet knew the service for Holy Sunday which has been suggested as a possible source, but stresses that Scripture is an equally, if not more, probable source for the association in the poem of God's covenants with Noah, Abraham and Moses, and that 'we must assume that the poem is in organisation essentially the work of the Anglo-Saxon poet.'.[20] At the same time, the development in certain sections clearly owes a great deal to the existing heroic narrative tradition.

Hence it may be supposed that, in Old English, an immediate liturgical starting-point might lead to a wider context of scriptural imagery and reference which would be incorporated into the vernacular tradition where compatible. The relative importance of these possible influences would vary, but together they suggested that certain episodes should be selected and developed. The attraction lay in extending the significance of the episodes through the historical network of images and references provided by the Bible and made current by Biblical commentaries, and through the contemporary images and associations provided by vernacular poetry. Although no Old English poem has the 'Creation-to-Judgement' structure, the fact that Anglo-Saxon poets, influenced by a variety of considerations, took for their subjects many events later dramatised in the cycles suggests that the cycles should be considered not as a new beginning but rather as the outcome of a long vernacular evolution which began before the *Quem Quaeritis* had developed into liturgical drama and which was not wholly distinct from (or wholly dependent upon) the liturgy. This long interaction of liturgy, scripture and poetic tradition had already made certain episodes more familiar to writers and their audience and made them obvious candidates in a sequence of Biblical subjects for vernacular treatment. In England particularly, a long and thriving religious vernacular tradition may have been a factor in the emergence of the Corpus Christi cycle as a characteristically English form.

If we seek the 'Creation-to-Judgement' framework necessary for the cycles, we may find it, as Kolve has done, in the long vernacular Middle English works, such as the *Cursor Mundi*, which are believed to have influenced the cycles and which depend upon earlier Latin works such as those of Peter Comestor (themselves looking back to a tradition evident in Bede and Orosius, for example). That vernacular works showing a development towards an extended chronological framework appear in Middle English rather than in Old English literature is perhaps explained by two general trends in English vernacular literature after the Norman Conquest. The first trend is towards a wider and more comprehensive chronological perspective. We may compare the treatment of the isolated incident in the *Anglo-Saxon Chronicle* in prose, or in the late historical narrative poems of *The Battle of Brunanburh* and *The Battle of Maldon*, with the wider time-scale that appears in vernacular poetry in, for example, Layamon's *Brut*, or in the insistence on a well-defined sequence of days, seasons and generations which we find in *Sir Gawain and the Green Knight*, roughly contemporary with the earliest cycles. Time assumes a new importance. The second trend referred to is linked to the first through the chronicle-romances: it is the emergence in secular literature of the long romance narrative.

Middle English religious narrative poems in the vernacular show the influence of a variety of traditions. The predominantly scriptural influence is seen in works such as *Genesis and Exodus*, a work based upon Peter Comestor's *Historia scholastica* but covering only certain events in Genesis and Exodus. Its scope, from the Creation to the death of Moses which is briefly related after the episode of the Moabite women, corresponds almost exactly to that of the Chester Old Testament plays without the prophet-sequence. Inevitably, certain key figures appear – some important in the play-cycles, like Noah, Abraham and Moses, and others not important, like Jacob (a minor appearance in the Towneley cycle) and Joseph; the episode of Cain and Abel is undeveloped in the poem. Yet what is most significant is where the poem stops, and why; the poet says that he will tell:

> Quhu lucifer, that deuel Dwale,
> . . .
> And held hem sperd in helles male
> Til god srid him in manliched,
> Dede mankinde bote and red,
> And unspered al the fendes sped,
> And halp thor he sag mikel ned.   [20–6][21]

This might be a statement of the theme of a Corpus Christi cycle, even though the poem does not deal with the life of Christ. It is arguable that the poet's concern with a divine purpose led him to select and develop certain episodes which, explicitly or implicitly, prefigured New Testament events.[22]

If, on the other hand, we examine the *Cursor Mundi*, a work utilising the temporal framework stressed by Kolve, we find that the poet sees his task in a different way:

> Men ȝernen iestes for to here
> And romaunce rede in dyuerse manere
> Of Alisaunder þe conqueroure
> Of Iulius Cesar þe emperoure
> Of greke and troye þe longe strif
> Þere mony mon lost his lif
> Of Bruyt þat baron bolde of honde
> Furste conqueroure of engelonde
> Of kyng Arthour þat was so riche
> Was noon in his tyme him liche.   [1–10][23]

This poet saw his work in terms of the literature of entertainment and, like the dramatist, had to popularise his subject-matter and inject into it a greater degree of narrative interest than is characteristic of a purely doctrinal work.[24] This narrative interest, which is a way of holding the attention of an audience accustomed to secular narratives, involves a concern with motivation and cause-and-effect which requires a greater emphasis upon the literal representation of events. Whereas in the poems on Old Testament incidents in Old and Middle English the Passion-sequence may be implied, in poems like the *Cursor Mundi* it duly takes its place in the account of events.

The chronological organisation and narrative emphasis are likewise characteristic of the play-cycles and are both aspects of a new literalism which distinguishes the cycles from the liturgical plays. The cycles and the religious narrative poems of the thirteenth and fourteenth centuries are part of a new zeal for lay instruction; their subjects had been made familiar to lay audiences through their treatment in a long vernacular poetic tradition, but these same subjects were now treated in a new way. As in the *Cursor Mundi*, so in the cycles a wide chronological framework is utilised; the play-audiences knew, as they watched the Old Testament scenes, that the Passion-sequence was only a few wagons away, to be presented vividly before their eyes in due course.

Yet despite these obvious links between the vernacular poems and the cycles, the dramatist's medium is not that of the poet, and treatment of the same subject by dramatist and by poet may produce very different effects. Hence it is finally important to consider whether the chronological-typological framework of long vernacular poems could be used with the same effect in the play-cycles.

The 'Dramatic' Approach

A Biblical event may have typological significance and its action-narrative may equally attract a poet working in a narrative tradition and a dramatist seeking a visually realisable plot. But poets may stress other aspects of a subject than the narrative, seeking a compatibility of mode and subject. A dramatist also has to seek a compatibility of mode and subject, and not all Biblical subjects can be dramatised – at least not without considerable modification. The sacrifice of Isaac is given in a few lines in *Genesis and Exodus*,[25] corresponding to three verses in the Biblical account;[26] but in drama the episode is expanded and realised, in visual as well as verbal terms, in a dialogue between Abraham and Isaac which has no parallel in the Bible or in poetry. In the Chester play, this dialogue develops from Isaac's bewildered questions, through his horrified pleading when he learns that his own father is to kill him, to his expressed resignation on hearing that this is God's will, after which the dialogue continues for a further hundred lines as Isaac delays his father by questions.

This dialogue could readily be approached from a didactic standpoint. The sacrifice of Isaac prefigures the sacrifice of Christ. Isaac's ingenuous questions reflect a genuine and Christlike concern for others, corresponding to Christ's own concern, at His Passion, with the fall of Jerusalem, the forgiveness of His foes, the future well-being of His Mother. The laments of Abraham are a planctus-like counterpoint to the action. Kolve draws attention to Isaac's appeal to Jesus for mercy, a further indication of the link,[27] and the Expositor makes this meaning plain.[28] This is not merely a naturalistic dialogue between father and son; its purpose is primarily thematic and the incident has meaning mainly in relation to the Passion.

Yet the same dialogue is open to other interpretations. Dramatically, the emotion of Isaac is a natural response, the assertion of a natural justice against the unnatural act of a father killing his son, and, as a climax, of a loving father ordered to commit this 'sin' by a supposedly loving God. The prolonging of the dialogue suggests that Isaac is deliberately creating questions and trying an emotional appeal, subtly disguised as humble obedience, to weaken Abraham's resolve. The result is a struggle in Abraham between paternal love and duty to God which constitutes an important part of the modern dramatic appeal of the play. It also has the effect of delaying, and hence intensifying, the sacrificial climax to the play.

Are these two interpretations compatible? This is a matter for individual response, but I feel that they point in different directions. Although, allegorically, the Isaac-play is an assertion of the working-out of God's plan at the Crucifixion, naturalistically, the stress on human suffering becomes a critical comment on the same plan. When Abraham says:

> O my sonne, I am sory
> To doe to thie this great anye:
> Gods Comaundment do must I,
> His workes are ay full mylde.   [293–6]

the inadequacy of the expression – *I am sory, this great anye* – intensifies the sense of suppressed anguish, while in this context *His workes are ay full mylde* is patently untrue and can hardly be said without bitterness. It is this kind of emphasis which makes tragedy possible in a Christian framework – we lose sight of the wider doctrinal context.

The problem is even greater when the emotional emphasis is linked to a tone markedly out of keeping with the doctrinal significance of the play. Doctrinally, among its possible significations, the Flood could be a prefiguration of the Judgement.[29] Dramatically, it could evoke a picture of human terror, like the account in *Cleanness* where the images of human helplessness and suffering overshadow the idea of divine justice. But the cycles, limited in numbers and space and time, concentrate upon a few figures, Noah and his family. In Towneley, in particular, there is a sustained argument between Noah and his wife which results in physical violence. It is possible to regard Mrs Noah as typifying an antediluvian discord, an image of the sin which God is punishing, and to argue that the play asserts the theme of order at a family level – on board the Ark Mrs Noah calms down and typifies the restoration of authority which follows the Flood. But the echoes of scenes of domestic strife from the fabliau are strong, and Noah is comically ineffectual in his dealings with his wife, in contrast to his dignified dialogues with God.

The Herod Play also illustrates the discrepancy between doctrinal purpose and naturalistic effect. The Chester Herod, like the Herod of other cycles, is a raging tyrant, relying upon brute force to assert his authority and torn by inner fears and uncertainties. He could be a symbol of the sinful disorder of the pre-Christian world. This disorder is presented at a personal level in Herod's inner conflicts; at a social level in that his personal disorder results in disorder in his realm, of which the Slaughter of the Innocents is one mainifestation – knightly power turned to unchivalric ends. But from a naturalistic standpoint, Herod is the choleric man made comic by his anger, undignified and ineffectual, and the comedy of his presentation becomes the main feature of the play.

There are many other such plays, but the main 'problem-play' is surely the Towneley *Secunda Pastorum*. From a purely literary stand-point the success of the play should lie in the balance of comic and serious scenes; but the comic element, particularly the character of Mak, seems to acquire so much weight and importance that it obscures the Nativity section. Doctrinally, a unity can be postulated for the play. It presents a theme of disorder – the chaos of a realm under a disordered ruler (Herod) and characteristic of a sinful world with no redeeming Saviour. The disorder at the top of the social ladder, in Herod and his knights, is manifested also in the misery of the shepherds lower down the scale. At this level, Mak is the agent of disorder, a magician casting a spell on the shepherds to steal their lamb. The forgiveness of Mak is a necessary prelude to the Nativity scene, and the lamb as baby is a thematic reversal of the Christ-child as sacrificial Lamb. So the first part of the play is the thematic reversal and type of the second, important, not only as secular comedy but also as the prefiguration of a central episode, the Nativity. Mak's lamb produces disorder, but the Lamb of God will restore harmony.

Evidently this co-existence of naturalism and doctrine is inseparable from the nature of the Corpus Christi plays themselves. The thematic significance of a play depends upon the relation of the play to the wider context of medieval religious thought, especially in relation to Biblical exegesis, which might be familiar to the audience. Structurally, it depends not upon the individual episode but upon the connexion between the episodes, upon the total framework of the cycle which exists to serve doctrinal ends. By this approach, we are much closer to a modern concept of a play than in the liturgical drama, but the dramatic effect is still secondary. The prophets and the plays of Moses have a secondary importance in cyclical structure, according to Kolve, because they do not have doctrinal centrality in conformity to his twin principles of selection, not because they are incapable of satisfactory dramatic development or presentation (which they are). At best, we respond on two levels – to the immediate emotional impact of the presentation and to its wider analogical significance in the cyclical structure. Structural unity is not necessarily the same as thematic unity, although the attraction of Kolve's approach is that it indicates a means of relating the two, although neither necessarily produces dramatic unity.

To counteract any tendency to regard the cyclical framework as providing an adequate structural and thematic unity, I would emphasise not only the tension between tone and doctrine in, say, the plays of the Flood and of Abraham and Isaac, but also the effect produced by passing from one to the other. Doctrinally, the picture of God's wrath gives way to the picture of God's love, but the dramatic transition is from comedy to tragedy. Such variations in emphasis and tone run throughout the cycles and leave the impression not of a unified structure but rather of a sequence of distinct dramatic episodes, each separately conceived.

This impression is strengthened when we examine the production of the cycles in the Middle Ages. Were the postulated civic registers collections of plays independently commissioned by individual guilds, or were the guild-texts individual copies from a centrally written register? Notes in the York plays suggest that some guilds were performing plays of which no record was officially made,[30] and at Chester, during the revision of 1575, the Smiths submitted two versions of their play for approval.[31] If we believe that revisions of plays were the responsibility of the guilds, it is easy to see how the individual episode could develop at the expense of overall structure. This problem can be exemplified from the manuscript of the Towneley Plays which is clearly a compilation. At some time, it is postulated, this cycle borrowed a number of plays, with minor variations, from the York Cycle,[32] and at another time some six plays, it is claimed, were rewritten by a single author, distinguished by his own stanza-form and dramatic style, and usually called 'The Wakefield Master'. There are two ways of regarding these theories. Perhaps Wakefield borrowed its cyclical base from York and employed one man to redraft certain plays and modify the total thematic structure. Or perhaps the Wakefield authorities decided to stage a cycle but left the responsibility for texts to the guilds. The poorer guilds took plays from York, but the richer ones could afford to employ their own writer, a man who produced powerful and entertaining work which enhanced the status of the guild that performed it; nor need this last development have taken place when the cycle was originally formed.

Certainly, as towns rose and fell in prosperity, the structure of the cycle changed. The York cycle was modified on a number of occasions because the economic decline in the town had so impoverished some guilds that they could not afford to present their play. For example, in 1419 the Ironmongers complained of the expense of staging *Mary Magdalene* and some time in the 1430s they gave it up. In 1431 the Goldsmiths were unable to produce two plays, so their play of Herod was transferred to the Masons who wished to give up their play of *Fergus*. In 1422 four pageants were combined to give a single play of the Condemnation, and two to give the Crucifixion play. The result of these changes, a result produced by economic and not artistic considerations, is to distort the structure of the cycle and the possible internal unity of the individual episode. The principle of these revisions is evidently to retain the doctrinal framework of the cycle even at the expense of dramatic unity. Chester and York both have plays of the Creation; but the fact that Chester combines Creation and Fall with the story of Cain and Abel, while York devotes six plays to Creation and keeps *Cain and Abel* separate, is bound to affect the dramatic impact of the Creation.

Wagon-staging would necessarily reinforce the episodic nature of the cycles, unlike the modern performances at York and Chester, where the performance on a fixed set by a limited group of actors emphasises cyclical structure and individual characterisation. By mounting each play on a wagon and conceiving each separately, the total cyclical frame is broken. With a different Christ, Herod or Pilate in each episode, characterisation in performance was limited to the individual play and there could be no overall consistency in portrayal. Moreover, the analogical structure might well be offset by the immediacy of the performance. It is to be expected that in the civic community the actors were known personally to many, that despite the emphasis upon production, one performance a year was not likely to produce an acting 'style'; and the closeness of actors and audience, particularly when the actors descended to street-level, would intensify the sense of reality. The actors were manifestly ordinary human beings 'pretending'. This may well have prompted the Wycliffite complaints that the plays were blasphemous.[33] The high cost of production, seen in guild-accounts, no less than the ambitious theatrical effects often required,[34] may have been an attempt to master the problem of maintaining the dignity of high subjects under these difficult conditions. It is possible to regard the wrestling-match of the Chester Shepherds, the 'necking-scene' between Pilate and his wife at York, or Pilate's cheating tactics with the torturers at Towneley[35] as manifestations of sinful disorder; but the immediate physical representation suggests a literal event rather than allegory, much as it tends to do in overtly allegorical morality plays where real vice takes over the centre of interest from abstract virtue.

The liturgical plays were written for a limited number of clerics on a fixed set. This method of fixed set/limited-cast production was used for the morality plays and in France for vernacular religious plays, and it is by far the best method dramatically. The theme of the cycles is likewise better conveyed by the fixed set, which emphasises dramatic unity. Far more ambitious effects are possible on a stage where complicated scenery and machinery can be erected and where the actors are at a remove from the audience; and also where a character is portrayed by the same actor throughout. And the cost of fixed-set production must have been lower than that for wagon-based drama – fewer actors, fewer costumes, less scenery, and no expense in maintaining a wagon and renting a house to keep it in during the rest of the year. But wagon-staging had one point in its favour – its inclusiveness.

Apparently any guild that wished and could afford it could be involved in play-production. The casts concerned are quite large – the total speaking numbers required for York are about 320, Chester about 270, Towneley about 250,[36] and even the two extant plays from Coventry require 38 characters – and this does not include walk-on parts, like the men who carried the animal-images into the Ark at Chester or the soldiers who capture Christ in Gethsemane or the 'extras' who must have been used for crowd-scenes. To these should be added the 'behind-the-scenes' staff – those who made the costumes, auditioned the actors, prepared the wagons and pushed them through the streets. This was, from a civic point of view, a great communal event in which many members of the community had a personal stake, and it was therefore like the village folk-play in its social function. A football match rather than a play might be a better modern analogy.

However we regard the cycles, we should be aware of the difficulties in applying to them modern ideas of 'play' or 'drama'. While critics since Chambers may have oversimplified the historical evolution of medieval drama, their studies have suggested that the cycles were the meeting-point of a number of influences, not all of which would be acceptable in a modern concept of drama. The cycles were tied to a particular background of Biblical exegesis, to a certain poetic tradition, to a unique set of social conditions. A reading of any cycle does not support the view that they propounded doctrines totally unacceptable to the post-Reformation Church, particularly in the uncertain years of the sixteenth century, or that they could not have been 'Protestantised' with very little effort; but in people's minds they were very much tied to the ethos of the old Church. At the same time, one has only to look at the new concern with artistic unity that the Renaissance brings into England, the first effects of which are already evident in the work of Chaucer and of the *Gawain*-poet, to see that the play-cycles are built upon a completely different principle of form and cannot readily be approached as literary drama. Moreover, changes in the character of both towns and guilds tended to make the concept of a community drama sponsored by the guilds more difficult to realise. Entertainment by participation develops towards the modern idea of entertainment by spectacle, with the rise of theatres where the audience is passive rather than active and the players are professional actors. The secular stage is less the product of a gradual process of 'secularisation' than of independent but related changes in the idea of religion, literature and entertainment which were not reconcilable with the Corpus Christi plays.[37]

SOURCE: article in *Leeds Studies in English*, 3 (1969), pp. 47–61 – a modified version of a paper read to the Liverpool University Medieval Society in May 1967 and to the English Language Post-Graduate Seminar at Leeds University in February 1968.

[Reorganised and renumbered from the original. For short-form references to works, see Abbreviations List, p. 8, above – Ed.]

1. [Ed.] For works by Chambers, Young and Craig, see Abbreviations.

2. The liturgical background is regularly incorporated into introductory accounts of the medieval drama for students; see, for example, the introduction to R. G. Thomas, *Ten Miracle Plays*, York Medieval Texts (London, 1966).

3. [Ed.] For works by Hardison and Kolve, see Abbreviations.

4. The need for studies of local conditions in approaching the play-cycles is argued by Arthur Brown, 'The Study of English Medieval Drama', in J. B. Bessinger & R. P. Creed (eds), *Franciplegius: Medieval and Linguistic Studies in Honor of F. P. Magoun Jnr*, (New York and London, 1965), pp. 265–73.

5. For a full account of the meaning of *drama* and *play*, see *OED*.

6. *Dialogue* could refer to the form of a literary work in Middle English but not (so far as I am aware) to one feature of a more complex form (e.g. dialogue *v.* action); see *OED* and *MED*.

7. Craig, p. 20.

8. Chambers, II, p. 69.

9. This is the traditional picture of 'development', although Hardison has rightly stressed that the development is not necessarily a chronological progression from simple to expanded forms (Hardison, Essay I).

10. An inevitable weakness of studies of the cyclical form is that they minimise the individual emphasis given to the same event in different cycles. The concentration upon grace in *Ludus Conventriae*, upon the fulfilment of divine purpose in *Chester*, upon human foible in *York* and vital sin in *Towneley*, produces very different dramatic and doctrinal effects both within the whole cycle and in the individual plays.

11. I take examples from *Chester* because the cycle is one in which I am particularly interested; it is typical of the medieval cycles in exemplifying certain dramatic features.

12. Kolve, p. 56.

13. Ibid., p. 100.

14. R. K. Gordon, *Anglo-Saxon Poetry*, rev. edn (London, 1954), p. 133.

15. B. F. Huppé, *Doctrine and Poetry: Augustine's Influence on Old English Poetry* (New York, 1959), p. 206.

16. Ibid., p. 209.

17. Ibid., p. 209.

18. S. B. Greenfield, *A Critical History of Old English Literature* (New York, 1965; London, 1966), p. 149.

19. R. B. Burlin, *The Old English Advent: a Typological Commentary* (New Haven, Conn., and London, 1968), p. 3.

20. E. B. Irving, Jnr, *The Old English Exodus* (New Haven, Conn., 1953), p. 16.

21. *The Middle English Genesis and Exodus*, re–ed. O. Arngart, *Lund Studies in English*, 36 (Lund, 1968); line 21 is missing in the manuscript.

22. Arngart, op. cit., suggests that this opening statement of theme results merely from the fact that 'The author was following his source unreflectingly' (p. 9). He sees the major consideration in selecting and developing incidents in the poem as the poetic form: 'The poet on the whole followed Comestor quite closely . . . except that . . . he concentrated on the main themes of action and incident that were best adapted for rendering the epic form' (p. 9).

23. *Cursor Mundi* (*The Cursur o the World*), ed. R. Morris, EETS, O.S. 57 (London, 1874).

24. On the 'entertainment function' in Latin works comparable with *Cursor Mundi*, see B. Smalley, *English Friars and Antiquity in the Early Fourteenth Century* (Oxford, 1960) ch. I, 'The English Public', and particularly p. 20.

25. *Genesis and Exodus* (1321–30).

26. *Book of Genesis*, xxii, verses 9–11.

27. Kolve, p. 73.

28. *Chester*, Diemling, IV (461–76).

29. Cf. *Matthew*, xxiv, verses 36–9.

30. See introduction to *York*.

31. For a full discussion of the problem, see G. Frank, 'Revisions in the English Mystery Plays', *Modern Philology*, xv (1917–18), pp. 565–76.

32. For a discussion of the postulated relationship, see M. C. Lyle, *The Original Identity of the York and Towneley Cycles* (Minneapolis, 1919). Miss Lyle's theory has been questioned; see *Wakefield Pageants*, p. *xxii*, n. 2.

33. See Kolve, ch. II.

34. See Salter, pp. 54–80.

35. *Towneley*, XXIV.

36. M. Rose, *The Wakefield Mystery Plays* (London, 1961), pp. 26–30, compares the cast-numbers for *Towneley* and the estimated population of Wakefield in 1377 in the course of his argument for fixed-set production of the Towneley Cycle. It is no part of the present paper to argue the case of 'scaffold' versus 'pageant' staging but merely to note that a consequence of wagon-staging would be the reinforcement of an already established episodic structure. It may also be noted that further 'unnatural breaks' in overall cyclical structure might occur when the cycle was played over a number of days, as at Chester.

37. [Ed.] In the original article, David Mills expressed thanks to members of the Liverpool and Leeds groups (see SOURCE, above), and particularly to Professor J. E. Cross (Liverpool) and Professor A. C. Cawley (Leeds).

2. THE CORPUS CHRISTI PLAYS

V. A. Kolve   The Drama as Play and
Game   (1966)

... The Latin liturgical drama of the Church was almost entirely
sung or chanted, and the performers themselves (the priests and the
choir) were often the only audience of the piece. The first episode to be
dramatised by the Church was the visit of the Marys to the tomb on
Easter morning; of the four hundred-odd texts extant of this dramatic
episode, that of the *Concordia regularis*, a tenth-century manual
directing Winchester usage, has particular interest: 'Aguntur enim
haec ad imitationem angeli sedentis in monumento atque mulierum
cum aromatibus venientium ut ungerent corpus Ihesu.'* [1] Even at
this early date, the Church conceived of dramatic action as something
performed *ad imitationem*, although most of the generically descriptive
words that came to be used did little more than emphasise the formal,
liturgical element: titles such as *ordo* or *officium*, and plays designated
only by their subject, such as *De Peregrino*, are common and have no
specifically dramatic connotation. More suggestive of genre are
similitudo, exemplum, miraculum and, most common of all, *repraesentatio*.
(The records can be studied in Karl Young's *Drama of the Medieval
Church*.) [2] Though these plays continued to be performed until the
Reformation, the most elaborate texts had all been composed by the end
of the thirteenth century; [3] and it is a striking fact that the vernacular
cycle-drama, which came into existence in the last quarter of the
fourteenth century, in naming itself rarely used an English translation
of any of these words. Instead, it employed English equivalents of a
much rarer term, *ludus*, which seems to have been used only in late
Latin plays – in the *Ludus breviter de Passione*, the piece entitled *Incipit
ludus, immo exemplum, Dominicae Resurrectionis* (both from the *Carmina
Burana* manuscript of the thirteenth century), the superb Beauvais
play of Daniel (*Incipit Danielis ludus*), and a play of the twelfth century
by Hilarius, the *Ludus super iconia Sancti Nicolai*. [4] As a generic term, its
lack of precision has tried the patience of distinguished scholars. Thus

* Translation: These things are done in imitation of the angel seated in the
tomb and the women coming with spices to anoint the body of Jesus.

Chambers has written that *ludus* is 'a generic term for "amusement"', and the special sense of dramatic play is only a secondary one',[5] and Young has called it 'a designation rendered generally ambiguous through its common association with popular revelling'.[6] Yet this very ambiguity may prove an entrance into the medieval idea of theater, for it is this word *ludus*, in its English equivalents 'play' and 'game', that becomes the ubiquitous generic term for the vernacular drama.*

Certain vernacular words not deriving from *ludus* are used on occasion. 'Processe' and 'processyon' occur in the (non-cycle) Digby Plays, implying in the first instance little more than a formal arrangement of speech and action, and in the second, the act of playing the *Conversion of St Paul* at three different stations with the audience following it to each, in procession.[7] A more common word is 'pagent', used to describe both the wagons on which some cycles were played and the episodes staged on them. Manuscripts of the Chester cycle preface each new play with the Latin form, *pagina*; its English equivalent is sometimes used in the Digby plays and it occurs frequently in the Proclamation to the *Ludus Coventriae*.[8] It had a secondary sense of trick, deceit or merry game.[9] The word 'shewe' was also in use, both as substantive and as verb, and involved conceptions such as revealing, displaying, demonstrating.[10] The term 'miracles', very common in contemporary notices of the drama, clearly should indicate subject rather than medium, but it was applied so loosely that the protesting Wycliffite preacher uses miracles as a blanket term for plays of the Passion, the Antichrist and the Doom, as well as for plays of miracles performed by Christ and the saints.[11] Each of these terms is important, but none rivals the Englished *ludus* in frequency or suggestiveness.[12] The Corpus Christi drama was spoken of as 'play' or 'game'.†

The gathering of evidence that the English Middle Ages used the word 'play' for a dramatic performance might seem tedious and unprofitable. Yet evidence of medieval usage does have value, for the word has gone dead; its specialised dramatic sense is now largely divorced from its root. Some of its original force can be restored by quoting several contexts in which it is used (it is the commonest

---

* Similarly, the vernacular drama in France called itself *jeu*, and in Germany, *spiel*.

† 'Game' as a substantive could also mean simply 'pleasure'. 'Play' and 'game' were both used to mean amorous sport, and heaven and hell could both be described (with differing connotations) as places of 'play' or 'game'. The only usages of interest here are those that are demonstrably generic in force.

generic term of all) and I shall then bring forward 'game' usages to confirm the richer meaning of 'play' evident in passages such as these. From the Chester Banns:

> you bakers, see that the same wordes you utter,
> as Christ hym selfe spake them, to be A memoriall
> of that death and passion which in play ensue after shall.[13]

And from the Chester *Prophets*:

> Moe prophetis, lordinges, we might play,
> but yt wold tary much the daye;
> therfore six, sothe to say,
> are played in this place.[14]

From York, when Herod lays a trap for the three Kings, and is content to await their return thus:

> Go we nowe, till þei come agayne,
> To playe vs in som othir place.[15]

From the Proclamation to the *Ludus Coventriae*:

> In þe xxiij[ti] pagent palme sunday
> in pley we purpose ffor to shewe.[16]

And from the same Proclamation:

> the mawnde of god þer xal they play.[17]

Of Mary, from a prologue by *Doctor* later in that cycle:

> how sche was assumpte · here men schul be pleyand.[18]

And as a final example, stage directions from that cycle's *Passion* play:

here enteryth Satan in to þe place in þe most orryble wyse · and qwyl þat he pleyth þei xal don on jhesus clothis · and ouerest A whyte clothe and ledyn hym A-bowth þe place and þan to pylat be þe tyme þat hese wyf hath pleyd.[19]

Many other instances could be cited, but these few will serve to alert us to a slight resonance of meaning no longer present in modern speech. The frequent description of action as being performed 'in play' is suggestive, and it is important, too, that the verb is always 'to play', where we might use 'to act', 'to produce', 'to perform'. This was so because drama was conceived *as a game*, and was frequently identified by that word as well. In England in the Middle Ages, one could say 'We will play a game of the Passion' and mean what we mean when we say 'We will stage the Passion'. The transition from one to the other is more than a semantic change; it is a change in the history of theater.

'Game' usages are crucial to an understanding of the medieval conception of drama. Because even the twelve-volume *Oxford English Dictionary* takes no clear notice of this usage, evidence for it must be presented in some detail.[20] From the Proclamation to the *Ludus Coventriae* comes this description of the play of *The Fall*:

> and þan almythy god ffor þat gret dyspite
> Assygned hem grevous peyn · as ȝe xal se in game
> In dede.[21]

In a concluding passage, the whole cycle is designated so:

> whan þat ȝe come þer xal ȝe sene
> this game wel pleyd in good a-ray
> Of holy wrytte þis game xal bene
> and of no fablys be no way.[22]

The word is twice used to describe the earliest extant morality play, *The Pride of Life*, as here by the play's prolocutor:

> Nou beit in pes & beit hende,
>   & distourbit' noȝt oure place
> ffor þis oure game schal gin & ende
>   Throgh Jhesu Cristis swete grace.[23]

And the long and beautiful morality play called *The Castell of Perseverance* concludes with this speech by God:

> all men example here-at may take,
>   to mayntein þe goode, & mendyn here mys:
>   þus endyth oure gamys![24]

There survives a short play from the early sixteenth century entitled a 'Cristemasse game, made by Maister Benet Howe. God Almyghty seyde to his apostelys, and echon off them were baptiste, and none knewe of othir'.[25] Similarly, John Skelton's morality play, *Magnyfycence*, probably to be dated 1516, closes with an address to 'ye that haue harde this dysporte and game'.[26] Sixteenth-century records from Bungay, Suffolk, dealing with the Corpus Christi drama in that town, speak of the 'game gear', the 'game booke', the 'game pleyers',[27] and of 'ye game on corp's xxi day'.[28] In Harling, Norfolk, payments were recorded in 1457 for the 'Lopham game' and the 'Garblesham game', in 1463 for the 'Kenningale game', and in 1467 (clearly a variation on the same) for the 'Kenyngale players' (Lopham, Garboldisham, and Kenninghall all being towns near Harling).[29] In 1493, the churchwardens of St Nicholas's Church, Great Yarmouth, were paid for a 'game' played on Christmas Day.[30] Bishop Bonner in 1542 enjoined that no 'common plays, games, or interludes' be

permitted in holy places.[31] And as late as 1605, in Ben Jonson's
Volpone, Nano the dwarf announced an entertainment to be performed
by himself, the eunuch and the hermaphrodite, with the words, 'Now,
room for fresh gamesters' (I ii). Finally, to establish the currency of
the term throughout the centuries that saw the birth and the full
maturity of the vernacular religious cycles, there are two drama
fragments, the first of them dated by Robbins as not later than 1300
and possibly written twenty-five years earlier. It is a prologue, and
includes these lines:

> nu sittet stille and herknit alle
> zat hur no mis ting ev bifalle
> and sittet firme and wel a-twe
> zat men moyt among ev go
> þey zat beut igadert fale
> ne maknet nayt to lude tale
> hit uer ev bot muchel scame
> for to lette hure game.[32]

The second, from the sixteenth century, is an epilogue that concludes
with an appeal for money:

> Souereyns alle in same ȝe that arn come to sen oure game
> . . .
> Vnto holy chirche to ben in-cressement
> alle that excedith þe costes of oure play.[33]

'Play' and 'game' are here used interchangeably, in exact apposition,
just as in these lines from *Magnyfycence*:

> For though we shewe you this in game and play,
> Yet it proueth eyrnest, ye may se, euery day.[34]

It is clear that the 'play' usages cited earlier also carry with them this
reinforcing sense of 'game'.

Some of the formulas in which these words customarily occurred,
and some of the ideas associated with them, provide further and
especially important clues to the medieval idea of theater. Then, as
now, play or game could describe children's pastimes, adult sports
and elaborate jokes alike: elements of pleasure, diversion or gratuitous action are always involved. Both words were used as antonyms of
'serious', as in the *Cursor Mundi* description of Lot's terrible warnings
to the citizens of Sodom:

> Bot al þat loth to þaim can sai
> þam thoght it was not bot in plai.[35]

Another example is the *Gawain* poet's description of his hero as he

rides out to keep his promise in a Christmas 'game' which may cost
him his life:

> Now rideӡ þis renk þurӡ þe ryalme of Logres,
> Sir Gauan, on Godeӡ halue, þaӡ hym no gomen þoӡt.[36]

Lydgate wrote, in his *Troy Book*, 'It is an ernest and no game', and in
the *Assembly of Gods* he used the phrase, 'Chaunge from ernest in to
mery play'.[37] Two kinds of human action and motive, fundamentally
different, were distinguished by these words, and from a conception of
drama as play and game – as something therefore not 'in ernest' – a
drama involving sacred personages and miraculous events could be
born.

In *Magnyfycence* we can find the antithesis used in both its general
and its generic senses. Counterfet Countenance explains his duplicity
in these terms:

> Counterfet eyrnest by way of playes.
> Thus am I occupyed at all assayes.

And later the dramatic world is itself offered as a game and play
analogue to a world in which actions *are* 'eyrnest', that is, to the world
of everyday reality:

> Beholde howe Fortune on hym hath frounde.
> For though we shewe you this in game and play,
> Yet it proueth eyrnest, ye may se, euery day.

We are thus shown truth 'vnder pretence of play'.[38] This polarity,
'play' and 'ernest', also explains the Wycliffite preacher's antagonism
toward the drama. His attitude is sombre: 'al holynesse is in ful ernest
men', and play, by nature not in earnest, is therefore both foolish and
false, and can offer nothing to men who wish to be holy. He mentions a
defense that men make for the drama: 'And sythen as ther ben men
that only by ernestful doynge wylen be convertid to God, so ther been
othere men that wylen be convertid to God but by gamen and pley . . .
now it is tyme and skilful to assayen to convertyn the puple by pley
and gamen'.[39] But he denies it out of hand: only things done in earnest
are relevant to truth and Christian life. We shall examine his other
arguments later; here it is enough to note that he defines the nature of
the drama just as the banns, proclamations and drama texts
themselves do, as 'play' and 'game', opposed to 'ernest'. He sees, too,
its kinship with the game amusements of children and men; the
drama is only one kind among others:

Dere frend, beholdith how kynde tellith that the more eldere a man waxith the
more it is aȝen kynde hym for to pleyn, and therfore seith the booc, *'Cursid be*

the childe of han hundred 3eer!' And certis the world, as seith the apostil, is now at his endyng, as in his laste age; therfore, for the grete ne3yng of the day of dome, alle creaturis of God nowe weryen and wrathen of mennus pleying, namely of myraclis pleyinge.[40]

Cursed be any man who has not put away childish things. The only scholar ever to pay close attention to this Wycliffite sermon was the late George Raleigh Coffman; he noted that in the course of it the preacher uses six specific examples of play: Sara's abstention from play and the company of players; Ishmael's playing with Isaac, which caused him to be driven into the desert; the playing of the followers of Abner and Joab, in which they destroy one another; the playing of the children of Israel before the Golden Calf; the playful mocking of Elisha by the children of Bethel, who were torn to pieces by bears in punishment; and David's playing before the ark of the Lord. That this variety of event was all designated by the same word seemed to Coffman incomprehensible, and he considered it an adequate reason for disregarding the whole treatise: 'A man who shows such a confused state of mind with regard to the use of important terms can certainly not be expected to give us a logical idea of what the dramatic type, Miracle Play, includes.'[41] But he is fighting the facts. The Latin drama of the Church had avoided the Crucifixion and had little connection with game. The church and the liturgy were its natural milieu. It was simple, dignified, ritualistic, limited in its means; it was called *ordo, processio, repraesentatio*. When the drama moved into the streets and the market place, into a milieu already the home of men's playing and games, it was redefined *as* game and allowed to exploit fully its non-earnest, gratuitous nature at the same time as its range of subject and its cast of sacred personae grew. It was a special kind of game, of course, its unique character clearly defined in a Latin-German dictionary, the *Variloquus* of Johannes Melber (*c.* 1479), where play itself is given as one of the meanings of *scena*: 'Etiam pro ludo capitur in huiusmodi loco facto ubi rusticus efficitur rex vel miles, et ludo peracto quolibet est sicut prius rusticus fuit.'[42] It is the kind of game in which a peasant is made a king or knight, and after it is over becomes once again a peasant.

My preliminary exposition is at an end. I have put forward evidence that the English Middle Ages described their religious drama as play and game; that this conception of genre involves the common medieval antithesis, 'game' and 'ernest'; that there was little fundamental distinction made between drama and other forms of men's playing. And I have argued that this conception of theater developed in response to difficulties intrinsic to the Corpus Christi story.

To go deeper into this matter, we must leave philology. The nature of drama conceived as a game needs also to be explored within a larger and more theoretical framework, and Johan Huizinga's admirable analysis of the nature of play, in *Homo ludens*, can serve us as a new point of departure. Once its implications have been examined, it will be possible to attempt a full-scale generic description of the Corpus Christi drama, to relate what we know about medieval staging to the dramatic theory I have been seeking to reconstruct in these pages. Huizinga wrote:

Summing up the formal characteristics of play we might call it a free activity standing quite consciously outside 'ordinary' life as being 'not serious', but at the same time absorbing the player intensely and utterly. It is an activity connected with no material interest, and no profit can be gained by it. It proceeds within its own proper boundaries of time and space according to fixed rules and in an orderly manner. It promotes the formation of social groupings which tend to surround themselves with secrecy and to stress their difference from the common world by disguise or other means.

It is . . . a stepping out of 'real' life into a temporary sphere of activity with a disposition all of its own. Every child knows perfectly well that he is 'only pretending', or that it was 'only for fun'. . . . The consciousness of play being 'only a pretend' does not by any means prevent it from proceeding with the utmost seriousness. . . . The inferiority of play is continually being offset by the corresponding superiority of its seriousness.[43]

These generalisations deserve to be read carefully. They are broad enough to cover all forms of drama, as well as children's games, athletic contests, dance marathons, or what you will. But the seriousness of 'ye game on corp's xxi day', as the Bungay records term it, goes beyond the absorption intrinsic to any form of play. In ways we have already examined, it 'imaged' sacred personae of the highest importance to man, and it sought to instruct in matters central to the salvation of souls: it was considered profitable game. Formal and repetitive in nature, it played year after year within a specifically limited time and place. Within those limits special conventions applied, creating a temporary world within the world of real life, and dedicating this created world to the performance of an act in some sense gratuitous to urgent daily concerns. Once this conventional world had been established, it was easily recreated until it became traditional. Like all play, this drama depended on formal order, without which progress within a game and pleasure from a game are alike impossible: anyone who breaks the rules spoils the game, makes it a poor and foolish thing. The formal order of the Corpus Christi game, its sequence of action, was determined by the playbook; failure to observe this order, an arbitrary limitation on the possibilities of

action, was considered an offense punishable by civic authority.
Records exist of fines paid by guilds and individuals for playing badly
or incorrectly, to the shame and displeasure of the community.[44] The
particular order that this game sought to create was not only
aesthetic, but historically true: it sought to pattern human experience, to give to the history of men an order that would reveal its
meaning.

Play and game thus creates a world within the real world, and the
dramatist's art relates the two worlds meaningfully to each other. But
the two need never be mistaken or confused. When the *Ludus
Coventriae* promises us 'the mawnde of god þer xal they play', we may
be sure that this is to be serious, all-engrossing play, but play
nevertheless, which is to say of an order of seriousness different from
the historical Maundy Thursday which is its referent. Similarly,
when the Chester Banns alert the city at Whitsuntide that the days
from Monday through Wednesday are to be devoted to the playing of
the cycle, and when the location of stations has been determined, a
formal world has been delimited within which the dramatic game can
be played. One may see how important was this sense of a world apart
by juxtaposing two late anecdotes concerning the devil. The fourth
tale of *A Hundred Mery Talys*, published in 1526, is entitled 'Of hym
that playd the deuyll and came thorow the waren & mayd theym that
stale the connys to ronne away', and concerns a player from a pageant
who wears his devil's costume while going home, frightening
everyone grievously.[45] A very different reaction can be found in the
reminiscences of Mrs Tattle in Ben Jonson's play, *The Staple of News*:
'My husband Timothy Tattle, God rest his poor soul! was wont to say
there was no play without a fool and a devil in't; he was for the devil
still, God bless him! The devil for his money would he say, I would
fain see the devil.'[46] Although Timothy Tattle enjoys seeing a devil
within the carefully circumscribed world of play, the villagers are
terrified when a refugee from that world suddenly enters the world of
real life.

Though the Wycliffite preacher shares with the dramatists an exact
sense of the drama as play, he understands differently how this play
world relates to the world of actual experience. He is unable to see the
dramatic artifact as something analogous, but in a root-sense
'unrelated', to real life: 'And therfore many men wenen that ther is no
helle of everlastynge peyne, but that God doth not but thretith us and
is not to do it in dede, as ben pleyinge of miraclis in sygne and not in
dede.' He believes the drama teaches men that hell is only a *locus* on a
pageant stage, and that the wrath of God is merely a dramatic
attitude, for it is obvious to any spectator that the damned souls are

not really punished in any Judgement Day pageant. This view grows out of his belief that only real action should occupy men, and that all else is falsehood, feigning and a work of the devil (three terms constantly equated in his mind): 'Not he that pleyith the wille of God worschipith hym, but onely he that doith his wille in deede worschipith hym.'[47] Here his argument is intrinsically more convincing, but it remains irrelevant. The duration of play is a momentary interval in, and abstention from, the real concerns of life; when the audience disperses they resume these concerns, the most significant of which for the Christian Middle Ages was the doing of the will of God. For a religious drama to have existed with the full approval of the Church, such a consciousness of the dramatic medium was necessary. The Wycliffite critic is interesting, not so much because he opposed the drama – a hyperzealous, Lollard fear of images and idolatry could lead to that very naturally, and the practical consequences of his opposition probably amounted to little – but because he often summarises the arguments of those who valued the plays, and because his own objections furnish an explicit contemporary statement of some of the difficulties that seem from the very beginning to have shaped the medieval conception of theater. His final answers are confused, because he thought action that was unreal was therefore untrue, clinging rigidly to two polarities: real and unreal, true and false. Whatever was false he considered to be an abomination to God and a peril to men's souls. In this he may have been right, but his categories are muddled: the world of play (and its mode of meaningfulness) lies outside the antithesis, truth or falsehood. This fact is common to children's games, knightly tournaments, champion wrestling, and all drama that has ever been.

Although any drama can be reduced to a game analysis, the medieval cycles furnish for the English theater the first major example of that genre, influencing in ways that have not yet been fully understood the great drama of the Elizabethan and Jacobean periods. And what is more, they furnish the purest, most explicit, and most comprehensively detailed example of a theater of game that has existed until our own time. After the Restoration, theater in England and elsewhere took a very different turn, reaching its climax in the heavily naturalistic theater of the early years of this century. Dryden, as early as 1672, had signalled this new direction, in claiming deception as the dramatist's aim; in his *Of Heroic Plays, An Essay*, he argued that trumpets, drums, cannons and sound effects offstage are essential 'to raise the imagination of the audience, and to persuade them, for the time, that what they behold in the theatre is really performed. The poet is then to endeavour an absolute dominion over the minds of the spectators; for though our fancy will contribute to its own deceit, yet a writer ought to help its operation.'[48] Until recently, we were heirs chiefly of this 'theater of illusion' – a very different kind of dramatic game. Though we never actually confuse dramatic action with real life, we are asked to grant it our maximum credence within the structure of the theatrical experience. Everything about the texts, the acting and the staging is carefully contrived to make the fact of 'theater' as unobtrusive as possible. The medieval drama required different habits of its spectators, and gave them a different kind of artistic experience in return. Today, playwrights like Brecht, Ionesco and Beckett have gone back to this older idea of theater or have worked in terms consonant with it. But the cycles can give us the thing itself in its first flowering, and if we would read them, stage them, and understand them properly, we must learn first of all to respond to the game nature of their action. In the pages that follow, I shall examine the relationship between this theory and the procedures and practices of the medieval stage.

The Corpus Christi drama took place in broad daylight, in the streets and open places of the town. The audience surrounded the playing area, as clearly visible to one another as the players were to them; occasional exits, entrances and even dramatic action took place on street level in their midst. Richard Southern's researches into the meaning of 'place' and *platea* in medieval dramaturgy have led him to an important conclusion: the 'place' was simply the area in front of the stage or scaffold, to which the actors might descend if necessary. It was never geographically localised, and there was no pretense that what went on there went on in an imagined locality relevant to the action. Action itself told the story, and it happened *there* in England, in front of and amid the spectators. In Southern's words: 'It was not until the Italian Renaissance that the place of a performance could become attired in costume like an actor and take a part in the drama – and scenery was born'.[49] The pageant wagon or scaffold would indicate the *locus* or *loci* of the action, but in terms of the 'place' itself these reference points were only conventions in a game: when Mary and Joseph travelled from Bethlehem into Egypt, the meaning of the action was clear, though the actual distance between the *loci* may have been only several yards.

Furthermore, this drama used actors from the community who were known to the audience in real life. From Coventry records we learn of 'Ryngold's man Thomas thatt playtt Pylatts wyff'; of wages 'payd to Robert Cro for pleayng God iij s iiij d'; and of fines levied by the Weavers' Guild in 1450 against Hary Bowater, who played

Simeon's clerk, Crystover Dale who played Jesus, and Hew Heyns who played Anne.[50] A few records in York suggest that occasional performances were graced by actors imported from outside: the visits of three players from Donnington, one from Wakefield, and four from London are noted in the mid-fifteenth century.[51] But this was the exception, not the rule; local, familiar faces in biblical roles would have made any fully developed kind of theatrical illusion impossible. Moreover, because each pageant wagon had its own complete cast to play its episode at each assigned station on the route, no single actor (except perhaps in the *Ludus Coventriae* Passion plays) performed the entire role of any major character. The York cycle, for example, employed in any given year no fewer than twenty-four different Christs in the adult episodes alone; the Chester and Towneley cycles both used eleven. This does not necessarily imply incoherent characterisation, for there were undoubtedly traditional approaches to the major roles; but it did serve as a powerful check against illusion.[52] These townsmen would have been astonished by Stanislavsky. They were ordinary men engaged in a certain kind of game, distinguished from their fellows only by a more generous mimetic gift. To take an extreme case, those who played God would not have sought (even for the duration of the pageant) to *be* God, nor to get inside His personality: such a notion would have seemed to them blasphemous and absurd. They presented not the character of God but certain of His actions. This approach encouraged a formal stylisation in both writing and acting wholly foreign to the chaotic world of real life.

Such a conception of theater also made possible the presentation of large, complex actions in swift and simple terms. In every cycle Noah builds the ark in front of the audience, either using prefabricated parts or wheeling a finished model onto the pageant stage; but always he claims it is taking him a hundred years, and the audience enjoys the speed with which the ark is actually readied as a kind of merry joke unique to the drama. The Chester stage direction makes the game nature of the action clear: 'Then noy with all his familie shall make a signe as though they wrought vpon the shipe with diuers instrumentis.'[53] When the ark is ready to be filled, painted boards representing the birds and the beasts are brought on; there are instructions that the verses and pictures should strictly accord in sequence.[54] The escape of Moses and the Israelites from Pharaoh and his forces was played with the same game literalness. In the *Exodus* I saw produced on a pageant wagon in front of York Minster in 1957, the Red Sea was a long linen cloth, painted with waves, and held facing the audience while Moses and the Israelites walked behind it; when Pharaoh and his men came in pursuit, it was thrown up and over them, and they lay 'drowned' beneath. The Israelites rejoiced in song as the wagon was pulled away. The action, strong, clear and delightful, probably represented something very close to medieval practice; records from Coventry specify, with no sense of incongruity, 'it. p'd for halfe a yard of rede sea vj d.'[55]

There was need for a kind of theater that could stage mythic actions as well, which could make phenomena never experienced in the normal course of things visible and dramatically 'real'. Because these plays were intended as 'quike bookis' for the unlearned,[56] they sought to make the whole of doctrinal meaning tangible in this way. Greban's *Le Mystère de la Passion*, written before 1452, begins by staging the creation of the world, a difficult but unavoidable subject, with a Prologue to explain that so far as possible it will be shown literally – shown, that is, in a way the spectators can apprehend through their *senses*:

> Mes la creacion du monde
> est ung mistere en quoy se fonde
> tout ce qui deppend en apprès:
> si la monstrons par mos exprès;
> car *la maniere du produyre*
> *ne se peust monstrer ne deduire*
> par effect, *si non seulement*
> *grossement et figuraulment;*
> *et selonc qu'il nous est possible,*
> *en verrez la chose sensible.*[57]
>
> [my italics]

Just as the halo around a saint's head in a picture imparts abstract meaning and gives the saint a kind of appearance familiar only in pictures,[58] so the medieval drama stages actions which, though unlike anything we encounter in ordinary human life, are nevertheless as 'real' as anything else in the play world. Thus the whole drama becomes charged with a mythic quality, where inner meaning is made as external as any other kind of outward appearance. Mary rides on an ass into Egypt, and she is physically 'assumpt' into heaven: in this drama, both actions *happen*, and they happen in equally literal ways. God was played by a man, but He was distinguished from the order of men by a gilt face.[59] And, as in the visual arts, the profound mystery of the Trinity was established very simply: in the Chester play of the *Pentecost* the actors playing God the Father and Christ sit together to hear the prayer of the disciples that they be sent some comforter, and when God the Father speaks He refers to *His* incarnation, even though the incarnation was performed by the Son at his side. It is *Deus Pater* who says:

> But while I was in that degree,
> in earth abyding as man should be,
> chosen I haue a good menye,
> on which I must haue mynd.[60]

When His long speech of recapitulation is finished, the stage direction reads, 'Tunc Deus emittit Spiritum sanctum in spetie ignis'.[61] The doctrine of the Trinity has been made visible as three-in-one, the most mysterious of its membership – the Holy Ghost – being shown as fire, probably in the form of a hank of burning hemp lowered from above.

In all the cycle plays there is much mechanical to-and-fro-ing between earth and heaven. When the York Jesus is about to ascend into heaven he says, 'Sende doune a clowde, fadir' and a cloud comes down; He gets into it and is hoisted aloft out of sight.[62] The action was not designed to resemble reality, but rather to translate it into a game mode, a play equivalent. It is possible that the guilds staged the seven days of the Creation with movable charts, decoratively painted, as we might illustrate a lecture,[63] for part of the compact implicit between the medieval audience and dramatist was the acceptance of such devices as signifying reality. Even music in these plays was symbolic, and was never used simply for atmosphere or emotive effect. In the words of its best student:

It is there, like God's beard of gold, or the horned animal heads of the devils, because it signifies something. It is easy to be misled by the directions which require music to be played, or sung, at some of the great dramatic moments. The point was not to increase dramatic tension or to 'soften up' the audience, but *representation*. 'Heaven is music', so at the crises in the drama when heaven actively intervenes, music too intervenes.[64]

The need to instruct in doctrinal truth, to clarify and make visual certain important meanings that were spiritual and mysterious in nature, undoubtedly played its part in shaping the medieval conception of theater: it had to be a medium in which these things could 'happen'. This necessity liberated it, and greatly increased its expressive potential.

Never was a suspension of disbelief invited; instead, the game episodes were played in their turn, and in the Chester cycle and the *Ludus Coventriae*, characters like *Nuntius, Expositor, Contemplacio* and *Poeta* served to direct them, introducing new actions and making doctrinal comments. Their function is to enclose the action, whether natural or mythic, in a frame of commentary which puts the playing unmistakably at a distance from reality. The Chester *Expositor*, for example, really does control the game – hurrying here, moralising there, now briefly narrating a story that cannot, because of time, be played, and occasionally stepping forth to address the audience directly on what they have been watching together. The French medieval drama often used a *meneur* (or *maître*) *du jeu*, and we know from a miniature by Jean Fouquet that he could be in the very middle of the action, holding the playbook in one hand and a baton in the other, conducting the game.[65] We know also that the *meneur du jeu* often spoke the moralisations and sermons of the play.[66] It is possible that the Chester *Expositor* or the *Poeta* of *Ludus Coventriae* moved among the actors in this same fashion, although no evidence exists one way or the other. What matters is that a similar conception of genre is involved, one far removed from that later kind of theater in which the happenings on stage, once under way, have the air of being autonomous, inevitable and independent of author or director. . . .

SOURCE: extract from the chapter 'The Drama as Play and Game' in *The Play called Corpus Christi* (Stanford, Cal., and London, 1966), pp. 11–27.

NOTES

[Reorganised and renumbered from the original. For short-form references to works, see Abbreviations List, p. 8 – Ed.]

1. Chambers, II, p. 309.
2. See especially Young, II, pp. 407–10.
3. Ibid., p. 397.
4. Ibid., p. 408; see also I, p. 684.
5. Chambers, II, p. 104.
6. Young, II, p. 408.
7. *Digby*: *Herod* (20, 559); *St Paul* (155–7).
8. *Chester*, Diemling, passim; *Digby*, *St Paul* (657); *Ludus Coventriae*, Proclamation, and also XXL (287–8).
9. See *OED*: 'pageant' (sense 1c); also *A Hundred Mery Talys*, ed. Herman Osterley (London, 1866), pp. 67–8.
10. See, for instance, *Chester*, Banns (118), *Ludus Coventriae*, Proclamation (10–11, 28).
11. The evidence is set out by George R. Coffman, 'The Miracle Play in England – Nomenclature', *PMLA*, XXXI (1916), pp. 448–65. He emphasises that 'miracles' was a popular, not an official, word for the plays. Because he fails to take the Wycliffite's categories seriously, his paper reaches (rather bewilderingly) what he calls 'negative results'.
12. Erwin Wolff – 'Die Terminologie des Mittelalterlichen Dramas in Bedeutungsgeschichtlicher Sicht', *Anglia*, LXXXVIII (1960), pp. 1–27 – fails to notice this central fact. He, too, has been misled by the infrequency of the

Latin *ludus* into thinking its English derivatives unimportant. He concludes that 'pageant' represents the greatest liberation of the drama from its liturgical beginnings, simply because it means both wagon and spectacle.

13. *Chester*, Banns (133–5); see also I (185–8).

14. Ibid., V (409–12); see also VI (177–9).

15. *York*, XVII (211–12); see also XL (191–2).

16. *Ludus Coventriae*, Proclamation (308–9).

17. Ibid. (314).

18. Ibid., XLI (25).

19. Ibid., XXX (465 s.d.).

20. The *OED* records a possible theatrical sense in contexts relating to Greek and Roman antiquity (4b); two special combination-forms, 'game-play' and 'game-player' (17), and the entry given for 'gameley' are unequivocally so defined. But 'game' in the fully naturalised, theatrical sense displayed here is unrecorded. Glynne Wickham's first volume of studies of the Elizabethan stage has an interesting discussion of *plega*, *pleg-stów*, and *pleg-hús*; see Wickham, 2, p. 166ff, and my note 30 below.

21. *Ludus Coventriae*, Proclamation (46–8).

22. Ibid. (518–21).

23. *Non-Cycle Plays*, p. 91 (109–12); see also p. 88 (55–8).

24. *Macro*, p. 186 (3644–6). 'Game' words are used to describe the main action of the play as well, p. 157 (2688, 2697); for other examples see *York*, XXIII (103–4), and *Everyman* (808–9), ed. A. C. Cawley (Manchester, 1961).

25. In *Specimens of Old English Carols*, ed. Thomas Wright, Percy Society, 4 (London, 1841), p. 28.

26. *Magnyfycence* (2566–7).

27. Chambers, II, p. 343.

28. The record for 1543, which Chambers overlooked, was noticed by Lawrence Blair, 'A Note on the Relation of the Corpus Christi Procession to the Corpus Christi Play in England', *Modern Language Notes*, LV (1940), p. 93.

29. Chambers, II, p. 368.

30. Wickham, 2, p. 361 (n. 21). Wickham and I discovered the importance of 'game' independently, each of us having finished our work before learning of the other's researches. We use very little of the same material, though our findings reinforce each other; for students of the later period, and for anyone interested in the continuity of the tradition I attempt to define here, Wickham's study is essential.

31. Lily B. Campbell, *Divine Poetry and Drama in Sixteenth-Century England*, (Berkeley, Cal., 1959), p. 225.

32. Rossell H. Robbins, 'An English Mystery Play Fragment Ante 1300', *Modern Language Notes*, LXV (1950), p. 32 (1–8).

33. 'A Sixteenth-Century English Mystery Fragment', ed. Rossell H. Robbins, *English Studies*, XXX (1949), p. 135.

34. *Magnyfycence* (1948–9).

35. *Cursor Mundi*, p. 168 (2815–16).

36. *Sir Gawain and the Green Knight*, ed. J. R. R. Tolkien and E. V. Gordon (Oxford, 1930), p. 22 (691–2).

37. Cited by the *OED* under 'earnest' (sense 2) and 'play' (sense 7), respectively.

38. *Magnyfycence* (427–8, 1947–9, 2548). The whole sequence of speeches from line 2505 to the end is interesting in its use of new generic terms.

39. 'A Sermon against Miracle-plays', ed. E. Matner, *Altenglische Sprachproben* I, Part II (Berlin, 1869), p. 229.

40. Ibid., p. 241. An earlier preacher also held all play to be potentially a snare of the devil in that it fostered idleness; see *Old English Homilies of the Twelfth Century, Second Series*, ed. R. Morris, EETS, o.s. 53 (1873), p. 211.

41. G. R. Coffman, op. cit. (note 11, above), p. 458.

42. Quoted by Mary H. Marshall, '*Theatre* in the Middle Ages: Evidence from Dictionaries and Glosses', *Symposium*, IV (1950), p. 380.

43. J. Huizinga, *Homo ludens* (London, 1949), pp. 13, 8. Benjamin Hunningher, in *The Origin of Theatre* (Amsterdam, 1955), pp. 14–16, has also used Huizinga, along with Frazer and others, in order briefly to suggest the connection between play, ritual and theater in primitive cultures, in connection with his study of the origins of the early Latin drama of the Church.

44. See, for example, the Beverley records in Chambers, II, p. 340.

45. *A Hundred Mery Talys*, pp. 7–11.

46. From the 'Intermeane' after Act I; quoted in A. P. Rossiter, *English Drama from Early Times to the Elizabethans* (London, 1950), p. 62.

47. Matner, op. cit. (note 39, above) pp. 230–1, 231.

48. Quoted by Bertram Joseph, 'The Elizabethan Stage and Acting', in Boris Ford (ed.), *The Age of Shakespeare* (Harmondsworth, 1955), p. 150. This admirable essay should be read by anyone interested in the history of theatrical conventions.

49. Southern, p. 236.

50. *Corpus Christi Plays* (11, 12–3, 107).

51. *York*, pp. xxxvii–viii.

52. Prosser, pp. 54–5, notes that any major character would have been played by several persons, and suggests that this should prevent us from speaking of any complete cycle as 'one play'. I think this perhaps posits too modern (and relative) a notion of dramatic unity. The need to divide production responsibility among the guilds was an immediate cause, but it happily suited the needs of the genre and story as well, creating a different but not necessarily inferior kind of dramatic coherence.

53. *Chester*, Diemling, III (112 and note), MS Harl. 2124 has it in Latin some few lines earlier.

54. Ibid. (160 s.d.).

55. *Corpus Christi Plays*, p. 97. See M. Rose, *The Wakefield Mystery Plays* (London, 1961), p. 146.

56. Matner, op. cit. (note 39, above), p. 234 (8).

57. Arnoul Greban, *Le Mystère de la Passion*, ed. Gaston Paris and Gaston Raynaud (Paris, 1878), p. 6 (239–48).

58. Northrop Frye, *Anatomy of Criticism* (Princeton, N.J., and London, 1957), p. 135.

59. See Chester records in Salter, p. 76.

60. *Chester*, Diemling, XXI (199–202).

61. Ibid., XXI (238 s.d.).

62. *York*, XLVIII (175).

63. Representations of the Creation by manuscript illuminators could easily have been translated into stage devices, at once simple and beautiful. See, for example, Margaret Rickert, *Painting in Britain: the Middle Ages* (London, 1954), Plates 92 and 101; also M. R. James (ed.), *Illustrations of the Book of Genesis* (London, 1921), fol. la, lb. Items in Coventry records concerning the 'makyng of iij worldys' and a fee for 'settyng the world of fyer' and for 'kepyng fyre' clearly suggest that the end of the world was shown literally; see *Corpus Christi Plays* p. 102. Also Frank, p. 172, and Anderson, pp. 141–2.

64. John Stevens, 'Music in Medieval Drama', *Proceedings of the Royal Musical Association*, LXXXIV (1958), p. 83.

65. The miniature which shows a performance of the *Martyre de Sainte Apolline*, is reproduced in Gustave Cohen, *Le Théâtre en France au Moyen Age* (Paris, 1928), Vol. 1, Plate III. See Anderson, pp. 74–8.

66. Frank, p. 170.

Donna Smith Vinter   Didactic Characterisation: the Towneley *Abraham* (1980)

An early fourteenth-century vernacular sermon, possibly introduced into a Palm Sunday liturgical procession or more probably, from internal evidence, delivered by a preaching friar 'at, or rather outside, a large secular cathedral',[1] takes as its voice that of Caiaphas, the high priest.[2] Establishing his credibility by assuring his audience that he addresses them under holy auspices, this 'Cayphas' invokes the convention of game that V. A. Kolve has demonstrated to underlie the mystery drama.

> A welsooþ sawe soþlich ys seyd
> Ech god game ys god y-pleyd
> Louelych & lyȝt ys leue
> þe Denes leue and alle manne
> To rede and synge ar ich go hanne
> Ich bydde þt þou ne greue.   [31–6]

Richard Axton has singled out this isolated text as an example of 'the solo "Spiel" of audience address [which] forms a basic type in the folk tradition' of play-acting.[3] If this is an attempt at dramatic impersonation, however, the message of Caiaphas's sermon is both appropriate and inappropriate to his historical character. He is of course a logical choice to explain Palm Sunday, since not merely was he present at the time, but he also himself made the unwitting prophecy of the redemptive effect of Christ's death: 'You do not understand that it is expedient for you that one man should die for the people, and that the whole nation should not perish' (John xi.50). Yet he is not the psychological choice. Historically he was one of Christ's enemies, and the sermon-poem does not attempt to resolve this antinomy by suggesting that he has in any way undergone a conversion: he is in hell.

> Whar fore ich & annas
> To fonge Ihesus of Iudas
>   Vor þrytty panes to paye
> We were wel faste to helle y-wronge
> Vor hym þt for ʒou was y-stonge
>   In rode a gode fridaye.   [49–54]

A significant attempt is made, however, to locate this Caiaphas in time. After he testifies that he was sent to hell for his part in the crucifixion, he continues:

> þe prophecie þt ich seyde þar
> Ich hit seyde þo as a star
>   Ich nuste what ich mende
> Ich wende falslyche jangli þo
> Of me þat wyt naddych no
>   bot as Ihesu sende.   [61–6]

Caiaphas is looking backwards, with a new historical understanding of himself. His voice is thus not what it once was, for he now like an obliging narrator explains the old dramatic irony and explicates the hidden meaning of the words which as an unwitting accomplice of the Redemption he formerly spoke. His sermon develops the full penitential meaning of Palm Sunday for the contemporary Christian. We may say, then, that the historical Caiaphas and a more recent, trans-historical Caiaphas are merged in this game-playing sermon-giver.

It is instructive to check the fragment of a medieval homiletic or liturgical event against the method of later characterisation in the English cycle drama. No such gross, didactically motivated violations of historical verisimilitude or psychological probability are to be found there. The opposite is manifestly true. To a greater or lesser degree, the plays flesh out the biblical outlines of action and character, drawing on centuries of Latin and vernacular expansions and explications of the holy text. Primarily they fill in and develop what might have been the human motives of the agents, investigating, for example, Joseph's probable reactions to Mary's pregnancy.

However, it is also true that the mystery playwright had to confront a modified version of the alternatives presented in the Caiaphas sermon. Looking backwards like Caiaphas on the completed shape of the epic story, he would know his character first of all in a static and morally determined way – as saved or damned, as a victim or personification of some deadly sin or a hero of some virtue or grace of God. Yet he would also know that character as a participant in an evolving story, and would strive, for didactic purposes, to illustrate the psychological motives and moral choices that finally shaped his soul.

It is in this territory, therefore, bounded by fixed pictorial images of God and devil, saint and sinner, on the one side, and a concept of the psychodynamics of the moral life on the other that one can look to test the obligations and the skill of these dramatists in putting words into the mouths of their received characters. Indirect confirmation that these were in fact the terms in which the playwrights were likely to have apprehended their craft comes from the early fifteenth-century treatise on the ten commandments, *Dives and Pauper*. Discussing the first commandment, Pauper explains how holy images are to be used and understood. When Dives observes that saints and apostles did not in real life dress in the glorified way they are often depicted, Pauper replies:

Þat is soth. Þe ryche peynture betokenyȝt þe blisse þat þey been now inne, nought þe aray þat þey haddyn vpon erthe, for manye of hem, as Seynt Pouyl seyȝt, wentyn in wol feble aray, in gotys skynnys, in bauseynys skynnys wol nedy, ful of anguyshe and dyshese: Circuierunt in melotis & pellibus caprinis egentes angustiati afflicti [Heb. ii.37]. Neþeles ymagis stondinge in chirchis mai be considered in two wises, eþir as þei representen þe state of seintis of whom þei ben ymagis as þei lyuyden in þis lijf & so þei ben to be peintid in such maner cloþing as þo seintis vsiden whilis þei lyuyden heere, or ellis þei mai be considerid as þei representen þe state of endeles blisse in whiche seintis ben now, & so þei ben to be painted riali & solempneli, as þe cherubyns þat representiden þe aungelis þat ben in heuene wer maid of gold, Exo. xxv. Neþeles in al such peinture an onest meen, neþer to costlew bicause of þis consideracioun ne to vile for þe former consideracioun, me þenkiþ, is to be kept, for seyntis louyden an onest meen in al her lyuyng.[4]

The middle way that Pauper advocates here between the historically authentic and the hypostatised bears closely on both the problems and the solutions of the medieval playwrights in drawing their characters.

Caiaphas and Pauper suggest that one might investigate modes of characterisation in the mystery plays by testing the voices in which a character speaks. Briefly, to what extent does he speak as he has been hypostatised in the Church's memory – as emblematic of a particular moral stance or determined by a salient action? And to what extent is he given a morally more flexible voice and the process set forth of his response to God's intervention in his life? An expository aside in *Cursor Mundi* betrays the attitude that might keep the comprehensive authorial viewpoint from researching the human emotions of such a figure. The narrator here has in a sense already fused his character Abraham with the way he is remembered in hagiography.

> In that tyme that I of mene
> þe folke was good þe world was clene
> So good beþ hit neuer I-wis
> So mychel of welþe so mychel of blis.
>
> [Trinity MS., 3107–10][5]

It certainly has to be acknowledged that at the root of all the characters in the mystery plays is an epic or narrative conception. That is, the point of view on character and action is inescapably that of a narrator looking back on a completed action and telling his story, as it were, in the past tense. Not only was the playwright constrained in elaborating character by the allegorical and typological weight that the characters' actions had come to bear, but he was equally influenced in his portrayal by the need to make transparent the tropological value of his characters' lives. He followed his narrative sources in accomplishing this goal by reading backwards into their lives the effects of the good or evil actions for which they had earned praise or infamy. Simply, spiritual fate became character, their ends became their beginnings. Because, for example, Judas betrayed Christ and did not repent, he is viewed from the epic perspective as without grace from his very birth: his action is generalised to constitute his character. So does he describe himself in the Towneley manuscript fragment, *Suspencio Jude*:

> My fathers name was ruben, right;
> Sibaria my moder hight;
> Als he her knew apon a nyght
>   All fleshle,
> In her sleyp she se a sighte,
>   A great ferle.

> her thoght ther lay her syd with-in
> A lothly lumpe of fleshly syn,
> Of the which distruccion schuld begyn
>   Of all Iury;
> That Cursyd Clott of Camys kyn,
>   fforsoth, was I.   [7–18][6]

Cursor Mundi perceives Cain in similar terms:

> Þe firste childe þat euer she bare
> Was caym cursed ful of care
> And aftir him I wol ȝou telle
> A blessed childe hiȝt abelle
> Þis abel was a blessed blode
> And caym was þe fendes fode
> Was neuer wors of modir born.   [Trinity ms., 1051–7]

Thus the one-time sinner of the bible has become in tradition the habitual sinner. We can hypothetically reconstruct the mental process at work by noticing that between the informational clause which a Middle English metrical paraphrase of the Old Testament has added to Genesis –

> Soyn Eue consauyd and bare a chyld,
>   Cayn, *that sythyn so cursyd was*
> Be cause of Abell meke and myld
> That he slow with a cheke of a nase[7]

– and the passage from *Cursor Mundi*, 'sythyn' has been deleted.

But there was another way to view this time before the Redemption and the destinies of men – like Cain, Abraham and Judas – that it contained. For in the rich circular and oxymoronic logic of the Christian apprehension of time, the time before Christ and the time after Christ can be seen to correspond. They do so at the hands of the medieval playwrights, who deny themselves few opportunities to suggest the contemporaneity of the stories they tell. St Augustine's commentary on Psalm 148 makes the distinction that is operative in dramatic characterisation, not between the Old and New Testaments, but between the insecurity of this world and the resolution of the next:

... Propter haec duo tempora unum quod nunc est in tentationibus et tribulationibus hujus vitae, alterum quod tunc erit in securitate et exsultatione perpetua, instituta est nobis etiam celebratio duorum temporum, ante Pascha, et post Pascha. Illud quod est ante Pascha, significat tribulationem in quo modo sumus: quod vero nunc agimus post Pascha, significat beatitudinem in qua postea erimus.[8]

[There are two times, one that is going on now, in the temptations and tribulations of this life; and the other which shall be then, in eternal security and joy. For this reason we celebrate two times: the time before Easter and the time after Easter. That which is before Easter signifies our present tribulations; that which is after Easter, our future bliss.]

In these terms, 'our present tribulations' stretch from creation to Doomsday. A sermon for the Nativity in the *Speculum Sacerdotale* describes the Old Testament spiritual climate in terms that are really of perennial application: 'For fro the tyme that Adam hadde synned vn-to the tyme that the saveoure come there was grete discorde be-twix God and man, betwix man and angels, betwyx man and man, betwix spirit and flesche.'[9] This description of alienation from God and yet of a kind of active moral ferment might well apply to the timeless world of a morality play like *The Castle of Perseverance* before its final resolution in spiritual triumph.

In one sense, as far as the purely human characters of the mystery plays are concerned, time is only this Old Testament – unredeemed – time of tribulation and discord. And yet in another sense the audience that watches and that knows the end of the story knows that all time is post-Easter, that time has been redeemed, and that the story of Abraham, for example, must be understood in terms of that victory.

The epic imperative, therefore, does not constrain the playwrights to produce monumentally flat and boring characters, as the plays themselves amply attest. A dramatic interest in conflict and process can still be brought in by the front door. The same tropological imperative which fixes character can also stimulate an interest in the stages or degrees of development by which the world-historical attitude for which we remember the figure matures.

'Attitude' is a key word here and, it seems to me, captures exactly the nature of the medieval playwrights' interest in their characters. As students of the drama are aware, the word is one to which Bertolt Brecht has seminally drawn our attention by his insistence on the centrality of 'gest' to his concept of epic drama.[10] This is not the place to renew the debate on the usefulness of Brechtian theory and practice for elucidating medieval dramatic aesthetic.[11] But I shall defend the heuristic value of 'gest' as a tool for clarifying the relationship between idea and psychology in the mystery playwrights' elaboration of character.

Brecht, of course, intended above all to yoke didacticism and drama, 'to communicate, together, stories and ideas'.[12] Throughout his career as a dramatist and dramatic theorist he emphasised the importance of *story* in the drama, and in maturity he came to see that his opinion was actually shared with Aristotle's *Poetics*: 'according to

Aristotle – and we agree there – narrative is the soul of drama.'[13] He finally even acknowledged that his epic theatre was not such a radical departure from the western dramatic highroad and that the label might even be abandoned, having 'fulfilled its task if the narrative element that is part of the theatre in general has been strengthened and enriched'.[14]

This concern with story led him to advocate a fundamentally episodic and paratactic plot structure in which meanings brought out by the temporal development of an action are supplemented by meanings derived through the possibilities of deliberate comparison of episode with episode, much of this comparison highly visual in nature. By this construction the audience is enabled to 'make comparisons about everything that influences the way in which human beings behave'.[15] What Brecht advocates, therefore, seems to resemble the cumulative double perspective that inheres in the cycle drama: individually focused scenes whose succession also places the spectators at a distanced and superior angle of vision. One critic has even considered the special quality of Brecht's plays to result from the conjunction of a dramatic, immediate perspective and a Marxist 'anticipatory look backward' from a future golden age,[16] the latter an interesting parallel to the much discussed 'Christian perspective' of medieval drama.[17]

But more central to our purpose is Brecht's analysis of what happens within each episode of an 'epic drama'. In his view, a scene should be reducible to its basic gest, the outline or inscape of its consequential action, the verbal and physical postures that capture the essence of the relationships or the attitudes within the scene:

Each single incident has its basic gest: *Richard Gloster courts his victim's widow. The child's true mother is found by means of a chalk circle. God has a bet with the Devil for Dr Faustus's soul. Woyzeck buys a cheap knife in order to do his wife in*, etc.[18]

What Brecht offers, then, is a defense of a 'flat' drama that is also highly dramatic in the sense of 'kinetic'.[19] It is kinetic because it concentrates its energies on this gestic delineation of dramatic encounters between human beings, 'for it is what happens *between* people that provides them with all the material that they can discuss, criticise, alter'.[20] It is flat not only because structurally the scenes are meant to relate laterally, comparatively to one another as well as causally or dramatically building to tension, complication, and final resolution, but also as the result of the writer's concern to portray within each episode the characters' attitudes as they are lucidly externalised in gesture and therefore formally graspable as an image of human interaction. Psychologically shallow, the scene eschews the discovery of hidden depths in a character or his actions as merely distracting. The gest thus describes an embodied message, the conjunction of the kinesis of story and the flatness of idea.

Let us take the Towneley version of the story of Abraham and Isaac to illustrate how a similar apprehension of gest underpins a medieval playwright's drawing of character in action. This rendition of the Old Testament story has met with variable fortune at the hands of critics. Praised by John Gardner for 'the truth and richness of its emotion and the complexity of its thought',[21] it has also been dismissed by Rosemary Woolf as 'inferior'. She maintains:

In the medieval plays of Abraham's sacrifice . . . it is Isaac who is the hero rather than Abraham. Therefore, although according to the literal narrative the point of the sacrifice is the testing of Abraham's faith, the dramatic structure of the plays instead directs our interest and attention to Isaac's consent. . . . The only play in which Isaac's deliberate self-offering is not emphasised, either by a long speech or in the form of a recurrent motif, is the Towneley play, and, apart from some moving lines, this play is in every way inferior to the others.[22]

But besides the fact that all versions can be shown to invest considerable dramatic energy in portraying the choice Abraham is presented with and indeed to suggest that in killing Isaac Abraham would be plunging a sword into his own heart,[23] it is circular reasoning to observe that Isaac is at the center of dramatic interest and to use that observation as a stick to beat the play in which he is not. Moreover, for my purposes here, which are not primarily evaluative, the Towneley play is interesting precisely as it does focus on Abraham, demonstrating how the English cycle drama could mediate between dramatic and narrative, human and heroic comprehension of such a figure.

Cursor Mundi may stand as an example of heroic narrative elaboration on Genesis xxii. Additions to the spare biblical account are chiefly didactic interpolations stressing Abraham's exemplary character. Very little is made of Abraham's emotional dilemma, his ambivalent response to God's command, and there is no imagined dialogue between Abraham and Isaac to bring out the human suffering of the incident. Isaac asks the biblical question about the meaning of Abraham's actions, but he is given no opportunity to recognise what is happening to him before the angel intervenes:

> Sir he seide where shal we take
> þat beest oure sacrifise to make

Siþ we wiþ vs brouȝte noon
God he seide shal sende vs oon
Wiþ þis he stood þe childe ny
And drowȝe his swerde priuely
Þat þe childe were not war
Ar he had done þat char.   [Trinity ᴍꜱ., 3165–72]

But when the mystery playwrights slow down this account in order to elaborate it, they by no means abandon the heroic perspective on Abraham that it implies – the portrait of him as it might have been mounted in a stained glass window. In their suppositions of what Abraham must have thought and said, they never have him ask why God has commanded him to sacrifice Isaac, nor is his dilemma ever what choice he will make. In this sense his character is a static one, anticipating and incorporating the end of his actions in their beginning. Because his obedience is always assumed, the prolonged emotional suspense before the angel's intervention is never about the outcome of the action. But suspense in drama depends on the drawing out of an emotion, in this case Abraham's anguish and Isaac's natural fear, and very rarely on surprise about the issue.

The dramatists do draw out the affective aspect of Abraham's plight, knowing that they must fulfill the dramatic requirement that their characters be men and women like ourselves if we are to respond to their creations in any other than a purely cerebral way. But as the morality drama again testifies, moral and emotional life tend to be identified in medieval dramatic psychology as aversions and affections cluster around or are inspired by moral leanings of the soul. It is in these terms that the playwrights dwell on Abraham's suffering – to make humanly, and therefore morally, accessible both the difficulty and spiritual rewards of his obedience. They are not primarily concerned to imbue a humanly improbable obedience with psychological verisimilitude so much as to make 'a statement of the virtue of obedience . . . in concrete human terms'[24] in the sympathetic exploration of Abraham's and Isaac's feelings.

Any appreciation of Abraham's character must take care to balance these two emphases – the ideal and the human. Woolf, for example, is guilty of overstressing the heroic and typological side of Abraham when she states:

The dramatists . . . show in Abraham reasoned obedience tempered by natural human feeling. Since he is a type of God the Father he can feel no conflict nor judge the situation as a tragic dilemma. The dramatists are concerned only to show what the cost of obedience can be. Just as Noah had done, though in far less tempting circumstances, Abraham instantly expresses obedience to God's will.[25]

It is confusing to assert that Abraham feels no conflict. The dramatists did not have Abraham's typological value so strongly in mind as to forget his humanity, and his natural human feeling makes for a strong emotional conflict in all versions. The interesting critical problem becomes to examine how the structuring of these scenes permits such emotion to be expressed and felt without ever implying that Abraham or we think that his faith and obedience are not secure from the very beginning.

The answer, it seems to me, is to be found in an understanding of how the plays achieve for Abraham a single, externalised gest in which each of his attitudes or responses to God's command completes and gives meaning to the other. Simple though it finally be, this gest is composed by a sophisticated manipulation of Abraham's voices. As might be said of character in dramatic literature generally, the character of Abraham is in reality built up by portraying a series of his stances, vis-à-vis the other characters in the play and vis-à-vis us, the spectators.

In the course of the Towneley play Abraham establishes a relationship with God and also a relationship with the human world around him – Isaac, the servants and Sara, as her offstage presence is suggested by the dialogue. Thirdly, he is constantly presenting or indicating the facts of these relationships to us, the audience, before whom he assumes a stance both expository and intimate. We participate in both the divine and human demands made on Abraham, we know him through them, and we rely on him to demonstrate how they may be reconciled.

The action begins with Abraham's prayer to God to have mercy on unregenerate humanity:

> Adonay, thou god veray,
>   Thou here vs when we to the call,
> As thou art he that best may,
>   Thou art most socoure and help of all;
> Mightfull lord! to the I pray,
>   Let onys the oyle of mercy fall,
> Shall I neuer abide that day,
>   Truly yit I hope I shall.   [1–8]

But, in a common ploy of such speeches, these devotions soon modulate into a monologue on mankind's sorrowful history since Adam's fall, a monologue which also has the intrapersonal quality of meditation or soliloquy. God is now referred to in the third person rather than addressed in the second, and Abraham's direct, confidential relationship is with the spectators:

> Mercy, lord omnipotent!
>   long syn he this warld has wroght;
> Wheder ar all oure elders went?
>   This musys mekell in my thoght.   [9–12]

His subsequent narrative of the 'mervels' [34] of world history to date
is of course a didactic recapitulation for the benefit of the audience,
with such narrative indicators as, of Noah's flood, 'That was a wonder
thyng to se' [28]. But it is a tale also told to involve us in the sadness
that it brings to Abraham's heart. His mood is part of its content:

> when I thynk of oure elders all,
>   And of the mervels that has been,
> No gladnes in my hart may fall,
>   My comfort goys away full cleyn.   [33–6]

The weight of this sorrow stimulates another direct appeal to God:
'lord, when shall dede make me this thrall?' [37], which is again
supported by an expository gesture towards the audience – 'An
hundreth yeris, certis, haue I seyn' [38] – and then by another
indication that Abraham, a man of sorrows, is to be understood as
engaged in a kind of soliloquy: 'Ma fa! sone I hope he shall / ffor it
were right hie tyme I weyn' [39–40].

In short, through a speech by Abraham which seems to depend on
at least three objects of address, the spectators are made both to feel
for Abraham as a man, their representative in this pre-Paschal dark
night of the soul, and to acknowledge his patriarchal powers both to
teach them and to intercede for them. He is an image of authority and
of weakness. As a character he manages both to call forth a certain
empathy from the audience and to impress them with a magisterial
distance.

None of the other versions which open with a 'portrait' speech –
York, *Ludus Coventriae*, Brome and Northampton[26] – establishes such a
sorrowful tone, but they all in a similar way imply the dependency of
Abraham on God. In each of these plays he thanks God for his
blessings, and in particular for Isaac. The audience, aware of what is
coming, must feel an apprehensive pity for him. This is especially
striking in *Ludus Coventriae* where Abraham unknowingly but
explicitly lays out the terms of his future dilemma. To vivify what
Abraham says about their mutual affection, Isaac is present during
his father's opening monologue. When he goes, Abraham prays in one
breath,

> Ther may no man love bettyr his childe
> þan Isaac is lovyd of me
> Almyghty god mercyful and mylde
> Ffor my swete sone I wurchyp þe   [57–60]

and in the next,

> Dere lord I pray to þe Also
> me to saue for þi seruuaunte
> and sende me grace nevyr for to do
> thyng þat xulde be to þi displesaunte.   [65–8]

One can almost catch the narrator behind the ordering of these speeches, saying in effect, 'Abraham loved Isaac, but he loved God more'. In the context of the play, however, the speaker is unaware of their portent and stands dramatically vulnerable. Narrator and character are present but subtly discriminated for the audience to appreciate.

In the Towneley play, God appears above after Abraham's soliloquy to announce, in the conventional monologue of the self-contained Being, that he will test Abraham's faith as a prelude to helping Adam's unhappy descendants. Although this speech does not explain God's arbitrary and, from a human point of view, irrational command, it effectively answers Abraham's prayer that mankind be succoured. It also implicitly adumbrates the Anselmian logic of the redemption: the effects of mankind's bad faith and insufficient love in Adam can only be reversed by Christ's infinitely greater testimony of truth and love.[27] Abraham's sacrifice will not only be a type of this munificent one, but in itself an efficacious act. (This typological understanding is not the one commonly acknowledged – Abraham's sacrifice as a prefiguration of God's sacrifice of his only son and Isaac therefore the proto-Christ – but the play's dramatic logic is more subtle than the schema.)

And so Abraham fittingly answers God in a voice that does not waver. 'All men schall take exampyll hym be / My commawmentys how they schall fulfyll', predicts God in the Brome play [45–6]. Abraham responds to God's command by swearing instant obedience, and in Towneley even praising God as well:

> A, lovyd be thou, lord in throne!
> hold ouer me, lord, thy holy hand,
>   ffor certis thi bidyng shall be done.
> Blissyd be that lord in euery land
>   wold viset his seruand thus so soyn.
> ffayn wold I this thyng ordand,
>   ffor it profettis noght to hoyne.   [74–80]

That the firmness of Abraham's attitude, his resolved 'I will', never alters is what gives the drama its epic quality. The play is flat, as Abraham is flat, because they both demonstrate an unchanging obedience.

But Abraham has a second response. The moment God retires in the Towneley play, Abraham's tone changes: 'This commaundement must I nedis fulfill / If that my hert wax hevy as leyde' [81–2]. This is not a speech which in a more naturalistic or illusionistic convention we would assume that God was not meant to overhear. The play does not pose that issue, concerned as it is with the action on the level of externalised attitudes. Abraham is not concealing his emotional reluctance from God. Rather, the drama now simply adjusts its focus to the human sphere where God's commands must be dealt with. The dramatist wants especially now to establish Abraham as an index of human reaction and to bind the audience sympathetically to him.

Abraham shows himself even more human in imagining, as he now does, how frightened Isaac would be if he knew of God's injunction. Moreover, the full force of that 'if he knew' is deliberately obtained when Abraham immediately calls Isaac to him. Isaac, of course, does not know what his fate is to be and so activates the elementary dramatic irony implicit in the encounter – in that both Abraham and the spectators are aware that Isaac is unaware of the context in which he speaks – when he at once affirms, 'I luf you mekill, fader dere' [95]. In an exchange fuelled by Isaac's innocence and Abraham's foreboding sorrow, Abraham takes up the topic, playing the old gentle game of a parent, 'I wonder how much you love me?' Isaac's answer, 'more then all that euer was maide' [99], the child's fulsome hyperbole, is here calculated by the playwright to wring Abraham's heart. Yet this little scene has also been engineered by Abraham himself, its implicit demonstrator, who now sends Isaac away in order to be 'alone' to tell of his now fiercer agony:

> Now well is me that he is past!
> Alone, right here in this playn,
>   Might I speke to myn hart brast,
> I wold that all were well ful fayn.   [108–11]

He finishes, however, 'Bot it must nedis be done at last' [112]. Abraham has effectively illustrated for us the tenderness of the bond that is about to be snapped. At the same time, the Towneley playwright has also been using this first appearance of Isaac to recall Abraham's own immediate and unstinting testimony of faith in God when God in effect asked 'How much do you love me?' The love and pain of this second father-son encounter are released only within the foregone, epic conclusion of the absolute priority of filial obedience, not to mention of the world's redemption, over 'all that euer was maide'.

In Brechtian fashion the play's main gest or attitude may therefore be reduced to Abraham's enacted statement, 'Although ... , I will ...'. In the Towneley version he asserts,

> This nyght will I begyn my way,
> þof Isaac be neuer so fayre,
> And myn awn son, the soth to say,
> And thof he be myn right haire,
> And all shuld weld after my day,
> Godis bydyng shall I not spare;
> shuld I that ganstand? we, nay, ma fay!   [112–8]

These 'thofs' are paralleled in other versions, for example by the 'ʒit' of *Ludus Coventriae*:

> Now goddys comaundement must nedys be done
> All his wyl is wourthy to be wrought
> but ʒitt þe fadyr to scle þe sone
> grett care it causyth in my thought
> In byttyr bale now am I brought
> my swete childe with knyf to kylle
> but ʒit my sorwe avaylith ryght nowth   ·
> for nedys I must werke goddys wylle.   [89–96]

Mirk's *Festial* also remembers the essence of the story in these terms:

Þen Abraham, þogh he loued his sonne moche and had behest of God to haue gret yssu by hum, neuerþelese he toke hym anon wythout grucchyng, and ʒede to þat hulle, and made Isaak to ber wod to bren hymself wyth.[28]

As John Gardner points out,[29] Towneley is unique in that throughout Abraham's subsequent action of preparation for the sacrifice, his revelation of its victim to Isaac and his gentle but firm refusals to heed Isaac's questions and pleas for forgiveness, he never actually tells Isaac the reason why he must be sacrificed. The withholding from Isaac of this information and his bewildered entreaties intensify the anguish of the encounter, for father and son are shown mutually to cause each other to suffer. In fact, if anything the play's focus is really more on Abraham's agony, not understood by Isaac but with which the audience is therefore all the more vividly complicit. And so as Abraham breaks away from Isaac, 'blinded by tears' as Pollard's note has it, we are once more taken into Abraham's confidence where his overwhelming reluctance to slay his son is fostered by thoughts of his wife's grief and the nearby dramatic image of Isaac lying motionless, terrified but obedient.

The human world in which Abraham lives and the divine world which has so shatteringly intervened are thus both given their due in Abraham's reconciled response, 'Although . . . , I will . . .'. It is these moments which stress his torment, his 'although', that are part of Abraham's unique relationship with the spectators, who are aware that they are much closer to his pain than even Isaac can be. There is in a sense a resolute public Abraham and a privately distressed one. This use of varieties of intimacy is, of course, of the very essence of the dramatic medium. What is specially medieval is the way the playwright refrains from using what we might call these 'levels' of Abraham's response to create an action or a characterisation of doubtful outcome or of psychological depth. He is interested only in reinforcing the outline of Abraham's full dramatic gesture, a horizontal rather than a vertical concern, one might say. In this goal the playwright is aided by his creation, for Abraham himself does not merely 'live' his reactions but like a helpful narrator indicates them to us, the spectators, at key points in the action.

The form of the play, then – Abraham's humanly anguished hesitation which interrupts but does not cancel his heroic and flat determination to complete the task – is its content. His whole response to God's command, 'Although . . . , I will . . .', is in Brecht's sense the play's gest, its clear meaning. That is, finally, why God can forestall the outcome in the Towneley play with the words, 'I know well how he meant' [240].

Of the other versions, Northampton offers the best clue to the dramatic implication of the Towneley God's statement 'I know well how he ment'. In that play God sheds some additional light on his *modus operandi* in subjecting Abraham to such an ordeal. Recalling man's original sin God says,

> But ȝit siþ he haþ displesid me, I haue made proviaunce
>   Þat anodre of his kynd shal plese me ayeyne,
>   Þe which haþe euer be my seruaunt in al manere obseruaunce:
>   Abraham is his name, my man þat cannot feyne,
>   But evyr hathe be trewe.   [9–13]

As an act of moral renewal God will therefore test the foreknown 'trewe' man, setting a gratuitous test whose main object is one of demonstration:

> Of al þing erthely, I wot wel, he loueþ him best;
>   Now he shuld loue me moste, as reson wold and skylle,
> And so I wot well he doþe, I dyd it neuer mystrest.
>   But ȝit, for to preue hym, þe truþe wol I fele.   [18–21]

The same rationale of compensation for sin is present as in the Towneley drama, but this explicit reference to the demonstrative quality of the test is an important clue to what has determined the presentation of Abraham in all versions.

To account for God's foreknowledge of the outcome of a seemingly cruel test, St Augustine explained God's object to be not to prove Abraham's love to himself, but to prove it to Abraham:

... dixit Deus per angelum, *Nunc enim cognovi quia times Deum*; non quia tunc Deus cognovisse intelligendus est, sed egisse ut per Deum ipse Abraham cognosceret quantas haberet vires cordis ad obediendum Deo usque ad immolationem unici filii ...; ut ideo cognovisse diceretur, quia ipsum Abraham cognoscere fecerat, quem poterat latere fidei suae firmitas, nisi tali experimento probaretur.[30]

[... God said by an angel, 'For now I know that you fear God'; not because it was to be understood that God then came to know, but that he made it come about that through God Abraham himself came to know what strength of heart he had to obey God, even to the sacrifice of his only son. . . . So that it was therefore said that God knew because he had made Abraham himself to know, who might well not have recognised the firmness of his own faith if it had not been proved by such a trial.]

Rabanus Maurus perpetuates this interpretation:

Nam et alibi scriptum est: *Tentat vos Dominus Deus vester ut sciat si diligatis eum* (Deut XIII). Etiam hoc genere locutionis, *ut sciat*, dictum est, ac si diceretur, ut scire vos faciat quoniam vires dilectionis suae hominem latent, nisi experimento etiam eidem innotescant.[31]

[For it is also written in another place: *The Lord God puts you to the test that he may know if you love him* (Deut. xiii). Certainly it is stated in this manner of speech, *that he may know*, as if to say, in order to make you know, since the strength of his love lies hidden to man, unless indeed it is made known to him by trial.]

Although none of the plays makes such an idea explicit, their focus on the human cost of the sacrifice Abraham is prepared to make puts at the center of the drama his own emotional recognition of his dependent and loving relationship to God. They all in effect work to demonstrate this bond to Abraham, as must be felt in performance when a powerful force of tension is released in his prayer of joy and gratitude:

> A my lord god to wurchep on kne now I fall
> I thank þe lord of þi mercy
> now my swete childe to god þou kall
> and thank we þat lord now hertyly.   [*Ludus Coventriae*, 233–6]

The Towneley Abraham thanks God with what might appear

unseemly haste, in two lines [271–2], but expresses the same overwhelming emotion by rushing to Isaac's side to share the comfort with his son. And of course the ending of this play has been lost, where presumably we would have found father and son worshipping God together.

This building to Abraham's emotional discovery is what gives the audience a sympathetic entrance to his exemplary behavior, and it is the aesthetic justification for the characterisation of him in the Towneley play as the man who suffers. Abraham's initial prayer is answered as he and the spectators together pass through a symbolic death, both learning its cost and discovering the victory that it wins.

And the demonstration for the benefit of Abraham has also been a demonstration for the benefit of the audience: especially in a didactic theatre must moral disposition be tried by action, illustrated by gest. Medieval moral theology too demanded such an externalising tactic. Although it located moral decisions in the human heart, 'for there is no serteyne pes but to men of good wille',[32] it also held the conviction that these decisions could only be known by their consequences: 'bot for also moche as man seeth not the herte as oure lord Jesu / god and man / dide / and so he may not knowe it bot in party as by tokens withouteforth. . . .'[33]

It is this cooperation of factors in the drama therefore – a fixed conception of character as pre-determined by his subsequent actions combined with a lively awareness of the kinesis of the moral life of an individual, an audience-oriented dramaturgy which calls upon the character to be also partly the narrator of his own actions and emotions, and an attention focused on the significant outline of attitude and action, or attitude *as* action, the Brechtian gest – that enables the playwrights of the cycle plays to create speaking pictures in which didacticism and drama are indistinguishable.

Source: article in *Comparative Drama*, 14 (1980), pp. 117–36.

NOTES

[For short-form references to works, see Abbreviations List, p. 8 – Ed.]

1. Richard Axton, 'Popular Modes in the Earliest Plays', in Neville Denny (ed.), *Medieval Drama*, Stratford-upon-Avon Studies (London, 1973), p. 30.

2. Carleton Brown, 'Caiaphas as a Palm Sunday Prophet', in *Anniversary Papers by Colleagues and Pupils of George Lyman Kittredge* (Boston, Mass., 1913), pp. 105–17. Brown prints the text of the sermon from Sloane MS 2478, fols 43–44v.

3. Axton, op. cit., p. 30.

4. *Dives and Pauper*, ed. Priscilla Heath Barnum, EETS, o.s. 275 (London, 1976), p. 94 (fol. 25v). At the first 'Napeles' I have amplified this quotation by using the main BYL manuscript group reading given in Barnum's notes.

5. *Cursor Mundi*, ed. R. Morris, EETS, o.s. 57 (1874; rpt London, 1961).

6. This quotation is from *Towneley*, XXXII: for *Abraham*, see *Towneley*, IV.

7. *Middle English Metrical Paraphrase of the Old Testament* [233–6], ed. Herbert Kalen (Göteborg, 1923).

8. St Augustine of Hippo, *Ennarrationes in Psalmos*, in *Omnia Opera*, ed. J. Migne (Paris, 1841–49), IV, col. 1937.

9. *Speculum Sacerdotale*, ed. Edward H. Weatherly, EETS, o.s. 200 (London, 1936) p. 5.

10. One of the most useful of Brecht's discussions of this idea may be found in the essay 'On Gestic Music', in *Brecht on Theatre*, ed. and trans. John Willett (New York and London, 1964), pp. 104–6. An early statement by Brecht prefigures the idea in the term 'moral tableau', ibid., p. 38.

11. See the following: E. Martin Browne, 'Producing the Mystery Plays for Modern Audiences', *Drama Survey*, 3 (1963–64), p. 6; Martin Stevens, 'Illusion and Reality in Medieval Drama', *College English*, 32 (1971), pp. 448–64; Merle Fifield, 'Quod Quaeritis, o discipuli', *Comparative Drama*, 5 (1971), pp. 53–69.

12. Browne, op. cit. (note 2), p. 6.

13. *Brecht on Theatre*, op. cit., p. 183.

14. Ibid., p. 281.

15. Ibid., p. 86.

16. Darko Suvin, 'The Mirror and the Dynamo', in Erika Munk (ed.) *Brecht* (New York, 1972), pp. 91–2.

17. See, for example: Hardison, pp. 284–92; John R. Elliott, 'The Sacrifice of Isaac as Comedy and Tragedy', *Studies in Philology*, 66 (1969); George Steiner, *The Death of Tragedy* (London, 1961), pp. 331–3.

18. *Brecht on Theatre*, op. cit. (note 10, above), p. 200.

19. For the traditional opinion which saw in the narrative organisation of medieval drama an essentially undramatic flatness, see: Madeleine Doran, *Endeavors of Art* (Madison, Wisc., 1954), pp. 372–3; George Kernodle, *From Art to Theatre: Form and Convention in the Renaissance* (Chicago, 1944), p. 14.

20. *Brecht on Theatre*, op. cit., p. 186.

21. John Gardner, *The Construction of the Wakefield Cycle* (Carbondale, Ill., 1974), p. 58.

22. Rosemary Woolf, 'The Effect of Typology on the English Medieval Plays of Abraham and Isaac', *Speculum*, 32 (1957), pp. 813, 816.

23. Cf. the discussion of the 'self-sacrifice' of Abraham in Gustav Dreifuss, 'The Figures of Satan and Abraham', *Journal of Analytic Psychology*, 17 (1972), pp. 171.

24. Arnold Williams, 'Typology and the Cycle Plays: Some Criteria', *Speculum*, 43 (1968), p. 684.

25. Woolf, op. cit., p. 147.

26. For other versions of *Abraham*, see: *York*, x; *Ludus Coventriae*, v; Brome and Northampton in *Non-Cycle Plays*; *Chester*, Mills, iv.

27. St Anselm, *Cur Deus Homo*, i, xxv, in J. Migne (ed.), *Patrologia Latina* (Paris, 1844–64), cLVIII, cols 399–400.

28. John Mirk, *Festial: A Collection of Homilies*, ed. Theodore Erbe, EETS, e.s. 96 (1905; rpt New York, 1973), p. 77.

29. Gardner, op. cit. (note 21, above), p. 63.

30. St Augustine of Hippo, *De Trinitate*, iii, ix, in *Opera Omnia*, op. cit. (note 8, above), viii, col. 884.

31. Rabanus Maurus, *Commentarium in Genesium*, iii, iii, in *Patrologia Latina*, op. cit. (note 27, above), cvii, col. 566.

32. *Speculum Sacerdotale*, op. cit. (note 9, above), p. 9.

33. *The Mirrour of the Blessed Lyf of Jesu Christ*, trans. Nicholas Love, ed. Lawrence F. Powell (Oxford, 1908), p. 124.

Rosemary Woolf   'The Wakefield Shepherds' Plays'   (1972)

. . . It would, of course, be a mistake to read the Chester shepherds' play as though it were similar in design to the plays of Flood where the surface realism is founded on solid religious allegory. It is immediately clear that there is no typological characterisation in the shepherds' play: the shepherds are not Cain nor the boy Isaac. Whilst there are hints at religious allegory that cannot be ignored, the dramatist's main purpose is obviously to depart from the previous stylisation of character, which might seem to show the Christ-Child born into a world aesthetically removed from the contemporary and familiar. Sin and virtue are reduced to size; Gartius is a dutiful shepherd, but his attitude to life, which resembles Autolycus's 'I care for nobody no, not I', is as indicative of an unredeemed world as is the lazy shepherds' preoccupation with food and stupid self-esteem. All therefore equally need the unrealistic conversion to priestly orders that is brought about by their recognition of the Christ-Child.

In so far as there is any plot in the Chester shepherds' play before the biblical story begins it lies in the wrestling-match: in other words the author has invented action by drawing upon the common sports of the peasant community. The Wakefield Master proceeds differently in that briefly in the *Prima pastorum* and lengthily in the *Secunda pastorum* he dramatises the type of plot that in France was the subject of independent farces. The secular plot of the *Prima pastorum* is that of the Three Wise Men of Gotham, which now survives only as a story in jest-books.[1] Within it, however, as a short inset, is the story of Moll and her pitcher, which is the subject of a lost French farce,[2] and which a little later Gil Vicente, the Portuguese dramatist, incorporated in a Nativity play composed for performance on Christmas Day.[3] The plot of the *Secunda pastorum* now has only a close parallel in a late eighteenth-century ballad,[4] but in type it resembles the plot-type involving ingenious trickery which is used in many French farces, including the most famous of them all, *Maître Pathelin*.[5] Plots of this kind were evidently floating ones, appearing in exempla, novellae, jest and farces.[6] There is thus no way of telling precisely from what source or genre the Wakefield Master borrowed his plots, but . . . he in all likelihood knew the genre of the French farces, and must therefore have been conscious that he was adapting the material of farce to a religious context.

The interesting point is of course the manner in which these plots are adapted to their new context. The theme of the Wise Men of Gotham as also of Moll and her pitcher is foolishness and make-believe. These elements the Wakefield Master heavily underlines, using the second of the plots to illuminate the first. According to the jest, two shepherds quarrel over the issue of whether one of them may bring back the flock of sheep that he is about to buy over a certain bridge, part of the foolishness consisting in the fact that these sheep are as yet unbought. In the *Prima pastorum* this is elaborated: the first shepherd who has lost his sheep through *rot*, has scarcely any money to buy more sheep at the fair to replace them, yet in the quarrel he asserts that he will bring back a hundred sheep – a provocatively large number – and, further to enrage the other, acts the part of driving them on, 'Go now, bell weder'. The entire illusoriness of the situation is emphasised by the third shepherd, who sets himself up as a wise man and tells the story of Moll and her pitcher to illustrate their folly: the shepherd's hundred sheep are thus as much in the imagination as Moll's dreams of wealth, all lost when she dropped the pitcher. The third shepherd, however, is just as foolish, for to make a more telling illustration, as in the jest, he empties his sack of meal, which he then demonstrates to be as empty of meal as the heads of the other shepherds are empty of wits. At this point the author of *A Hundred Mery Tales* draws a moral: 'This tale showeth you that some man taketh upon him to show other men wisdom when he is but a fool himself.' The Wakefield Master at the same point introduces the character of Garcio to draw the same moral:[7]

Now god gyf you care, foles all sam;
Sagh I never none so fare, bot the foles of gotham.
Wo is hir that yow bare, youre syre and youre dam,
had she broght furth an hare, a shepe, or a lam,
    had bene well.
Of all the foles I can tell,
ffrom heven unto hell,
ye thre bere the bell;
    God gyf you unceyll.

Like the Chester Gartius, Garcio is in the employ of the shepherds, and his attitude to them is yet more pointedly contemptuous. It is again he who is looking after the sheep, and when he invites the shepherds to come and see for themselves how flourishing they are, the shepherds prefer to sit down and eat the grotesque abundance of provisions that they have brought with them. After that they are weary, and when the angel appears, far from watching their sheep they are fast asleep. The turning point in the *Prima pastorum*, however, comes much sooner than in Chester, for, once the angel has announced the Nativity, the shepherds become learned men, as they are in the *Ludus Coventriae*, and they interpret the angel's message in the light of the prophecies. The third shepherd is even able to quote the prophecy of Virgil's shepherd in the fourth eclogue in Latin. Their salutations of the Christ-Child and their offering of simple gifts mark the climax of their devotion. As in Chester, there is no psychological continuity between the foolish, lazy, grumbling shepherds of the first part and the devout worshippers of Christ in the second.

More than half of the long *Secunda pastorum* is taken up by the plot of the sheep-stealing, which is contrived as a burlesque of the Nativity and antecedent themes.[8] It is as though the world before the Incarnation contained not types of the Redemption but deformed adumbrations, or, to put the matter with less seriousness, the whole episode could be considered a witty pretence at typology. There are, to begin with, clear equivalences between the plot and characters of the sheep-stealing episode and the sequence of the annunciation to the shepherds and the visit to the Christ-Child which follows. Mak (the sheep-stealer) tells the shepherds when they wake up of the supposed birth of his child; in the cottage when the shepherds arrive are Mak, the hen-pecked husband and ostensible father, his wife who has been feigning the pains of childbirth, and a lamb in the cradle. Then in the unmasking episode (which the dramatist must have invented since it is the nature of the plot that the trickster should be successful),[9] the fraud is discovered through the third shepherd's kindly wish to give the child a present: the affectionate term, 'Lytyll

day starne' by which he refers to him, is of course later used of the
Christ-Child and is a title proper only to Him.

The Mak episode has been compared to the sub-plot of Elizabethan
drama or the anti-masque.[10] The parallel with *A Midsummer Night's
Dream*, for instance, is interesting but there is the important difference
that, whereas the antics of Bottom and his companions follow upon
the serious love story, the sheep-stealing in the *Secunda pastorum*
precedes the religious matter that it buffoons. The placing of the Mak
episode is in fact important, for, whilst in one way it provides a type or
rather, like the Fall of Man, an anti-type of part of the Redemption, it
also pretends to be in itself a fulfilment of earlier typological patterns.
This is particularly clear in the relationship of Mak and his wife. Mak
in his cottage is obviously a debased version of St Joseph, and like St
Joseph he sees himself in the role of the unhappily married man. But
his wife, who is the leading partner in the fraud, to some extent casts
herself as the second Eve. Thus whilst Mak complains about the
sufferings in an evil marriage, his wife is given to *sententiae* about the
virtues of women: 'Yit a woman avyse helpys at the last' (her
comment upon the good advice that she has given about the trick) or
'Ffull wofull is the householde / That wantys a woman'. Other figures
should similarly be seen in a twofold relationship: for instance, the
sheep purporting to be a baby anticipates the baby who was
symbolically a lamb, but it is also a grotesque fulfilment of the lamb
offered by Abel and the sheep offered in place of Isaac.

The Wakefield Master has set the story of Mak within a fairly
straightforward treatment of the three shepherds. In contrast to the
other plays these shepherds are genuinely suffering from oppression,
truly poor and actually looking after their sheep: they are not feasting,
wrestling or quarrelling. It is not that their complaints are to be taken
entirely straight. The second shepherd who has a monstrously ugly
wife ('She is browyd lyke a brystyll, with a sowre loten chere') and who
warns the young men in the audience against marriage, is the
undignified husband of anti-matrimonial satire; whilst the first
shepherd who complains that taxes and the oppression of the
gentlerymen have made him too poor to cultivate his land is speaking no
more than a half-truth. But, while the shepherds' explanations of
their predicament are slightly comic and rebound upon themselves,
that they live a life of hardship is plain, and their sufferings cast light
upon the sufferings of the Christ-Child. At the end of the play the
second shepherd says compassionately of the Christ-Child, 'he lygys
full cold'; but earlier in the play the effects of cold had been described
in realistic detail: the shepherds complain that their feet are numb in
their boots, their eyes water, and their hands are chapped. To

emphasise the Christ-Child's sufferings through cold was, as we have seen, part of the meditative tradition, but it is only in this play that the actual sensations of cold are made alive to the imagination by describing them with such unelevated precision. Since the shepherds in this play deserve through their sufferings the comfort of the revelation of the Nativity, it is fitting that their speeches of adoration should be the most moving; and, whilst this is partly through their poetic quality, it is also partly because they are rooted in the earlier presentation of the shepherds: they do not have to become entirely new and different men before they worship the Christ-Child.

Whilst the shepherds in the *Secunda pastorum* are treated with more evident devotional purpose than in the *Prima pastorum* or Chester, the play is undoubtedly dominated by the Mak episode, and it is therefore not surprising that the author only supplied it as an alternative.[11] For, though the episode has a religious orientation lacking in the comic sequences of, for instance, the Rouen *Nativité*,[12] it could easily be missed by the unsophisticated, who would then understand it only as simple farce. To understand it this way would of course be great impoverishment: though quite well done, the dramatisation of the fraud is much inferior to the urbane *Maître Pathelin*, and of course crude beside Chaucer's narrative comedies. But, when understood within a religious framework its subtlety and literary self-awareness are reminiscent of Chaucer's manner and one wonders whether it may have been written for performance on some special occasion when it would have a fitting audience.

The dramatist's tone in his treatment of the shepherds in the *Secunda pastorum* is less ambiguous than in the *Prima pastorum* or in Chester, though at the point at which the third shepherd appears to accuse the others of being niggardly employers, it is less certain, and, as in the *Prima pastorum*, the shepherds are not guarding their sheep but asleep when the angel appears. In general it can be said that the authors of these three plays have put the shepherds into a morally intolerable position. In historical terms they are small farmers rather than shepherds, and their employment of a boy or groom to look after the sheep on their behalf is a practical arrangement since it leaves them with the necessary time to cultivate the arable land which they would own or hold on lease. But within the play this customary and sensible arrangement becomes morally odd, for it is necessary that the men should be called shepherds and that they should be abroad at night. But since their night wanderings serve no practical purpose, it gives them a vagabondish air and leaves them with time for senseless quarrels and feastings. It is now very difficult to recapture how this would have seemed or exactly what the authors' intentions were. In

Wakefield, which had grown prosperous on the cloth industry, many of the audience must also have been small farmers, and the fact that the shepherds are unnamed (or have *ad hoc* names), in contrast to Cain, who is the historical Cain first and a farmer second, must have increased their appearance of contemporaneity. Furthermore, whilst some of their grumblings about the oppression of the rich must be taken with a certain reserve (they have a slightly archaic air in that they would fit the social conditions of the late fourteenth century more appositely than those of the mid-fifteenth) and they perhaps reflect equally upon the grumbler and the rich, the complaints about maintained men are evidently genuine satire of contemporary abuse. It is clear, however, that there is no idealisation of poverty as the meditative tradition would have required: the dramatists had as sharp an eye as Langland for the portrayal of the grumbling and lazy poor. All the elements of social satire, fantasy and farce yield in every play to the idealised picture of the adoration of the Christ-Child, and this contrast is evidently the primary purpose of the design of the plays. But nowadays it is impossible to recapture the precise mood of the first part of the contrast, for whereas in other plays the key to their understanding lies in other forms of literature, in these it fairly certainly lies in life. . . .

SOURCE: extract from chapter 'Nativity Plays, II' in *The English Mystery Plays* (London, 1972), pp. 188–93.

NOTES

[Reorganised and renumbered from the original. For short-form references to works, see Abbreviations List, p. 8 – Ed.]

1. *A Hundred Mery Tales*, ed. P. M. Zall (Lincoln, Neb., 1963): no. 24, pp. 87–8; *The Mad-Men of Gotham*, in W. C. Hazlitt (ed.), *Shakespeare Jest-Books* (London, 1864), III, pp. 4–5. For the identification of these analogues, see H. A. Eaton, 'A Source for the Towneley *Prima Pastorum*', *Modern Language Notes*, XIV (1899), pp. 265–8.

2. Cf. L. Petit de Julleville, *Répertoire du théâtre comique en France au moyen âge* (Paris, 1886), pp. 311–12.

3. Gil Vicente, *Obras completas*, I (Lisbon, 1942), pp. 127–63; cf. N. Shergold, *History of the Spanish Stage* (Oxford, 1967), p. 41.

4. *Sir Walter Scott's Minstrelsy of the Scottish Border*, ed. T. F. Henderson, IV (Edinburgh, 1902), pp. 389–94; cf. the appendix by E. Kölbing in *Towneley*, pp. *xxxi–xxxiv*.

5. A. Banzer – 'Die Farce Patelin und ihre Nachahmungen', *Zeitschrift für neufranzösische Sprachen und Literatur*, X (1888), pp. 93–112 – included the Mak episode in his survey of imitations of *Pathelin*. There is undoubtedly a family

resemblance between the sheep-stealing episode and *Pathelin* and other French farces which turn upon fraudulent tricks of similar style.

6. The story of Moll, for instance, is common in collections of *exempla*; cf. G. H. Gerould, 'Moll of the *Prima Pastorum*', *Modern Language Notes*, xix (1904), pp. 225–30.

7. It has been ingeniously suggested by A. C. Cawley – 'Iak Garcio of the *Prima Pastorum*', *Modern Language Notes*, lxviii (1953), pp. 169–72 – that Iak Garcio and the third shepherd are identical. This theory, which if true would require substantial emendment of the text, rests largely upon literary judgement: Cawley speaks of 'the absence of any good reason for bringing him [Garcio] into the play at all', whereas on our interpretation his presence is part of a carefully conceived design.

8. See, for instance: M. M. Morgan, ' "High Fraud": Paradox and Double-Plot in the English Shepherds' Plays', *Speculum*, xxxix (1964), pp. 676–89; F. J. Thompson, 'Unity in The Second Shepherds' Tale', *Modern Language Notes*, lxiv (1949), pp. 302–6.

9. Cf. T. M. Parrott, 'Mak and Archie Armstrang', *Modern Language Notes*, lix (1944), pp. 297–304, who rightly points out that in all versions of the trick oath, the deception is successful. If the trickster is to be punished, as in *Pathelin*, this is brought about by some further twist in the plot.

10. Cf. H. A. Watt, 'The Dramatic Unity of the *Secunda Pastorum*', *Essays and Studies in Honor of Carleton Brown* (New York, 1940), pp. 158–66.

11. The modern custom of referring to the two plays as the *Prima* and *Secunda pastorum* is misleading in its implication that both were performed, which is a very unlikely hypothesis. The MS incipits refer to the *Prima* as *Pagina pastorum* and the *Secunda* as *Alia eorundem*, which bears out the more probable hypothesis that the *Secunda* was provided as an alternative.

12. *Mystère de l'Incarnation et Nativité de nostre Sauveur et Rédempteur Jésus-Christ, représenté à Rouen en 1474*, ed. P. Le Verdier, ii (Rouen, 1885), pp. 101–34, 147–58, 192–201.

Eleanor Prosser   The *Woman Taken in* *Adultery* Plays   (1961)

In the three extant plays on the Woman Taken in Adultery (unfortunately the Towneley play is lost), we . . . find that didacticism and drama are not in conflict. On the contrary, doctrine was precisely the tool needed to make a simple and unfocused narrative into an exciting drama, as well as vivid sermon.

The biblical account (John viii.3–11) could only loosely be

considered a story of repentance. In an attempt to trick Jesus, the scribes and Pharisees bring an adulteress before Him, hoping that He will reject the old Mosaic law of stoning and thus condemn Himself. Jesus stoops, writes on the ground, speaks his charge – 'He that is without sin among you, let him first cast a stone at her' – and again writes. Stricken in conscience, the Jews depart, and the woman is left alone with Jesus. There is no indication that she repents. He asks who has condemned her and her only words are, 'No man, Lord'. Jesus answers, 'Neither will I condemn thee. Go, and now sin no more'. The major point in the account is the lesson derived from the behavior of the Jews: let not the guilty condemn. However, the dramatic emphasis soon shifted from the Jews to the woman herself.

The Chester and York plays are little more than direct renditions of Scripture, but in both there are significant additions. Again, as in the Chester treatment of Cain, we see the playwrights' awareness of the homiletic nature of the mystery cycles. They knew that the audience was so trained by the Church that it would respond to any story, whether recounted or enacted, as an *exemplum*. Just as a playwright must make clear why Cain could not repent, so he must make clear why the adulteress could be forgiven.

The Chester version, in play XII, *The Temptation*, is the earlier and the more successful. At the close of the scriptural sequence recounted above, the Woman is given a speech that at once clarifies her state as a penitent and returns attention to the basic scriptural theme:

> A! lord, blessed must thou be,
> that of mischefe hath holpen me!
> from hence-forth synne I will flee,
> and serue thee, in good fay.
>
> ffor godhead full in thee I see,
> that knoweth all workes that done be;
> I honour thee, knelinge on my knee,
> and so I will doe aye. [265–72]

There is no contrition, no confession – merely a brief statement of purpose to amend. The first stanza, then, together with her act of kneeling, could serve as signs to the audience of completed repentance, a reminder that Christ does not forgive an unrepentant sinner. The second stanza returns the focus to the main line of action: Jesus's knowledge of the hidden sin of the Jews. The play closes as an expositor summarises the action to point the scriptural theme: let not the guilty condemn.

Whereas the Chester playwright solved his problem without destroying unity, the playwright of York XXIV, *The Woman Taken in*

Adultery, got caught between the two themes. As a result, he rides an uneasy seesaw. Here the warning sign to the audience is unmotivated. The Chester Woman's free promise to amend is consonant with Jesus's exhortation 'Go and sin no more'. At York, however, Jesus is given a line signalling full remission of sin – 'Of all thy mys I make the free' [68] – although the Woman has had no lines indicating penitence. Her answer is merely a brief speech hailing Him with love for saving her from sin and shame. Thus the York addition is forced in.

Moreover, in contrast to the Chester version, the Woman's speech at York closes on thanks for remission of sin. Attention has been shifted to a repentance theme that is, at best, incidental to the main plot. The playwright realised this fact and added a colloquy between Jesus and His disciples: first, the disciples praise Him for His mercy to the guilty; second, Jesus repeats the scriptural lesson about the Jews. Though the two themes are loosely allied, each has a different focus. As a result, the effect of the play, both thematically and dramatically, is two-fold.

Both plays reflect a growing concern with the doctrine of repentance, and one might expect to find the secondary theme gradually becoming dominant. The York play is transitional, an inept job of splicing. In the Hegge *Woman Taken in Adultery*, play xxiv, the playwright entirely refocuses the action upon the greater of the themes – the road to Salvation – and by so doing creates an exciting and effective religious drama.

In an opening exhortation by Jesus, the scriptural theme is carefully made subordinate to the repentance theme, and the audience is prepared for an 'everyman' drama – not history, but a personal experiencing of the mystery of Redemption. The sermon opens with 'Man for thi synne take repentaunce' [1], and includes many of the familiar doctrinal points: no sin is too great; for love of man, Christ paid his ransom; for love of Christ, man should turn to Him and ask mercy. Again and again, 'Only ask mercy' is stressed. And just as Christ will have mercy, so man must have mercy on his neighbor. Thus the theme of the Jews is made subordinate and the unified theme established: man need only *ask* for mercy.

The play opens at the point of attack as the Pharisees and scribes plan to trick Jesus by some false quarrel. They are not introduced as out-and-out villains; rather, they believe Jesus to be a hypocrite and want to open the eyes of the people by shaming Him. Suddenly 'Accusator' rushes across the *platea*. In high glee, he reports that a young man has just entered the chamber of a local harlot. What sport it would be to rout out the adulteress, to catch her in the act! The Jews are delighted with the idea. It will be great fun (note the gradual revelation of their evil); moreover, they can use her to trick Jesus. They eagerly rush to the house and break down the door.

Their timing has been perfect, for a young man frantically rushes forth – his breeches in hand and boots untied. Among the rare fragments of approval accorded the Hegge cycle, this is one of the bits often cited. Gayley, for example, commends it as a welcome comic interpolation. Such rare humor as 'the unaffected precipitancy of the young man taken in adultery who escapes *Calligis non ligatis et braccas in manu tenens* . . . must have leavened the general didacticism of the cycle with some flavor of actuality'.[1] In his view, the comic was merely stuck in as 'relief'. Others approve the scene as sensationalism *qua* sensationalism: again, as a welcome relief, breaking the general pall of tedium. Actually, the action – and it was undeniably comic – serves four specific dramatic purposes.

First, we now can have absolutely no doubt about the Woman's guilt. In the other plays she is merely posited as an adulteress, a pawn in the lesson on the Jews. Here she is made very real, and we anxiously await her entrance. Second, by revealing the character of her partner in sin, the playwright subtly suggests the character of the Woman. There is no sympathy for the young man. He is defiant and violent, and exits cursing. Moreover, he is comic, and thus we cannot pity him because of any misplaced sentiment. The writer has eliminated any possibility of true young lovers pathetically trapped in a clandestine affair, and when the Woman enters, we expect an abandoned whore. Third, the scene further reveals the character of the Jews. The young man is wild, and, dagger in hand, he threatens to kill anyone who stops him. The picture is ludicrous if we remember that he is awkwardly juggling breeches and dagger and tripping over bootlaces. The only danger is that he will go sprawling, but the Jews curse him and retreat. Obviously, they are cowards as well.

Fourth, and most important, the young man's exit does not serve as 'relief' in any sense of the word. The comic scne is a grotesque device to heighten contrast. When the Woman enters, as she does almost immediately, the serious is a violent shock. The Jews stand outside her door, taunting the 'stynkynge bych', hailing her forth in the vulgar language of the street:

> Come forth thou stotte com forth thou scowte
> com forth thou bysmare and brothel bolde
> com forth thou hore and stynkynge bych clowte
> how longe hast thou such harlotry holde.

> Com forth thou quene com forth thou scolde
> com forth thou sloveyn com forth thou slutte
> we xal the tecche with carys colde
> A lytyl bettyr to kepe thi kutte.   [145–52]

Against the comic scramble of the young man, against the orgiastic
rhythm and prurient sadism of this obscene chant, there could be no
greater contrast than the Woman's entering speech.

> A mercy mercy serys I yow pray
> Ffor goddys loue haue mercy on me
> of my mys-levynge me not be-wray
> haue mercy on me for charyte.   [153–6]

Her first words are a frantic plea for mercy for the love of God – and
we in the audience remember the opening exhortation of Jesus. If a
man but ask mercy, grant it in charity, for 'lyke as he is thou art
vnstabyl' [27].

But we have seen the full degradation of her accusers gradually
revealed, and, as we expect, her plea is in vain. 'Aske us no mercy it
xal not be' [157]. She squirms, twists, frantic with hysteria: she offers
to bribe them; she begs that, since she must die, she be executed
immediately, not killed in public where she will shame her friends
(she grasps at straws, trying to avoid stoning). In her final plea the
author carefully uses terminology that will keep the contrast between
man's vengeance and Christ's mercy clearly in mind: 'Stondynge
[Since] ye wyl not graunt me grace . . .' [169]. Her accusers only grow
more malicious, and the violence reaches a peak as, threatening to
beat her, they drag her across the *platea* to Jesus.

Again the contrast is striking. The noisy cluster of struggling
figures crosses to Jesus's station, where He stands, silent, writing on
the ground. The Jews self-righteously accuse her. Jesus writes on.
And immediately – before Jesus has said a word – the Woman has a
speech of full repentance.

> Now holy prophete be mercyable
> vpon me wrecch take no vengeaunce
> Ffor my synnys Abhomynable
> In hert I haue grett repentaunce
> I am wel wurthy to haue myschaunce
> Both bodyly deth and werdly shame
> but gracyous prophete of socurraunce
> this tyme pray yow for goddys name.   [209–16]

She is clearly made a penitent by the use of key points of doctrine: she
asks mercy (recall the theme and her first words to the Jews); she

confesses her guilt; she is contrite (note the pertinent 'in hert'); and she admits that she fully deserves her punishment. Her accusers' repeated demands for stoning, which follow immediately upon her speech of penitence, are thus put in true perspective.

Now Jesus speaks the scriptural admonition ('He that is without sin among you'), the Jews flee in shame, and Jesus and the Woman are alone. At this point, traditionally, Jesus should ask where her accusers are, but before He speaks the Woman repeats her plea, making her confession and contrition even more concise and adding a statement of amendment.

> Thow I be wurthy ffor my trespas
> to suffyr deth ab-homynable
> Yitt holy prophete of your hygh grace
> In your jugement be mercyable
> I wyl nevyr more be so vnstable
> O holy prophete graunt me mercy
> of myn synnys vnresonable
> With all myn hert I am sory. [257–64]

After this, Jesus asks about her accusers. She answers that they have fled in shame and again prays that He take compassion on her sorrow. Jesus asks who has condemned her. She answers, 'No one' – and once more puts herself at His mercy. Following each line of traditional dialogue, then, a speech of repentance is inserted. The result is not mere repetition. Rather, the completed act of repentance is spread out, eliminating the need for one long speech; and with each new point or each restatement of a point already made, the depth of her contrition grows. That is, the concept grows in the minds of the audience as more and more associations are awakened. Today we miss the fact that each speech is slightly different. But even if we are unaware of the progression in doctrine, the repeated pleas are highly effective dramatically. Jesus asks about her accusers but they no longer matter to her. She refuses to be deflected, and again and again, with mounting urgency, she prays for grace. The role would be a choice one for an actress even today.

Now Jesus speaks the traditional words of release and of exhortation to sin no more, and the Woman has a short prayer of thanks for 'grett grace' and of purpose to amend. The play closes as Jesus turns to the audience and briefly restates the theme: man need only ask for mercy and, if he is truly contrite, God will forget His wrath. An interesting reflection of the close tie between the audience and the drama is the fact that the actor drops his role as Jesus and closes with a prayer for the audience and for himself, as a member of it.

> Now god that dyed ffor all mankende
> saue all these pepyl both nyght and day
> and of oure synnys he us vnbynde
> hyghe lorde of hevyn that best may.   [293–6]

Thus the drama comes full circle as the citizens of the town also ask mercy.

To echo Salter, by the name of all that's mysterious, this surely is drama! And not because of an extraneous bit of comic sensationalism. The Hegge *Woman Taken in Adultery* is an exciting play because an imaginative artist developed a homiletic argument in dynamic action. Judged solely on technical grounds, the play is highly effective drama. Moreover, it is effective not in spite of its religious purpose, but precisely because of its almost perfect fusion of form and idea – of drama and doctrine.

SOURCE: ch. 6, 'The Woman Taken in Adultery', in *Drama and Religion in the English Mystery Plays* (Stanford, Cal., 1961), pp. 103–9.

NOTE

1. C. M. Gayley, *Plays of Our Forefathers* (New York, 1907), pp. 191–2.

Clifford Davidson   The Realism of the York Realist and the York Passion (1975)

A gifted amateur dramatist, whom scholars now identify as the York Realist, contributed eight complete plays (XXVI, XXVIII–XXXIII, XXXVI) to the Passion series in the York cycle.[1] These plays were probably written about 1425 to replace earlier plays[2] and thereby were designed to enhance the dramatic effectiveness of the Passion series. This remarkable playwright's style was recognised long ago by Charles Mills Gayley, who spoke of his work as belonging to a 'realistic period' and noted that the dramatist himself is distinguished 'by his observation of life, his reproduction of manners, his dialogue, and the plasticity of his technique: whether in presentation of the comic, or of the tragic and horrible, aspect of his narrative'.[3] Much more recently, J. W. Robinson has presented evidence to illustrate more specifically the nature of the playwright's concern for detail, for dramatic use of dialogue, and for realistic presentation of human behavior. Robinson's article, published in *Modern Philology* [in 1962–63] ...[4] is an important piece of criticism, though now perceptive scholars will recognise that there are many ways in which his interpretations need qualification. Most urgently, we need a more precise understanding of the York Realist's *realism*, especially since this term as used in literary criticism has come under increasing attack. Furthermore, any such understanding of the realism of this dramatist must then be balanced with an evaluation of the traditional and iconographic elements in his plays, for if we may borrow some words by Rosemary Woolf out of context, these scenes 'should not be . . . explained solely in terms of realism'.[5]

It is my contention that the York Realist, like many of the skilled artists and painters who were his contemporaries, believed primarily that he was giving new life to the symbolic pictorial narrative of the Passion. From the standpoint of aesthetic experience as well as of philosophical inquiry, the previous century had meant increased interest in *particulars*. While the painters and the York Realist perhaps did not completely share the thoroughgoing phenomenalism of the nominalists at Oxford, they nevertheless no longer tended to follow the older practice of eliminating the arbitrary individual detail from their work. Seemingly irrelevant details often provide the means through which an illusion of reality may be impressed upon the imagination of the audience. This tendency in art is perceptively identified by Erwin Panofsky as a 'modernistic rebellion' among northern artists who craved 'for volume and space as opposed to two dimensional patterns, for light and color as opposed to line, for concrete, particularised reality as opposed to abstract, generalised formulae'. This rebellion, according to Panofsky, is 'comparable indeed to the *philosophia moderna* of those nominalists who found the quality of real existence only in things "individual by virtue of themselves and by nothing else" '.[6] There is a turning to immediate experience, to detail, to individuality as sources for an affective art.

Thus, for example, in the York Realist's trial of Jesus before Herod, the monarch is individualised and at the same time is given a wonderful liveliness through his indecorous behavior, which is set forth in a unique manner. The king even invents his own language – '*Seruicia primet* such losellis and lurdaynes as þou, loo! / *Respicias timet*, what þe deuyll and his dame schall y now doo?' [XXXI, 236–7] – as he combines being offended (at Jesus's disregard for his royalty) with attempting to have fun at the Savior's expense. Thereby Herod, who assumes that Jesus is mad or a fool, illustrates the ultimate foolishness of those who reject salvation. In this way the York Realist, like the Northern [European] painters, brings together such elaboration of specific detail in a realistic manner with the system of symbolism and meaning with which certain scenes in Christian history had been imbued for centuries. In the work of the York Realist, iconography and realistic detail co-exist.

Another instance which illustrates the relationship between detail and meaning occurs when the York Pilate's attendant urges him to 'wasshe whill þe watir is hote' [xxxiii, 443]. Robinson is properly impressed by this detail. 'Other medieval dramatists (and more learned exegetes, too)', he insists, 'would not normally concern themselves with the temperature of the water in which Pilate washed his hands – the allegorical meaning, perhaps, but not the tempera-ture.'[7] Yet in both philosophy and art of the early fifteenth century, the tendency of the age was toward depiction of such seemingly irrelevant details as the concern of Pilate's attendant and the temperature of the water. As Meyrick H. Carré notes: 'One tendency of the new school of thinkers was the inclination to seek for reality in the individual thing in preference to the universal entity. Associated with this trend there appeared increased emphasis upon intuition or sensory apprehension in knowledge.'[8] While painting could never concern itself directly with such a sensory experience as the tempera-ture of the water, artists too were capable of showing great sensitivity through visual details. Thus in a miniature in the splendid *Hours of Catherine of Cleves*, dated 1430–40, the attendant pouring water over Pilate's hands is also shown to be very solicitous of his master's comfort, for he has a towel draped over his shoulder in readiness. In spite of the fact that both his hands are presently occupied with pouring the water, he will have the towel ready for Pilate when he needs it.[9] Surely the towel in the book of hours is the visual analogue of the beadle's care about the temperature of the water in the play. However, in neither instance is the symbolic meaning of Pilate's act of washing abrogated. Indeed, the vividness with which the symbolic act is dramatised is designed to draw attention to it and hence to underline its meaning.

Hence the York Realist in his concern for vivid details succeeded in filling out scenes and broadening his understanding of characters. For example, even a villain such as Judas appears in the York Passion as something more than a 'flat' character or symbolic representation of man's evil nature. Of course he is still the archetypal betrayer, but he is also a human being who *feels* envy and greed, then unfortunately reacts in such a manner that he will *act* on the basis of such feelings. Therefore he is plunged convincingly into tragedy and finally into a despair that will lead him ultimately to suicide and damnation. The scene in which Judas meets Caiphas and Annas will curiously take place at Pilate's mansion, to which he has trouble gaining entrance. The Janitor decides that he does not like Judas's appearance – 'Thy glyfftyng is so grymly / Þou gars my harte growe' [xxvi, 157–8] – and the lively exchange which follows draws heavily upon particularising details. Even after the betrayer had indicated that he has come to keep 'youre dugeperes' from possible injury [181–4], the Janitor with the typical officiousness of a bureaucrat must first consult with his lords before Judas may be let in. Then, utilising material from the popular sermon tradition, the York Realist gives Judas a *motive* for betraying Jesus. He wants the thirty pence he would have stolen had the precious ointment brought by Mary Magdalene been sold,[10] for as treasurer for the disciples he had made a practice of diverting a tithe to himself: 'The tente parte þat stale I ay still' [138].

Finally, in a triumph of realism, the York Realist arranges his portrayal of Judas's betrayal agreement so that this character is made to play a role which considerably narrows the distance between him and his audience's experience. Like a merchant, he offers a bargain to the trio Caiphas, Annas and Pilate. They begin questioning Judas closely about his offer in preparation for haggling over the price, and finally Pilate asks, 'Now, what schall we pay?' [xxvi, 229]. Of course they agree at once that Judas's price, only thirty pence, is indeed a great bargain. The eagerness with which they accept Judas's fee gives a moving impression of something most valuable sold for a ridiculously small price. (In the early fifteenth century, thirty pence [30d.] was not, of course, the infinitesimal sum that it would be today. York records show that in 1397 Robert Paton was paid two pence for working two days as a carpenter to repair a pageant. In 1501, when the York Realist's plays were still being played in York, the Coventry accounts show that two shillings sixpence [i.e., 30d. – Ed.] were paid for five yards of blue buckram.)[11] The horror and foolishness of what Judas is doing are not suppressed, but rather the dimensions of the drama are expanded so that the scene with its bargaining may more effectively capture the attention of the members of the audience, many of whom were themselves merchants. A new scope has surely been added to the story of Judas's betrayal through the introduction of realistic details which make the biblical event come to life as a dramatic experience designed to affect a particular audience.

The extent of the York Realist's attention to realistic detail and his use of such detail may be judged by comparison of the York scene in which Judas sells his Lord with the same scene in the Montecassino Passion. In the earlier liturgical drama from Montecassino, Judas merely makes arrangements for the betrayal in thirty lines of formalised verse.[12] The Montecassino Judas, who is purely evil, is not individualised as a character, and his actions seem to be little more than what would minimally be needed to transfer the scene of betrayal from the miniature in the *Codex Purpureus Rossanensis* or from the sculpture at Modena Cathedral into dramatic form.[13] The betrayer simply appears at the synagogue where he meets Caiphas, explains that he too sees Jesus as a threat, and offers to betray him. Caiphas responds with the money. While the aesthetic impact of a drama such as the Montecassino Passion can be very powerful when presented before an audience prepared to appreciate it, it is not popular drama and would surely have seemed lifeless and overly simplified to a crowd of flourishing tradesmen in a fifteenth-century city such as York. The York Realist, on the other hand, deliberately sets out to flesh out the bare story and to make it come to life. He is interested in the appearance of reality – an appearance of reality which will help to bring home to the audience the truths told in the story. Thus his work may be compared to the accomplishments of the Northern painters whose experiments with perspective assisted them to create a life-like quality.

In contrast to the liturgical drama and earlier vernacular plays, the work of the York Realist stands apart from that medieval aesthetic which, informed by *philosophical* realism, had encouraged the artist to attempt to capture the essential meaning of a scene or event without drawing upon unnecessary or unwarranted details. For this dramatist, as for nominalists such as William of Ockham, the key to reality is through 'immediate present experience'.[14] However, the York Realist refused to discard traditional iconography in his depiction of scenes from the Passion of Christ. He wants to have it both ways: he utilises particulars since these give life to the play, while at the same time, as will be shown below, he also relies heavily on traditional ways of communicating through iconography. Hence he inventively presents the sensual Procula amorously flaunting herself in Play xxx, though she is actually included in the drama for reasons which extend beyond realism for its own sake. She had been present in dramatic representations of this scene as early as the Montecassino play,[15] and now in the work of the York Realist represents individualised human concupiscence allied with external forces of evil against the Savior of men. Through his realism, the York Realist is able in this scene to elaborate upon the bare outline of events as told in their source, the apocryphal *Gospel of Nicodemus*. The elaboration is not frivolous, for it is designed to present the story with a greater sense of vividness and to relate its meaning more effectively to the lives of the members of the audience. Hence the York Realist sets out to create a more emotionally charged drama than had hitherto been presented at York. The final effect of this drama is not to focus attention only on the particulars, but rather to point to the truths of the Christian story as these are to be made applicable to the lives of all those who look upon the spectacle.

In the York Passion, the work of the Realist combines both its realism and its iconography toward producing a desired emotional response. The culmination of the Passion sequence in the event of the Crucifixion is orchestrated so that its appeal will be both to the head and the heart – but especially to the heart. Essentially this is not a drama written to support the optimistically rational theology of St Thomas Aquinas, but rather it shows more evidence of affinity with the popular exposition of Christianity as expounded by the Franciscans. The York Realist would seem to believe that religious drama ought not to stop when it has told its audience '*about*' the Passion; he wishes further to draw them into 'direct acquaintance with' a re-enactment of the historical events.[16] Thus apprehended, it involves a series of events toward which no viewer could be expected to remain coolly unemotional.

The high point of the Passion series comes, of course, at the Crucifixion, which received perhaps its most vivid prose description in St Bonaventure's contribution to the *Meditaciones vitae Christi*, a composite Franciscan work that directly or indirectly influenced the York Passion. In the *Meditaciones*, which was translated into English by Nicholas Love as *The Mirrour of the Blessed Lyf of Jesu Christ*, each detail of Christ's treatment is given minute scrutiny.[17] Such careful attention to particulars also marks the plays by the York Realist. Unfortunately, except for a few lines at the beginning of Play xxxiv, the Shearmen's 'Christ Led up to Calvary', neither the approach to the site of the cross nor the *Crucifixio Cristi* (Play xxxv) are by the York Realist.[18] When the Realist picks up the story in the excellent *Mortificacio Cristi* (Play xxxvi), he is able to do full justice to this final drama in the Passion series. Here at last is the end of the process which was begun when Judas agreed with the high priests and Pilate to betray his Master. At the beginning of the play, Christ is hanging on the cross, but not as an isolated figure. The whole scene of the Crucifixion is here spread out before the audience, with spoken dialogue and visual effect combining to create a vivid spectacle designed to impress itself upon more than the mere intellects of those who are watching.

The *Mortificacio Cristi* opens with the terrible liveliness of those who have condemned Christ and who now stand by to watch and jeer. Pilate, concerned about his sovereignty, speaks first: those who rebel against his authority may see what their reward will be if they will only look at the men on the three crosses. He is, nevertheless, sorry about Jesus who has been crucified because of the malice and envy of the high priests rather than because of any guilt. The two priests, however, have no such doubts: they mock Jesus for the statements he had made and for the miracles he had performed before his arrest. 'If þou be funne / Þou be Goddis sonne, / We schall be bonne / To trowe on þe trewlye', the sneering Caiphas tells him [xxxvi, 101–3]. But Christ on the cross *is* the suffering Son of God who patiently looks out from the perspective of the cross upon a turbulent and sinful world. The contrast between his enemies and the dying Lord emphasises the pain of hanging on the cross as well as his forgiving attitude toward all men. Everyone is implicitly invited to become acquainted with the physical suffering of his crucifixion, which he is enduring so that all men who are repentant may be rescued from their misdeeds.[19]

The presentation of realistic detail in the Crucifixion thus, as in the fashion of showing this scene among the fifteenth-century Northern painters, performs the function of stimulating an emotional response. The realism does not have its end in itself, but in the desire to make the audience *feel* what is being presented in the playing area, for only when the Passion and Crucifixion are felt can the iconography of the tableau have its desired effect. Such an effect would have been inconceivable, of course, in the early Christian centuries, the period when Christian iconography was slowly being developed as the sacred science of luminous and talismanic figures which point to the divine realities.

Only after the eleventh and twelfth centuries did the Crucifixion generally become the soteriological center of the Christian story.[20] Thus for the new order founded by St Francis of Assisi in the thirteenth century the cross was available as the emotionally-charged symbol of forgiveness which represented what was believed to be the central fact of Christian existence. By the end of the Middle Ages, as Émile Mâle has noted, *suffering* had replaced *love* as the central term which might be used to describe what is at the heart of religious art.[21] Christ, by suffering on the cross, presents men with the gift of salvation; as Jesus tells them in the York play, 'On roode am I ragged and rente, / Þou synfull sawle, for thy sake, / For thy misse amendis wille I make' [xxxvi, 120–2].

The anguish that is evidenced in the York *Mortificacio Cristi* is completely missing from earlier representations of the Crucifixion such as the early fifth-century ivory in the British Museum which contrasts the death of Judas on the left with a stylised Christ on the cross at the right. Similarly, Anglo-Saxon ivories showing the Crucifixion stress neither the pain of this most inhumane form of execution, nor the visible effects of the Flagellation.[22] All this had long changed by the time of the completion of the fourteenth-century window which depicts the Crucifixion in the West end of the nave (south aisle) of York Minster. In this window, given to the Minster by Thomas de Beneston in 1338, Christ's arms are now painfully extended upward to the points on the cross where they are attached. Two Roman soldiers, one of whom seems particularly cruel in appearance, guard the victim, whose suffering appears here to be much in evidence. Yet the York Minster window does not reach the level of affective display that was achieved in the fifteenth century in, for example, the *Hours of Catherine of Cleves*, which contains a miniature[23] representing the Savior, his wounds still bleeding pro-fusely, at the time of his death. On each side of Christ, the two thieves, brutally tied with their arms stretched over the cross-pieces of their crosses, frame the central event, which is calculated to touch the emotions through its pathos. Even some of the angelic and animal figures in the borders of this illumination show sorrow or anguish.

The final stage in this development must surely be the central panel of the Isenheim Altarpiece by Matthias Grünewald early in the sixteenth century. At his death, the body of Grünewald's Christ is literally covered with sores from the ill treatment he has received. Thorns stick in his flesh from the crown of thorns which is still in place on his head. The terror of death as the termination of suffering is here mirrored in a manner that goes far beyond what must have been presented in the York *Mortificacio Cristi*. Nevertheless, the York play, too, was obviously in performance tending in the direction of such realism as we find in Grünewald. The scene depicted on stage must have been emotionally stirring.

The York Passion indeed is in the spirit of the *Meditaciones*, for it urges the Christian spectator to utilise the scenes which he sees as an aid to meditation. He is to meditate on the overwhelming affliction felt by the Lord. He is to have 'hyhe compassion' for the torments which he witnesses, for he will see Christ 'so tormented / that fro the sole of the foote, into the hyhest parte of the hede / there was in hym none hole place, ne membre withoute passion'.[24] As Joseph of Arimathea says in the *Mortificacio Cristi* when he approaches to take down the body, 'All mankynde may marke in his mynde / To see here þis sorrowfull sight . . .' [xxxvi, 365–6].

The audience's attention is carefully focused on the event and its significance when the York Realist dramatises the Reproaches of Christ to mankind (' Þus for thy goode / I shedde my bloode, / Manne, mende thy moode, / For full bittir þi bliss mon I by' [xxxvi, 127–30]. The Reproaches or *improperia* as they appear in the York play are, of course, liturgical in origin; as a form they are, in fact, 'extremely ancient', having appeared in England as early as the *Regularis concordia* in the tenth century.[25] In the hands of the York Realist, their conventional form actually increases their dramatic effectiveness, for at this point the audience receives more powerfully than elsewhere the impression that this is what it was actually like when Christ was crucified.

Similarly traditional in the *Mortificacio Cristi* is the Virgin's lament or *planctus*. Like the Reproaches, the *planctus* is characterised by the York Realist's concern for appropriateness and tact. Rosemary Woolf notes (p. 265) that the 'author allows the elaborate and harmonious stanza form to impose a shape upon the content of distress, so that the Virgin does not appear distracted and uncontrolled but has rather the reserves of dignity befitting her pre-eminence'. The Virgin remembers how 'full louely' Christ 'laye / In [her] wombe' [xxxvi, 133–4], and bewails the fact that this day she must be separated from him. She thinks of Jesus on the cross as 'þis blossome so bright' which is unhappily grafted to the tree of the cross, and complains that she has been smitten by a 'swerde of sorowe' [137–8, 159]. At the moment of his death, she tells him that her 'harte is heuy as leede' before she comes suddenly to the realisation that he is no longer living [262–4].

The striking emotionalism of the York Realist's presentation of the death of Christ is continued in his depiction of the Deposition. This indeed appears to be a scene that is intentionally sensational. Joseph of Arimathea and Nicodemus slowly and sorrowfully take down Christ's body after the suffering is completed.

> Be-twene vs take we hym doune,
> And laie hym on lenthe on þis lande.   [xxxvi, 378–9]

Yet, in contrast to the Wakefield Crucifixion's presentation of the mechanics of the Deposition, little attention seems to be wasted on such matters here. If Nicodemus pulled the nails which hold the body to the cross, as in the painted glass from St Saviour's Church, York (now in All Saints, Pavement), in an English alabaster now in the Victoria and Albert Museum,[26] and in the miniature in the *Très-Belles*

Heures de Notre Dame,[27] there is at least no indication for him to do so in the text of the York play, though in performance he may well have performed this function. The emphasis is on the manner in which the two men take Christ from the cross and lift him down between them, as in another alabaster sculpture also in the Victoria and Albert Museum.[28] As they lift him down, Joseph and Nicodemus show off the broken body of Christ and form a tableau which, if we may judge from the painting by Roger van der Weyden[29] or the miniature in the *Belles Heures* of the Duke of Berry,[30] must have been felt deeply by sensitive members of the audience. This way of presenting the Deposition goes back in the West to the *St Albans Psalter*, where apparently for the first time the 'incident itself . . . furnishes only a kind of substructure or pretext for the staging of a grandiose lamentation over the crucified Saviour in the Golgotha setting. Nicodemus seems to be less concerned with carrying out his work and completing the descent of the deceased than with presenting Christ's body and holding it in a position which affords to the mourners the best opportunity of showing their affection and grief'.[31] In the York *Mortificacio Cristi*, the mourners are members of the audience who have been drawn into the sorrow which is represented, for the Virgin Mary and others have left the stage at line 273. The scene is designed to bring tears to all eyes.

The handling of this scene in the York play has something in common with the details and the feeling of a passage in the York *Hours of the Cross* from a manuscript book of hours in the York Minster Library.[32] 'At þe tyme of euen-sang þai tok hym fro þe rod . . .', the text explains, then continues until the passage culminates in a statement linking the Deposition with one's own moral condition ('lord for þat ilk schame þat þu doun was tane / lat neuer my saul wit deydly syn be schlayne'). Following is the *incipit* of the Latin text from which the English is translated – a text that concludes with the *Adoramus te* which contains the *Responsorium* 'Qui[a] per sanctam crucem tuam redimisti mundum'.[33] In the York *Hours*, of course, the emotional effect of the scene would be dependent upon the quality of the individual's piety, while in the York play the paradox of a death designed to give men life is dramatised fully in an attempt to insure that all might not fail to feel the sorrow and meaning of this event. It is to be noted, for example, that once Joseph and Nicodemus have laid the body on the ground, they then raise it up once more before they take it to the grave which Joseph has prepared. Here is an opportunity for a visual effect beyond the reach of the ritualised York *Hours* – and it is an opportunity which is not missed.

As the vehicle for visual display, the York play's Deposition scene cannot be unrelated to another display of Christ's wounded and crucified body – the representation of the Trinity in the visual arts sometimes known as the *Corpus Christi*. Indeed, the York Realist has arranged for the showing of Christ in a pose similar to this familiar design as it was seen in a number of painted glass windows at York.[34] Furthermore, the Realist's purpose in showing off the body cannot be dissociated from the religious purpose behind the Corpus Christi windows,[35] nor is it unrelated to the Feast of Corpus Christi, which, of course, provided the occasion for the York cycle of plays. At the Deposition scene, therefore, the York Realist has in a sense summed up the entire Passion and Crucifixion. Thus was the audience reminded of the centrality of the sacrifice of Christ on the cross within the pattern of Christian history.

Of particular importance is the way in which the body of Christ is represented in the Corpus Christi subject, for the figure in painted glass may be taken as evidence of details the medieval audience expected to see. The unmutilated glass from St John's, Ousebridge, now in the north transept of York Minster, presents a Christ who has endured much suffering. The wounds are vividly depicted, and also include bleeding bruises all over his body from the flagellation ordered by Pilate. In any case, as noted above, it cannot be denied that both the windows and the Deposition scene in the play allow for showing Christ's body in approximately the same posture and generally for the same purpose.

The audience in the Deposition scene of the *Mortificacio Cristi* is clearly being invited to meditate on the whole meaning of Christ's Passion. Basic to the York Realist's understanding of the event is, of course, his belief that Christ in his Passion and Crucifixion gave his body for the salvation of the world. Such also is the message of the liturgy of the Feast of Corpus Christi. This liturgy contains many references implicitly linking Christ's body, sacrificed for men, with the continuing practice of the sacrifice of the Mass.[36] The showing of the body in the *Mortificacio Cristi* by Joseph of Arimathea and Nicodemus as they take him from the cross and again after he has been laid upon the ground may thus be regarded as a realistic presentation of the sacrificed divine body – a body which is present in essence in the host at Mass and which is also associated with the forgiveness of sin. The doctrine which links Christ's sacrifice with divine forgiveness is very clearly illustrated in a fourteenth-century illumination from a Carmelite Missal: the trinitarian *Corpus Christi* is seen above, with a priest baptising an infant below – i.e., performing a rite associated with removing the stains of sin.[37] And as John Thoresby, archbishop of York, wrote in 1357, 'the sacrament of the auter [is] cristes owen bodi in likeness of brede . . .' ('Eucharistia est unum corpus Christi', the official Latin proclaimed).[38] The play, like the rite, takes men back to the original event, but unlike the liturgical observance, it does so by encouraging men to use their imaginations when they place themselves at the foot of the cross on stage. Instead of asserting, as in the rite of the Eucharist, that the *reality* but not the appearance of the Crucifixion is present, the drama plays with appearances. Stage illusion is thus consciously manipulated so that people may see the appropriate details – bleeding hands, feet and side as well as the bloody marks of the torture and flagellation which Christ had previously suffered. The York Realist invites his audience to suspend its disbelief and thereby to discover experientially what it would have been like to look upon the historical event. This could never have been the case in the earlier liturgical drama where there is no attempt to combine realism with the symbolic action of the play.

The importance of a meditational experience of the kind encouraged by the York Realist in his contribution to the York Passion had been stressed in the *Meditaciones vitae Christi*, which (in Nicholas Love's translation) insists:

who soo desyreth with thappostle Poule to be Joyeful in the crosse of oure lord ihesu crist / and in the blessid passion / he must with hely meditacion theryn for the grete mysteryes & al the processe therof yf they were inwardly consydered with alle the inward mynde and beholdyng of mannes soule / as I fully trowe they shold brynge that beholder in to a newe state of grace. For to hym that wold serche the passion of oure lorde with all his herte and alle his inward affection there sholde come many deuoute felynges and sterynges that he neuer supposed before. [Sig. N3^v]

The Franciscan emphasis on an existential acquaintance with the realities of Christian life is here, and it helps to explain the York Realist's purpose in presenting realistic detail, carefully observed manners, and more psychologically accurate characterisation than previous drama in the Middle Ages. As an artist, he seeks to drive home the meaning of the Passion in a way that impresses itself upon the whole man and not merely his intellect. The result is an art which, like the preaching of the friars, turns realistic detail[39] to emotional effect – with a tendency to induce tears.

The realism of the early Netherlands painters was similarly able to bring tears to the eyes of pious beholders. A cursory look at a book of hours such as the *Hours of Catherine of Cleves* provokes admiration for the workmanship, the vivid and lifelike colors, the ingenuity of the borders, and so forth. But closer examination of the subjects illustrated in the illuminations demonstrates the extent to which the book exploited themes designed to make man remember his fallen nature and his mortality. The representations of the Passion, however, show a single unfallen man who *for our sake* allows himself to be sacrificed as an innocent victim. Here is an art designed to be wept over. Panofsky thus comments (1:2) with good reason that

there was a peculiar piety which seemed to distinguish the *intent* of Flemish painting from the more humanistic – and, in a sense, more formalistic – spirit of Italian art. . . . Michelangelo is said to have remarked, to the dismay of the saintly Vittoria Colonna, that Flemish paintings *would bring tears to the eyes of the devout* [italics mine], though these were mostly 'women, young girls, clerics, nuns and gentlefolk without much understanding for the true harmony of art.'

As the inheritors of Italian Renaissance formalism in art, we thus need to adjust our understanding of the realistic painters of the North, who did not strive for their realism for realism's sake.

The work of the York Realist also demonstrates that there was in the period between 1415 and 1430 in the North of England a similar concern which in intent wished to provide assistance to the imaginations of the men in the audience in order to bring them to an existential understanding of and relationship with the divine realities presented through the paradoxical *true illusion* of the play. This is a conclusion not contradicted by the external evidence. The Franciscan William Melton is generally given credit for successfully encouraging in 1426 the separation of the plays from the Feast day of Corpus Christi.[40] However, in spite of his concern that men not lose 'the benefit of the indulgences graciously conceded by Pope Urban IV to those who duly attended the religious services appointed by the canons', he nevertheless also specifically approved the playing of the plays. As the entry in the *York Memorandum Book* notes, Melton, 'coming to the city, had in several sermons recommended the Corpus Christi play to the people, affirming that it was good in itself and highly praiseworthy' ('affirmando quod bonus erat in se et laudabilis valde').[41] As a man trained in theology at Oxford (the *York Memorandum Book* identifies him as 'sacre pagine professor') and known as an effective preacher ('verbi Dei famosissimus predicator'),[42] Melton most likely would have approved of any drama intended to bring an audience to an aesthetic experience and understanding of the Passion. Surely Melton was a man less interested in 'the true harmony of art' than in inspiring people to respond existentially and emotionally to the scenes presented by the plays. Thus it is more than likely that he would have been sincerely respectful toward an art form that encouraged pious tears.[43]

The conscious purpose of the York plays was thus not to provide psychological release into dramatic game or entertainment. Indeed, such a response would seem to come under the categories condemned by the friar Melton when he spoke of 'strangers visiting the city at the festival not for the play alone, [who] joined in revellings, drunkenness, clamour, singing and other improprieties'.[44] The plays, however, were deliberately designed to impress feelingly upon the people the spectacle of the Christian story.

The realism of the York Realist may be defined, therefore, as a tendency intended to bring to life the meaning of the Christian story as formerly presented through a more strictly symbolic art. It is part of a larger impulse toward perspective and illusion in the arts of the fifteenth century, and it even in a sense looks forward to Coleridge's 'willing suspension of disbelief' as a dictum applied to the way the audience is meant to respond to the action on stage.[45] Audiences are encouraged to look upon the play as a meditational aid and, through the use of their imagination, to acquaint themselves experientially with the important facts and historical events of Christianity. In this drama, the symbolism of the earlier periods is not rejected, but is enveloped in a presentation that seems at once more modern and more emotional than anything which had come before.[46]

SOURCE: article in *Speculum*, 50 (1975), pp. 270–83.

NOTES

[Reorganised from the original. For short-form references to works, see Abbreviations List, p. 8 – Ed.]

1. These plays are written in skilful alliterative verse which has been studied by J. B. Reese, 'Alliterative Verse in the York Cycle', *Studies in Philology*, 48 (1951), pp. 639–68. To the plays in the Passion series may be added plays I, XVII, XL, XLV and XLVI. Reese, however, speaks of 'one or more authors' responsible for these plays (p. 668). But Craig (p. 228) prefers to believe in a single author at least for the alliterative plays in the Passion series.
2. The York Realist's work had not been added to the cycle in 1415 when Roger Burton, the town clerk, made up a list that describes the plays as they were then. Nor do they appear in a second list by Burton, most likely drawn up about 1422. See *York*, pp. *xix–xxviii*.
3. C. M. Gayley, *Plays of Our Forefathers* (New York, 1907), p. 158.
4. J. W. Robinson, 'The Art of the York Realist', *Modern Philology*, 60 (1962–63), pp. 241–51.
5. Woolf, p. 400. She is referring specifically to the scenes in which Judas argues with the Janitor and in which Pilate appears with Procula.

6. E. Panofsky, *Early Netherlandish Painting* (Cambridge, Mass., 1953), I, p. 35.

7. Robinson, op. cit., p. 243.

8. Meyrick H. Carré, *Phases of Thought in England* (Oxford, 1949), p. 145.

9. See John Plummer (ed.) *The Hours of Catherine of Cleves* (New York, n.d.), Plate 20. The towel, however, also appears over the shoulder of the attendant in an alabaster fragment at the Louvre. See W. L. Hildburgh, 'English Alabaster Carvings as Records of the Medieval Religious Drama', *Archaeologia*, 93 (1955), p. 80.

10. See *John*, xii. 3–6.

11. Extracts from T. Sharp, *A Dissertation* and R. Davies, *Extracts from the Municipal Records of the City of York*, in Wickham I, pp. 351–2.

12. Sandro Sticca, *The Latin Passion Play* (Albany, N.Y., 1972), p. 66.

13. See Robert R. Edwards, 'Iconography and the Montecassino Passion', *Comparative Drama* 6 (1972–73), pp. 275–9.

14. Meyrick H. Carré, *Realists and Nominalists* (Oxford, 1946), p. 110.

15. Sticca, op. cit., pp. 72–4.

16. Quotations from St Bonaventure, *The Mind's Road to God*, trans. George Boas (New York, 1953), p. *xviii*. The Franciscan principle of preferring 'direct acquaintance with, rather than descriptions of [things]' is extremely important for an understanding of the York Realist.

17. See the earliest edition of Nicholas Love's translation of *Meditaciones vitae Christi*, published by Caxton in 1486, beginning at sig. N3ʳ.

18. We have no way of knowing why the York Realist failed to replace the *Crucifixio Christi* with his own superior work. The extant play is, however, a very interesting example of dramatic art. Christ is fastened to the cross while it is on the ground. As in a famous painting by Gerard David, in a miniature in the *Holkham Bible Picture Book*, ed. W. O. Hassall (London, 1954), fol. 31v., and in an alabaster carving noticed by Hildburgh, op. cit. (note 9), p. 83, Plate XVIID, the cross in the York play has the holes for the nails drilled too far apart [XXXV, 107]. Christ's body must be stretched so that it will fill the cross. See also Kolve, pp. 188, 306.

19. Prosser, passim, stresses the late medieval doctrine of penance as central to the plays contained in the medieval cycles. The connection between the vernacular plays and the forgiveness of sins might be very close indeed, for, as Salter notes (p. 39), a statement on the cover of a play book containing the Chester plays (Harley MS 2124) links the promise of indulgences by the Bishop of Chester and by the Pope with attendance at the plays.

20. See Sticca, op. cit., pp. 42–5. In the earlier Middle Ages, the Resurrection had been the central event of the Christian story.

21. Emile Mâle, *Religious Art from the Twelfth to the Eighteenth Centuries*, English translation (1949; repr. New York, 1958), pp. 112–13.

22. *Catalogue of Early Christian Antiquities*, No. 291, reproduced in Ernst Kitzinger, *Early Medieval Art in the British Museum*, 2nd edn (London, 1955), Plate 7; John Beckwith, *Ivory Carvings in Early Medieval England* (Greenwich, Conn., 1972), figs 47, 67–72.

23. Plummer, op. cit. (note 9, above), Plate 26.

24. Trans. Love, op. cit. (note 17, above), sig. 07^r.

25. Hardison, pp. 131–2. See also the use of the Reproaches in *The Northern Passion*, ed. F. A. Foster, EETS, o.s. 145 (London, 1913), Pt. I, p. 191.

26. Hildburgh Collection A.15–1946.

27. *Très-Belles Heures*, fol. 216 (Panofsky, op. cit. [note 6, above], fig. 39). See also *Meditaciones*, trans. Love, op. cit., sig. Pl^r.

28. Hildburgh Collection A.49–1946. The Virgin, of course, is absent from the York Deposition.

29. See Gertrud Schiller, *Iconography of Christian Art* (Greenwich, Conn., 1972), 2, fig. 563.

30. Berry *Belles Heures*, fol. 149^r.

31. Otto Pacht, *The Rise of Pictorial Narrative in Twelfth-Century England*, (Oxford, 1962), pp. 30–1.

32. MS XVI, K, 6: *Hours of the Cross*, printed in *The Lay Folks Mass Book*, ed. T. F. Simmons, EETS, o.s. 71 (London, 1879), p. 86.

33. Ibid., pp. 83, 86.

34. See John A. Knowles, *Essays in the History of the York School of Glass-Painting* (London, 1936), p. 170.

35. The *Corpus Christi* subject was more or less the trademark of the prestigious Corpus Christi Guild, which was founded specifically for 'the praise and honour of the most sacred body of our Lord Jesus Christ', Knowles, op. cit., pp. 169–71.

36. See *Breviarum ad usum insignis ecclesie Eboracensis*, 1, Surtees Society, 71 (1880), cols 529–52.

37. Margaret Rickert, *The Reconstructed Carmelite Missal* (Chicago, 1952), Plate V.

38. *Lay Folks Mass Book*, p. 118–19.

39. On the realism in the sermons of the Franciscans, see G. R. Owst, *Literature and Pulpit in Medieval England*, 2nd edn (Oxford, 1961), pp. 23–41.

40. Chambers, II, pp. 400–1; Craig, p. 205; Wickham, 1, p. 122n.

41. Latin text in *York Memorandum Book*, ed. Maud Sellers, Surtees Society, 125 (Durham, 1915), 2, p. 156. Few scholars have noted the importance of this passage as a sign of approval of the plays.

42. Ibid.

43. Hysterical tears, such as the 'boisterous weeping' of Margery Kempe, was another matter; Melton refused to admit her to a series of sermons at Lynn unless she could control herself and refrain from such a distracting display.

44. *York Memorandum Book*, op. cit., 2, p. 156.

45. While I am convinced that what Glynne Wickham calls the 'emblematic tradition' continued to exert an immense influence in English drama well into the seventeenth century, so also am I convinced that we ought to look earlier in English drama for the beginnings of a practice that utilises in a conscious way the idea of the play as illusion designed to cast its spell over an audience willing to 'suspend disbelief'. For the York Realist, the play does not participate in Eternal Reality except as it casts its spell over the audience and

brings them to an 'acquaintance' with the facts of the Christian story as they must have taken place in history.

46. Research for this paper was supported by a Faculty Research Fellowship from Western Michigan University.

Stanley J. Kahrl   Of History and Time
(1974)

. . . Writing of the historical patterns of thought in Shakespeare's history plays, O. B. Hardison [has] proposed that: 'After all the qualifications based on order of composition, departures from the larger pattern and ambiguities of Tudor political theory have been accepted, the plays remain something more than a haphazard collection, and their unity is that of the medieval religious cycles.'[1]

Yet Hardison's proposal that the conception of history contained in the cycle plays of the Middle Ages could be a major influence on the later histories flies in the face of the received doctrines as to the sources and influences acting on the *genre* of the history play which supposedly makes its first appearance in the mid-sixteenth century. E. M. W. Tillyard admitted that the moralities had exerted 'a pervasive influence on all Shakespeare's history plays', but felt that even they had 'not had a great deal to do with the ideas about history' on which the later history plays were built.[2] What the actual influence of the moralities was he did not spell out. It is probable he had in mind some such influence as that proposed subsequently by Irving Ribner. Ribner – who specifically rejected the cycle plays as influencing the later histories because of their purportedly disorganised episodic structure[3] – proposed that 'The morality play structure was a perfect vehicle for executing the true historical function, for the morality was didactic and symbolic, designed to communicate idea rather than fact, built upon a plot formula in which every event was related to the others so as to create a meaningful whole'.[4] According to both Tillyard and Lily B. Campbell,[5] the historical ideas (that is, the historiography, which would provide the basis for the pattern Dr Hardison perceives) stemmed not from medieval drama but from such sixteenth-century works as the *Mirror for Magistrates* by way of *Gorboduc* and the later so-called 'chronicle plays'.[6] Neither Campbell nor Tillyard even mentions the cycle drama.

Certainly the conventions developed by the writers of interludes, as well as the historical orientation of such writers as Hall and Holinshed, had an influence on both the form and content of the *genre* of the Elizabethan history play. An equally formative influence, however, the cyclic view of history, derived in the first instance from conceptions of time developed in the early Christian period and later embodied in the English medieval mystery cycles. Campbell has claimed that 'It is on the assumption that history repeats itself that political mirrors of history can be utilised to explain the present'.[7] But this assumption is not one of the historical concepts peculiar to the Renaissance. Nowhere can medieval notions of the cycles of history be seen so well as in the civic plays which portray the history of the world from its creation until its end. Following the formal and explicit banning of plays on religious subjects by a succession of monarchs in the sixteenth century, however, the dramatists of the later sixteenth century were forced to develop an alternative body of historical narrative material for dramatic presentation, while still employing the dramatic conventions developed to present the earlier cycles of sacred history. When these dramatists had at their disposal a body of historical material as well-known to their audiences as sacred history had been known to their fore-fathers, then and only then could they create an analogous historical drama.[8]

To understand the correspondences between medieval and Elizabethan dramatic formulations of history we must review once again the conventions governing the form and content of the earlier plays. Both Sepet's older theory of the origins of cycle form as a 'budding out' of the Prophet plays and the more recent theory of Chambers, Young and, following them, Craig, that cycles consist of an assemblage of translated Latin liturgical plays plucked out of different liturgical feasts, have been modified in the light of V. A. Kolve's analysis of the historical conceptions governing cyclic form. . . . The purpose behind the institution of the feast of Corpus Christi in the first instance was 'to *celebrate* the Corpus Christi sacrament, to explain its necessity and power, and to show how that power will be made manifest at the end of the world'.[9] The manifestations of that power which give the cycles their underlying structure are the Three Advents of God into human history, listed in a medieval sermon as follows:

> Frendes, for a processe ye shull vndirstond that I fynde
> in holy writt iij commynges of oure Lord; the first was
> qwen that he com to make man; the secound was qwen he com
> to bie man; and the iij shall be qwen he shall com to deme man.[10]

These divine interventions into human history provide the conventional opening of the cycles, the plays presenting the life of Christ from the Nativity to the Resurrection and Ascension and the traditional ending in the Last Judgement. Here is the working of Divine Providence in its clearest form.

In addition to the anticipated scenes from the life of Christ, the cycles include other material, however. It is this other material which gives the Corpus Christi drama its cyclic quality. A group of plays dealing with scenes from the Old Testament regularly occur. Two principles appear to be at work in the process by which these scenes were selected. One such principle is that of the *exemplum*, where an historical event is simply adduced to point a moral. To this we will return later. Of more importance is the method of interpreting Old Testament figures in terms of the New, known as figural interpretation. Erich Auerbach, in his essay entitled simply '*Figura*', traced the development of the term *figura* down through the classical period to Quintilian, during which it developed meanings still current in discussions of poetic tropes and figures of speech. With Tertullian, however, another meaning develops, a meaning which derives its use from the practice of 'phenomenal prophecy'. A *figura* 'is something real and historical which announces something else which is also real and historical'. According to Auerbach,

figural interpretation establishes a connection between two events or persons, the first of which signifies not only itself but also the second, while the second encompasses or fulfils the first. The two poles of the figure are separate in time, but both, being real events or figures, are within time, within the stream of historical life. Only the understanding of the two persons or events is a spiritual act, but this spiritual act deals with concrete events whether past, present, or future, and not with concepts or abstractions.[11]

Figural interpretation differs from allegory, where the effort is to transform the historical events of the Old Testament into purely spiritual significations. An historical event treated as a *figura* can be considered separately from the immediate context in which it occurred, but it is never anything but a real event.[12] Thus in the 'Prima Pastorum' of the Wakefield Pageants in the *Towneley Cycle*, the foolish shepherds having become wise through revelation supply the spiritual links between events in the Old Testament and the Nativity.

> 1 PASTOR Of (the child) spake more: Sybyll, as I weyn,
> And Nabugodhonosor from oure faythe alyene;
> In the fornace where thay wore, thre childer, sene,
> The fourt stode before, Godys son lyke to bene.

> 2 PASTOR That fygure
> Was gyffen by reualacyon
> That God wold haue a son;
> This is a good lesson
> Vs to consydure.[13]
>
> [*Nabugodhonosor*: Nebuchadnezzar]

A. C. Cawley in his notes to this and related passages, indicates the traditional nature of such figural interpretation.[14]

Other traditional figural interpretations of the incidents from the Old Testament are regularly included in the cycles.[15] For example, the story of Cain and Abel is dramatised not just because it was the first murder, but also more importantly because the protagonists are *figurae* – Abel of Christ, in his capacity as the first martyr, and Cain of the envious Jews. The poet of the *Meditations of the Life and Passion of Christ* contrasted Abel's blood as crying for revenge with Christ's crying for mercy, a development of Hebrews xii.24.[16] This is the difference between the Old Law and the New. Or, the *figura* of Abraham and Isaac can be used to indicate not only that Isaac is a *figura* or type of Christ, but that Abraham's willingness to sacrifice his son makes it possible for God to sacrifice his in fact. The Expositor of the Chester version is the only one to underline the figural significance of this play, but his interpretation is clear:

> This deed you se done in this place,
> In example of Ihesu done yt was,
> that for to wyn mankinde grace
> was sacrificed on the rode.
>
> By Abraham I may vnderstand
> the father of heaven that can fand
> with his sonnes blood to break that band
> the Devil had brought vs too.
>
> By Isaac vnderstand I may
> Jhesu that was obedyent aye,
> his fathers will to worke alway,
> his death to vnderfonge.[17]   [*fand*: endeavour]

Not every Old Testament figure, however, appears in the cycles. The fiery furnace of Nebuchadnezzar may be cited by one of the prophetic shepherds, but it does not even appear in *The Play of Daniel*.[18] The principle of selection governing the choice of Old Testament figures to be included in the medieval English cycle plays derives from the fundamental postulates of medieval historiography, particularly the division of historical time into epochs or periods. R. G. Collingwood, in *The Idea of History*, proposed that the characteristics of Christian historiography which determined the medieval viewpoint were as follows:

(i) It will be a *universal* history, or history of the world, going back to the origin of man . . .

This is so because in the sight of God, all men are of equal importance.

(ii) It will ascribe events not to the wisdom of their human agents but to the workings of *Providence* preordaining their course . . .

(iii) It will set itself to detect an intelligible pattern in [the] general course of events, and in particular it will attach a central importance in this pattern to the historical life of Christ, which is clearly one of the chief preordained features of the pattern. It will make its narrative crystallize itself round that event, and treat earlier events as leading up to or preparing for it, and subsequent events as developing its consequences . . .

This is the thinking which lies behind the technique of figural analysis we have already noted.

(iv) Having divided the past into two, it will then naturally tend to subdivide it again: and thus to distinguish other events, not so important as the birth of Christ but important in their way, which make everything after them different in quality from what went before. Thus history is divided into epochs or *periods*, each with peculiar characteristics of its own, and each marked off from the one before it by an event which in the technical language of this kind of historiography is called epoch-making.[19]

The specific period or epochs chosen to be dramatised in the cycles were the seven ages of the world culminating in the sabbath of eternal rest with which St Augustine concludes *The City of God*.[20] St Augustine defines these ages as follows:

The first age, as it were the first day, is from Adam unto the flood, and the second from thence unto Abraham, not by equality of times, but by number of generations. For they are found to have the number ten. From hence now, as Matthew the evangelist doth conclude, three ages do follow even unto the coming of Christ, every one of which is expressed by fourteen generations. From Abraham unto David is one, from thence even unto the transmigration into Babylon is another, the third from thence unto the incarnate nativity of Christ. So all of them are made five. Now this age is the sixth, to be measured by no number, because of that which is spoken. 'It is not for you to know the seasons, which the Father has placed in His own power.' After this age God shall rest as on the seventh day, when God shall make that same seventh day which we shall be, to rest in Himself. . . But this seventh shall be our sabbath, whose end shall not be the evening, but the Lord's day, as the eighth eternal day.[21]

No epoch-making figure of the stature of Adam, Noah, Abraham and

David appeared in the age of the Transmigration into Babylon, Augustine's fifth age. Jechonias, the father associated with this age on the basis of Matthew i.11, is ultimately replaced by Moses and the Exodus on the basis of Bede's five-part division, 'based on the five hours in which the labourers in the vineyard were hired'. Bede's five periods were those of the Creation, Noah, Abraham, Moses and Christ; considering the prevalence of the Old Law–New Law dichotomy in medieval thought it is not surprising that Exodus replaces the Transmigration in many medieval divisions of history.[22] Whichever pattern is followed, the sixth age remains the same – contemporary history; in this pattern it can be treated as are all other epochs.

The conception of the seven ages of time, and the treatment of the Patriarchs as *figurae* explain the relations of the parts to the whole of the cycles. Reference to the present time of the audience, the time of the sixth age, could also be made through another application of history. For historical events not only relate to other events as announcements of God's providential plan: they can also serve as self-contained lessons for the present. *Any* event from the past can also become an *exemplum* for the present, providing an illustration of cause and effect with moral consequences. Cain in the Towneley Cycle may be murdering the first martyr, himself a type of Christ, but the character of Cain which the Wakefield Master develops is that of the medieval farmer who beats his servant and cheats on his tithes. God's refusal of Cain's sacrifice becomes a commentary on God's judgement of similar actions in the time present of the audience. Or there is the long list of imaginary characters whose names are in the book of Den, the Summoner, in the N-Town *Trial of Joseph and Mary*, all contemporary medieval English names, such as 'Symme Smalfeyth and kate kelle / and bertylmew the bochere'. The apparently anachronistic habit medieval dramatists have of developing their characters as medieval stereotypes derives not so much from a lack of historical imagination as from an historical view in which events in the present mirror events in the past. For the cyclic view of history implied by the theory of the seven ages leads to the belief shared by both medieval and Renaissance writers that in its patterns 'history repeats itself'. Thus not only sacred history, dramatised so to speak in 'medieval dress', but all forms of history hold precedents for the present, in so far as the patterns found there recur in the field of human action. It is but a small step from the Fall of Adam to the Fall of Princes. For the medieval dramatist, as for Ranulph Higden or Raphael Holinshed, the study of history had the double benefit of teaching God's purposes manifested in the epochs of history and inculcating moral lessons in the sphere of politics and ethics.

Both the figural and the exemplary applications of historical material can be seen at work in the drama of mid-sixteenth-century England. First, as regards the figural view of history, it is not difficult to see how the representation of one real historical event as announcing another later real historical event, originally applied to interpretations of the Old Law in terms of the New, could be extended to any two historical events within the cycles of time. Thus the dramatist of *Godly Queen Hester* employs the figure of Esther to illuminate the situation of Katharine of Aragon, just as a pageant writer had used the figure of King Ahasuerus to comment on Richard II nearly 150 years earlier.[23] A more instructive example of the figural use of history to interpret secular rather than sacred events, is Bale's *King John*. In the Interpretour's speech which divides the two acts Bale makes the following identifications:

> Thys noble kyng Iohan, as a faythfull Moyses,
> Withstode proude Pharao for hys poore Israel,
> Myndynge to brynge it owt of the lande of Darkenesse.
> But the Egyptyanes ded agaynst hym so rebell
> That hys poore people ded styll in the desart dwell,
> Tyll that duke Iosue, whych was our late Kynge Henrye,
> Clearly brought vs in to the lande of mylke and honye.
> As a stronge Dauid at the voyce of verytie,
> Great Golye, the pope, he strake downe with hys slynge,
> Restorynge agayne to a Christen lybertie
> Hys lande and people, lyke a most vyctoryouse kynge,
> To hir first bewtye intendynge the churche to brynge,
> From ceremonyes dead, to the lyuynge wurde of the Lorde.[24]

> [*Iosue*: Joshua]

This speech, written either under Edward VI or for the presentation of the play under Elizabeth, explicitly equates John and Henry VIII with illustrious Biblical predecessors. Each gains his identity from the type to which he corresponds.

But Bale's identifications go much further than this. John himself is a *figura* for Henry VIII; both are antagonists of Antichrist! The fulfilment of the figure only comes about fully with the second monarch.[25] Sedition promises that as a result of the tricks of the troop of vices, 'We iiij by owr craftes Kyng Iohn wyll so subdwe / That for iij C. yers all Englond shall yt rewe' [(i) 775–6]. When at the beginning of Act II [121–33] Clergye outlines how the interdiction will operate to bring John round, he is also indicating the forces that Henry VIII has overcome. Bale's handling of the vice roles – Sedition as Stephen Langton, Usurped Power as the Pope, or Private Wealth as Pandulphus – is an extension of Bale's figural handling of the major character. The type is recurrent, the individual is important only as a manifestation of the type at a particular moment in history. As a recent student of Bale's work has put it:

It is evident that Bale thinks of the evil characters as being first and foremost perennial representatives of evil; their occasional appearance as historical characters in a specific situation is used by way of *exemplum* to lend credence to their existence on a 'higher' plane.[26]

Bale, as is necessary in figural interpretation, insists on the historicity of the events he depicts, even if they are presented in the abstract forms of the morality rather than in the specific historical surroundings of the cycle drama. Nobility opines early in the play that 'kyng Iohn ys lyke to rewe yt sore / Whan ye wryte his tyme, for vexcyng of the clergye' [(i) 588–9]. As the play draws to its close, following John's poisoning, Verity assures the audience directly that 'Kynge Iohan was a man both valeaunt and godlye. / What though Polydorus reporteth hym very yll / At the suggestions of the malicyouse clergye? / Thynke yow a Romane with the Romanes can not lye?' [(ii) 2194–7]. Instead Leland is invoked to put things right. And as history the sad tale is also an *exemplum*, a cautionary tale for others beside the king. After Nobility has been rebuked by Imperial Majesty (Henry VIII himself?) for hearkening to Sedition, Nobility recalls,

> I consydre now that God hath for Sedicyon
> Sent ponnyshmentes great. Examples we have in Brute,
> In Catilyne, in Cassius, and fayer Absolon,
> Whome of their purpose God alwayes destytute,
> And terryble plages on them ded execute
> For their rebellyon.   [(ii) 2604–9]

These same 'examples' reappeared a number of times in the drama that was to follow, teaching not only Nobility to avoid the blandishments of Sedition. But of the two uses of history, the cyclic rather than the exemplary dominates Bale's thinking.

Few interludes from the end of Henry VIII's reign or those of Edward VI and Philip and Mary survive to indicate how typical was Bale's adaptation of older methods of interpreting history for his own polemic purposes. Clearly, whatever its ostensible subject, polemic drama was sufficiently widespread during the period to call for such acts as the *Act for the Advancement of true Religion and for the Abolishment of the Contrary* in 1543, which forbade 'interpretacions of scripture, contrary to the doctryne set forth or to be set forth by the kynges maiestie'.[27] That such interpretation could be somewhat more subtle than Bale's is suggested by the play of *Jacob and Esau*, properly praised by F. P. Wilson as a well-made play along classical lines,[28] but at the same time undoubtedly a studied Calvinist attempt to 'justify the seizure of power, and to insist that the seizure is reluctantly undertaken'.[29] Professor Bevington correctly observes that the play-wright 'is less concerned with informing his audience about Old Testament history than with seeing the original story as a type of current history'.[30] *Jacob and Esau*, though licensed in 1557–58, must belong, by its temper, to the period of Edward VI. I suspect that the biblical interlude, *The Tower of Babylon*, produced at court for Christmas 1548, was likely to have involved a cautionary example of some sort as well. In any event, the series of acts catalogued by Chambers,[31] and reviewed . . . by Wickham,[32] culminating in the act of 1559 which formed the basis for the Elizabethan control of the stage, all indicate that drama from this period had been consistently polemic. But it should be stressed that it was the specific applications of history, not the methods of interpretation, that had become offensive.

Much of the polemic drama was produced in the capital. In the provinces the older cycle plays were only polemic in that their production tended to be identified with Catholic sympathies. Hence the attempts to preserve the cycles by expunging offensive material, such as the Marian plays Martin Stevens believes were deleted from the Towneley Cycle.[33] But the end of dramatised biblical history was nearing. In the Act of 16 May 1559 Elizabeth charged the officers in the towns and cities

That they permyt (no plays) to be played wherein either matters of religion or of the governaunce of the estate of the common weale shalbe handled or treated, beyng no meete matters to be wrytten or treated vpon, but by menne of auctoritie, learning and wisedome, nor to be handled before any audience but of graue and discrete persons: All which partes of this proclamation, her maiestie chargeth to be inuiolably kepte.[34]

To be sure passing a law and enforcing it are two different matters.[35] Father Gardiner quotes a report solicited by the Privy Council in 1564 which indicated that 'of a total of 851 justices, only 431 were favourable to the government policy in matters of religion'.[36] Yet slowly but surely the Privy Council overcame such obstacles; the melancholy story of the suppression of the cycles as detailed by Father Gardiner is now thoroughly familiar.

What is of interest to students of early English drama is that where known replacements for the cycles are found they are still historical.

At Coventry an Oxford student named Smith was engaged to write a play on the *Destruction of Jerusalem*. A possible source is a book cited by Lily B. Campbell as an example of Reformation history. Joseph ben Gorion's history of the Jewish people was translated in 1558 by 'Peter Morwyng (or Morwen) of Magdalen College in Oxford' and ran through nine editions from then until 1615. In his preface Morwyng cites the value of this history as follows:

The history of the Jews could teach Christians useful lessons. . . . As when thou seest the Jews here afflicted with divers kinds of misery, because they fell from God: then maist thou be admonished hereby to see the better thine owne waies, least the like calamities light upon thee. . . . Thou shalt read here of terrible and horrible eventes of sedicion and rebellion . . . in so muche that nothing hastened their destruction so greatlye as their own doggishness and intestine hatred. Be thou warned therefore by their harmes, and take hede that thou maist avoid the like.[37]

Coventry's play was commissioned for 1584, and was played again in 1591. At Shrewsbury, Thomas Ashton, master of the free school, in 1566 produced a play on Julian the Apostate. At Lincoln the St Anne's day cycle was discontinued after 1555. Later, in 1564, the Common Council determined that a 'standing play of some story of the Bible shall be played two days this summertime'.[38] The play decided on in that year was 'the story of olde tobye', i.e., the new biblical history play was based on the apocryphal book of *Tobit*.[39] This play was produced until 1567. A surviving list of properties strongly suggests that 'the standing play of old Tobey' was a stationary production utilising many of the properties surviving from the earlier St Anne's day play, if not the Corpus Christi cycle which had become defunct earlier. In each case the history chosen appears to have been designed to fulfil traditional expectations in the audience without violating the injunction against treating matters of religion (that is, disputed doctrine) on the stage.

The plays at Coventry, Shrewsbury or Lincoln, like the play of *Samson* put on at the Red Lion Inn in 1567, or Thomas Garter's *The Most Virtuous and Godly Susanna*, also of the 1560s indicate that the first attempts to find alternative historical material were conditioned by the audience's expectations inherited from the past. Granted that the sacred history of the cycles was no longer safe from state control, might not biblical or early Christian history not directly associated with the Christian religion prove a safer substitute? In point of fact, it does not seem to have done so, any more than did *Gorboduc*. For to the Elizabethans, as to the medieval audience, all history is instructive, either in a figural sense, where one event announces the nature of one to follow, or in an exemplary sense, as a cautionary tale. Too many generations of glossators and commentators had worked over the corpus of biblical material for any of it to be innocent of applications to contemporary events, since it is the interpreter who makes history a matter for polemics. Thomas Norton and Thomas Sackville were just as guilty of violating the statute of 1559 as were writers of new biblical plays, for if *Gorboduc* does nothing else it deals with 'the governaunce of the estate of the common weale'. During the dramatic doldrums of the 1570s Harbage's *Annals* lists numerous titles drawn from classical history, demonstrating that Horestes and Cambises' vein proved for a while to be the safest to mine. Classical history and romance provided the bulk of the dramatic material produced until the end of the 1580s. By then the Elizabethan settlement was relatively secure; what had once been controversial could now be tolerated. English and biblical history alike return to the stage with *The Famous Victories of Henry V* in 1586, and *Job*, and Peele's *The Love of King David and Queen Bethsabe*, in 1587. But Peele's play was the end of a line. In the words of the play's most recent editor, *David and Bethsabe* stands alone in the Elizabethan period as an extant English play based completely on the Bible.[40] English, rather than sacred history, became the staple dramatic fare, but still a history conceived of in cyclic terms where both king and commoner could learn of God's purpose for man. In dramatising that history the Elizabethan playwrights had at their disposal the dramatic conventions developed to present cyclic patterns, namely the figural and exemplary conventions of the medieval mystery cycles. These conventions, rather than an Aristotelian plot, are what give the Elizabethan history plays their unity, and provided a means of easy communication between artist and audience. . . .

Source: extract from chapter 'Of History and Time' in *Traditions of Medieval English Drama* (London, 1974), pp. 123–34.

NOTES

[Reorganised and renumbered from the original. For short-form references to works, see Abbreviations List, p. 8 – Ed.]

1. Hardison, p. 290. The continued life of the cyclic view of history in Renaissance drama was originally proposed by E. Catherine Dunn, 'The Medieval "Cycle" as History Play: An Approach to the Wakefield Plays', *Studies in the Renaissance*, 7 (1960), pp. 76–89. Acceptance of her thesis has not, however, been rapid.

2. E. M. W. Tillyard, *Shakespeare's History Plays* (London, 1944; New York, 1946), p. 92.

3. Irving Ribner, *The English History Play in the Age of Shakespeare*, (Princeton, N.J., and London, 1957), pp. 28–9.

4. Ibid., p. 30.

5. Lily B. Campbell, *Shakespeare's 'Histories': Mirrors of Elizabethan Policy* (San Marino, Cal., 1947).

6. For a rejection of the term 'Chronicle play', see Ribner, op. cit., pp. 5–6.

7. Campbell, op. cit., p. 125.

8. See in this context Louis B. Wright's chapter on 'The Utility of History' in *Middle-Class Culture in Elizabethan England* (repr. Ithaca, N.Y., 1958), pp. 297–338.

9. Kolve, p. 48.

10. Ibid., p. 58. The reference is to the *Middle English Sermons*, ed. Woodburn O. Ross, EETS, o.s. 209 (London, 1940), p. 314.

11. E. Auerbach, *Scenes from the Drama of European Literature* (New York, 1959), p. 29.

12. Ibid., pp. 53–4.

13. *Wakefield Pageants*, 3 (350–8).

14. Ibid. (102–3).

15. Kolve, pp. 65–81, discusses a number of these interpretations.

16. Ibid., p. 67.

17. *Chester*, Diemling, IV (465–76).

18. *The Play of Daniel*, ed. Noah Greenberg (New York, 1959).

19. R. G. Collingwood, *The Idea of History* (London, 1946), pp. 49–50.

20. Dunn, op. cit. (note 1, above), pp. 78–9.

21. St Augustine of Hippo, *The City of God*, XXII, 30, ed. R. V. G. Tasker (London, 1945), lines 407–8.

22. Kolve, pp. 88–9.

23. For an excellent discussion of this play as an example of 'new and sophisticated techniques in the allegorising of biblical narrative', see David M. Bevington, *Tudor Drama and Politics* (Cambridge, Mass., 1968), ch. 7 on 'The Royal Divorce and Suppression of the Monasteries', pp. 86–95.

24. *John Bale's King Johan*, ed. Barry B. Adams (San Marino, Cal., 1969): I (1107–19).

25. See Bevington, op. cit., p. 99, for further discussion of this point. Bevington defines the technique employed by Bale as 'historical analogy'.

26. Thora B. Blatt, *The Plays of John Bale* (Copenhagen, 1968), p. 112. Adams, op. cit. (note 24, above), accepts Bale's historical conceptions as basically originating in the Apocalyptic thought patterns of 'sixteenth-century Protestant thinkers' (n. 32, pp. 59–65). This is too narrow a view.

27. Chambers, II, p. 222. Edward VI repealed the measure, but later lived to regret it.

28. F. P. Wilson, *The English Drama, 1485–1585* (Oxford, 1969), pp. 93–6.

29. Bevington, op. cit., p. 112.

30. Ibid., p. 109.

31. Chambers, II, pp. 218–24.

32. Wickham, II, pp. 54–97.

33. Martin Stevens, 'The Missing Parts of the Towneley Cycle', *Speculum*, 45 (1970), pp. 254–65.

34. E. K. Chambers, *The Elizabethan Stage* (London, 1923), IV, p. 263.

35. Joel Hurstfield has indicated some of the limits to the control Elizabeth could impose on her people in *Liberty and Authority under Elizabeth I*, inaugural lecture (University College, London, 12 May 1960), p. 9.

36. H. C. Gardiner, *Mysteries' End* (New Haven, Conn., 1946; repr. 1967), p. 70.

37. Campbell, op. cit. (note 5, above), p. 40–1.

38. Chambers, II, pp. 361–2, 394, 379.

39. A. F. Leach, 'Some English Plays and Players, 1220–1548', in *An English Miscellany* (Oxford, 1901), p. 227–8.

40. C. T. Prouty (ed.), *The Dramatic Works of George Peele: David and Bethsabe* ed. Elmer Blistein (New Haven, 1970), p. 175.

3. MORALITY PLAYS AND INTERLUDES

Robert A. Potter   Forgiveness as Theatre   (1975)

The greatest danger for mankind in the moralities is not in falling into sin (for all men sin) or yet in delaying repentance (for that can be amended), but in despairing of the possibility of the forgiveness of one's sins. In demonstrating first the necessity for repentance, and then the fact of its efficacy, the morality playwright seeks the participation of his audience in a ritual verification of the whole concept of the forgiveness of sins.

This verification begins with an obligatory introduction of mankind into the state of sin which is his legacy from Adam. An ingenious example of this method in action may be seen in the mock trial of *Mankind*. The nonsensical preamble of the scene suggests a manorial court, but the body of the 'trial' is in fact an elaborate parody-reversal of the sacrament of penance.[1] Mankind is instructed in the six deadly sins (lechery is excepted), and admonished to practice robbery and gluttony. In token of his changed condition he is given a new garment (a gallant's jacket in this case). The scene ends as all repeat 'Amen' in unison and run off to seek their pleasures before Mercy can intervene.

Sin in the moralities is depicted as a necessary stage in the education of Mankind, immediately pleasurable and virtually unavoidable. As a result, the state of innocence is usually brief in the moralities, sometimes to the point of being largely theoretical. A play like *Wisdom* (nearly one-third of which concerns the state of innocence) is the exception rather than the rule. Mankind in *Perseverance* falls and repents, only to fall once again. In *Mankind*, the ribald blasphemy of Nought, New Guise and Now-a-days expresses the inevitable temptations of the world in which Mankind finds himself. These characters' delight in their own evil is infectious, and once Mankind is seduced into sin by the Devil, he begs their forgiveness for previous injuries, repenting, like Faustus, of having thought of repenting.

The satire of the morality plays adheres to the conventions of medieval preaching tradition in exposing common social abuses. Clerical misconduct is denounced in *Everyman*, and Folly in *Mundus et Infans* is represented as a student of the law. In *Wisdom* the stage of sin is made specific in a pointed attack on abuses of the law and devices of maintenance, bribery, false indictment, perjury and jury tampering. This matter is staged in terms of a delightful disguising with dancing, song and minstrels' music.[2]

The sexual seduction of Mankind into sin is dramatised, either in a literal seduction scene (as with Mankind and Lechery in *Perseverance*) or by inference, with lemans, wenches and brothels indicated just offstage. Only *Everyman* lacks these strong suggestions, and even here the offer by Kindred of her maid as a companion for Everyman [360–4] may possibly suggest a sexual diversion. As Lucifer expresses it in *Wisdom*:

> Yowur fyve wyttys abrode lett sprede.
> . . .
> Beholde how ryches dystroyt nede;
> It makyt man fayer, hym wele for to fede;
> And of lust and lykynge commyth generacyon.
>
> [*Wisdom*, 453, 458–60]

The moralising of the moralities is not, then, a puritan denial of human nature; indeed, it is a dogmatic proclamation of the Adam in all men. And fortunately for all men, their sin may lead to remorse, that remorse may be converted to contrition, and thus they may be forgiven and saved. The dialectical thesis of the moralities, stated briefly, is that God has recognised human nature and carved out for it a path to salvation, through repentance.

In no two medieval morality plays is the presentation of repentance identically accomplished, but in all of them repentance is the climactic theatrical act. In most of the medieval plays an attempt is made to dramatise this transformation in the specific terms of the sacrament of penance.

In *The Castle of Perseverance* the component acts involved in taking the sacrament are delineated. The sequence begins when Mankind has thoroughly given himself up to the power of the World, embracing the seven deadly sins. Man's good angel laments the falling off, and Confession enters to offer assistance [1298]. Together they go to Mankind and urge him to repent. Mankind replies that they have come too soon, but Penance now enters (with a lance) and touches Mankind's heart, emblematically motivating the contrition necessary for repentance. The contrite Mankind begs Confession for mercy, and is informed of the choice which confronts him:

> If þou wylt be aknowe here
>   Only al þi trespas,
> I schal þe schelde fro helle fere,
> And putte þe fro peyne unto precyouse place.
>   If þou wylt not make þynne sowle clere
>   But kepe hem in þyne hert cas,
> Anoþer day þey schul be rawe and rere
> And synke þi sowle to Satanas
>   in gastful glowyne glede.
>
> [*Perseverance*, 1455–63]

Mankind confesses his sins [1468–93] and, in consequence, is absolved by Confession. To make certain that he will continue repentance, Mankind takes refuge in the castle Perseverance, accompanied by the seven virtues. His act of repentance is complete, except for the necessity of proving (or satisfying) the act of repentance by steadfastness. On this point Mankind fails; he falls prey to the sin of avarice, and dies in a state of sin. By crying out for Mercy at the hour of his death, however, Mankind enables Mercy to plead:

> If he dey in very contricioun,
> Lord, þe lest drope of þi blod
>   For hys synne makyth satisfaccioun.
> As þou deydst, Lord, on þe rode,
>   Graunt me my peticioun!
> Lete me, Mercy, be hys fode,
>   And graunte hym þi saluacion.   [3367–73]

As a result, through a combination of his own merits and God's infinite mercy, Mankind's soul is saved.

We have only the outline of the climax of *The King of Life*, and thus cannot be sure of its precise details. However the prologue indicates that following the vanquishing of Life by Death, and before the saving of Life's soul, a sequence of repentance intervenes. In the first place,

> Qwhen þe body is doun ibroȝt
>   þe soule sorow awakith;
> þe body is pride is dere aboȝt,
>   þe soule þe fendis takith.   [*K. of L.*, 93–6]

The soul's contrition is the immediate cause of the intercession of the Virgin Mary and of the soul's consequent salvation; in this respect *The King of Life* resembles *The Castle of Perseverance*. [One] theory, indeed, suggests that in its original form *Perseverance* was resolved by intercession of the Virgin rather than by the present debate of the four daughters of God.[3] A likely and unnoticed analogue for this lost portion of *The King of Life* is the Welsh play *The Soul and the Body* which includes a disputation between the soul and the body over who is responsible for their sinful life. The soul is arrested by the Devil, but saved by the intervention of Christ.

In *Wisdom*, the most carefully theological of the early moralities, the means of repentance is elaborately and precisely demonstrated. When the three faculties (Mind, Will and Understanding) have fallen into sin, Wisdom reminds them of the sure approach of death and shows them the image of their disfigured soul. Realising the peril of their common situation, the faculties and the soul call on God for mercy. Wisdom explains the process of ritual cleansing:

> By wndyrstondynge haue very contrycyon,
> Wyth mynde of your synne confessyon make,
> Wyth wyll yeldynge du satysfaccyon;
> Þan yowur soule be clene, I wndyrtake.

[*Wisdom*, 973–6]

The power of contrition is demonstrated in the departure of the soul's afflicting demons. The soul remains in a state of sin, however; and Anima, singing a passionate lamentation, leaves to reconcile herself to the church by making confession, accompanied by the three faculties. When the soul returns from confession, she has resumed her original beauty and resplendent costume. She now recognises Wisdom as Christ, without whom her sins would still be unredeemed. By the mercy of his passion, however, Christ has paid the price of her sins.[4] Through this satisfaction the sequence of penance is complete; Anima is now worthy of salvation:

> Ande now ye be reformyde by þe sakyrment of penaunce
> Ande clensyde from þe synnys actuall.
>
> . . .
>
> Now ye haue receyuyde þe crownnys victoryall
> To regne in blys withowtyn ende.

[1111–12, 1119–20]

It is one of the dramatic felicities of *Wisdom* that the divine basis for the soul's renewal (the passion of Christ) is presented without diverting the focus of the play from the soul's human situation. This purpose is emphasised in the soul's final speech, directed to the audience:

> Nowe ye mut euery soule renewe
> In grace, and vycys to eschew,
> Ande so to ende with perfeccyon.

[1159–61]

In *Mundus et Infans*, as in *Perseverance*, the necessity of repentance is determined by the cyclical evolution of Infans into Manhood and thence into old age. The process is carried forward by Folly, who leads

Manhood astray and later rechristens him Shame. In this condition
Manhood shuns Conscience and its promptings. Indeed, he is on the
brink of despair and suicide when he encounters Perseverance. It is
the function of Perseverance to explain the forgiveness of sins:

> Be-ware of Wanhope, for he is a fo.
> A newe name I shall gyve you to,
>   I clepe you Repentaunce;
> For, and you here repente your synne,
> Ye are possyble heuen to wynne,
> But with grete contrycyon ye must begynne.
>
> [*M. et I.*, 855–60]

Manhood's shame, in so far as it leads to despair, puts him in danger
of damnation. The same emotion, put to Christian use as contrition,
can elicit the grace of God:

> For thoughe a man had do alone
> The deedly synnes euerychone,
> And he with contrycyon make his mone
> To Cryst our heuyn kynge,
> God is also gladde of hym
> As of the creature that neuer dyde syn.
> AGE Now, good syr, how sholde I contrycyon begyn?
> PER Syr, in shryfte of mouthe without varyenge.
>
> [862–9]

Repentance is thus the solution and dénouement of *Mundus et Infans*.
The play's final scene involves the instruction of Age in the twelve
articles of faith and related knowledge which will help to confirm the
transformation effected by the sacrament of penance.

Even in *Hickscorner* and *Youth*, which dwell heavily on the state of
sin, repentance is the mechanism of the play's resolution. Youth
forsakes his companions Riot and Pride, and is given a garment of
repentance, 'beads for your devotion', and a new name: Good
Contrition. By the end of his play, the rascally Hickscorner has
disappeared, but his companions in vice (Freewill and Imagination)
are apprehended and brought to repent their ways. Freewill's
conversion is, in fact, accomplished by means of mental and physical
duress. Nevertheless, the formula is closely observed. Freewill begs
mercy for his sins and receives a new garment in token of his
repentance. He needs no change of name:

> For all that wyll to heven hye,
> By his owne frewyll he must forsake folye.
>
> [*Hickscorner*, 871–2]

Similarly, Freewill's colleague Imagination is led to repentance by imagining death and damnation. He, too, asks God's mercy and receives a new garment. In conclusion he acquires the more steadfast name of Good Remembrance, and the moral is applied to all present:

> And loke that ye forget not Repentaunce;
> Than to heven ye shall go the nexte waye
> . . .
> Unto the whiche blysse I beseche God Almyghty
> To brynge there your soules that here be present
> And unto vertuous lyvynge that ye maye applye,
> Truly for to kepe his commaundmente.
>
> [1016–17, 1021–4]

Everyman, the most artistically successful of the moralities, is also the most imaginative and philosophical in dramatising repentance in human terms. Here the consciousness of approaching death, which plays a part in the repentance scenes of *Perseverance*, *Wisdom* and the other moralities, is expanded into a controlling metaphor for the human situation. Within this metaphor damnation and salvation are present possibilities; behind the grim aspect of death (as in other treatises on the 'art of dying') lies the exemplary atoning death of Christ. The problem which *Everyman* presents with such daring and subtlety is the effort of dying mankind to find a solution for death. The solution, as it is systematically discovered in the action of the play, is not to be found in either external relationships (Fellowship, Kindred, Cousin and Goods) or internal attributes (Discretion, Strength, Beauty, Five Wits). Nevertheless, substantiated by external good deeds and informed by internal knowledge, it is possible for mankind to discover the theological answer to the dilemma. The solution leads, by way of repentance, toward putting the sequence of one's life and death in consonance with the redeeming life and death of Christ, and hence with the pattern of salvation.

The crucial transformation of Everyman is from a state of sin to a state of grace. This transformation is accomplished, in the central sequence of the play [463–654], by a closely detailed act of repentance. Everyman's repentance begins with contrition as a result of his estrangement from the external attributes upon which he had always depended – Fellowship, Kindred and Cousin, and Goods. With their departure he feels remorse:

> Than of my selfe I was ashamed,
> And so I am worthy to be blamed
> Thus may I well my selfe hate.   [*Everyman*, 476–8]

Because of this remorse he is able to recognise the perilous weakness of his Good Deeds and to be directed thereby to seek Knowledge. Having achieved this consciousness of his own spiritual illness, Everyman is ready to receive the specific doctrine of repentance. Knowledge leads to a higher state,

> Where thou shalte hele thee of thy smarte
> . . .
> Now go we togyder louyngly
>   To Confessyon, that clensynge ryvere.   [528, 535–6]

In the 'house of Salvation' Everyman finds Confession, a 'holy man' who accepts his contrition and prescribes a remedy for his illness in the form of penance. Everyman is to scourge himself, in remembrance of Christ's sacrifice and in petition for God's mercy. In a lengthy prayer Everyman acknowledges Christ as his redeemer and asks the intercession of Mary.

> . . . that I may be meane of thy prayer
> Of your Sones glory to be partynere,
> By the meanes of his passyon, I it craue.   [601–3]

Everyman completes the penance by scourging his body, in satisfaction of the sacrament. In doing so he makes the transition from a state of sin to a state of grace. The reality of this change is verified by three visible facts: first, Good Deeds, who has been hobbled by Everyman's sins, rises before the eyes of all to accompany Everyman on his journey; second, Knowledge provides Everyman with a penitent's garment in token of his contrition, which Everyman willingly puts on;[5] third, Everyman's book of reckoning, which previously had been rendered illegible by his sins, is now seen to be clear.

In full view of his audience, Everyman completes and demonstrates his repentance. The tension of the rest of the play lies in whether he will persevere in his state of grace or fall back into sin under the strain of approaching death. Everyman's inner attributes (Discretion, Strength, Beauty and Five Wits) are revealed to him and as quickly taken from him. Even the counsel of Knowledge is ultimately lost to him. Everyman, denied (like Christ) by all, yet sustained by his good deeds, and bound (with Christ) in the sacraments, dies in a state of grace. His last thoughts are of Christ's redeeming death, and his last words (from the sacrament of extreme unction) are Christ's last words:[6]

> *In manus tuas*, of myghtes moost
> For euer, *Commendo spiritum meum*.   [886–7]

By contrast, the author of *Mankind* is less concerned with human repentance than with the divine mercy which makes it possible. There is relatively little emphasis given to the specific mechanism of the sacrament of penance – the sequence of contrition, confession and satisfaction. Instead, the author of *Mankind* sees repentance as a kind of natural regeneration, in a world which is abundant with divine mercy. This identification is very carefully imagined in terms of the response of a particular audience.

Mankind was apparently written for performance by a touring company in rural Cambridgeshire and Norfolk.[7] On literary grounds, because of its lively and obscene low comedy and the aureate latinisms of its preaching, *Mankind* has frequently been mistaken for a degenerate text, and even regarded as an insincere travesty. 'Judged by the original standard of the morality play', writes Pollard, 'it is about as degraded a composition as can well be imagined'; W. K. Smart concludes firmly that *Mankind* is 'only *a sham morality* – with a slight morality framework that offers an excuse for the production of the play'.[8] A further critical difficulty has been in accounting for the undigested 'popular' elements in *Mankind*. As previously noted, the play is replete with borrowings from the tradition of folk drama – suggestions of a beheading cure, masked actors, and a collection. But the presence of 'popular' elements in a drama demonstrating the efficacy of Christian doctrine is no more evidence of a corrupted text than is the effusive rhetoric of its sermon speeches. On the contrary, we should expect to find just this blending of elements in religious plays which moved a fifteenth-century rural audience. *Mankind* shapes itself to the thoughts of such an audience in its smallest figures of speech ('the corn xall be sauyed, þe chaffe xallbe brente,' [life] 'is but a chery tyme',).[9]

The care of Mankind's soul is dramatised in agricultural terms from the first, as Mankind conscientiously tills his land and chases off his idle tempters. Tityvillus begins his seduction of Mankind by invoking sterility. He hides a board in the earth to make the soil barren and strews weeds in the field to ruin the season's crop. As a result Mankind gives up his labour and falls into sin, where he remains until rescued by his act of repentance.

The unity and validity of *Mankind* as a religious play have been well documented in a study by Sister Mary Philippa Coogan, who found an immediate source for the sermon speeches of the play in the *Jacob's Well* homilies. The comic scenes of *Mankind*, examined with a medieval tolerance and ingenuity, proved to 'carry almost the entire burden of teaching Mankind through experience what Mercy has presented to him in theory'.[10]

It is a priest with the name of Mercy who warns Mankind in the beginning about the forces of evil. These forces nevertheless lead Mankind into a life of sin, and in the process convince him that Mercy is dead. As a result Mankind concludes that there is no hope of salvation. When he hears that Mercy is in fact alive and looking for him, Mankind is overwhelmed with guilt. In shame he is ready to hang himself, with the assistance of Mischief and his colleagues in sin. The arrival of Mercy scatters the forces of Evil, but Mankind's remorse is such that he feels himself beyond redemption. Without a belief in the forgiveness of sins, Mankind is still in despair. Mercy, appearing, must convince Mankind (and the audience) of the reality and necessity for repentance. He explains the paradox by identifying mercy with natural regeneration:

> In þis present lyfe mercy ys plente, tyll deth
> makyth hys dywysion;
> . . .
> Aske mercy and hawe, whyll þe body wyth þe sowle
> hath hys annexion;
> . . .
> Be repentant here, trust not þe owr of deth . . .
> [*Mankind*, 861, 863, 865]

In a sterile merciless world, Mankind would be damned; with Mercy he may be forgiven and saved. Understanding this abundance at last, through his own experience, Mankind acknowledges his sins. Mercy instructs him in the means of avoiding sin and the necessity of perseverance. Mankind departs with the blessing of Mercy, and extends the hope of forgiveness and regeneration to include 'þis worcheppyl audiens':

> Syth I schall departe, blyse me, fader, her þen I go.
> God send ws all plente of hys gret mercy!
>
> [899–900]

Thus the presentations of repentance which we find in the moralities differ in their emphasis. *Perseverance*, *Everyman* and *Wisdom* tend to illuminate the particulars of the sacrament itself; *Mankind*, on the other hand, focuses on the spirit rather than the letter of repentance. One can even see in such differences the outlines of the two prevalent theories of penance in the fifteenth century – those of Alexander of Hales and Duns Scotus (emphasising the letter of the law) and of William of Ockham (emphasising the spirit).[11] Nevertheless, the unity of the plays is deep and specific. They are not documents of theological controversy but rather of a vernacular drama of ideas. Whatever their vast differences as works of art, *The King of Life*, *The Castle of Perseverance*, *Mankind*, *Wisdom*, *Everyman*, *Mundus et Infans*,

Hickscorner and *Youth* are as one in their praise and demonstration of repentance. The medieval morality plays are a single act, variously celebrated.[12]

Thus the traditional morality play is not a battle between virtues and vices, but a didactic ritual drama about the forgiveness of sins. Its theatrical intentions are to imitate and evoke that forgiveness. In a morality play the events in the plot unfold, not with the tension and surprise of melodrama, but with the relentlessness of tragedy – toward a happy ending. It is a didactic drama, not in the melodramatic sense of containing a moral, but in the Brechtian sense of embodying one. Human life, in the sequential actions of the morality play, is a dialectical pattern, a linear problem which unfolds its own solution.

The morality play is acted out on the stage of a world where man is born to rule, bound to sin, and destined to be saved. To its audiences, and to their consciences, the plays reveal that the fall out of innocence into experience is unavoidable, theologically necessary, and solvable, through the forgiveness of sins. The action is thus an affirmation of the life process and the ultimate rationality of the human predicament.

SOURCE: extract (section 3) from chapter 'Medieval Plays: The Repentance Drama of Early England' in *The Early English Morality Play* (London, 1975), pp. 47–57.

NOTES

[Reorganised and renumbered from the original. For short-form references to works, see Abbreviations List, p. 8 – Ed.]

1. Coogan, p. 97.
2. The discussion in *Wisdom* encompasses lines 685–776. The legal satire continues until 873, the entrance of Wisdom. On the basis of these references, John J. Molloy has suggested that *Wisdom* is an Inns of Court play: *A Theological Interpretation of the Moral Play, 'Wisdom, Who Is Christ'* (Washington, D.C., 1952), pp. 191–2.
[Texts quoted in this extract are: *Wisdom, Castle of Perseverance* and *Mankind*, in *Macro*; *King of Life* (usually entitled *Pride of Life*), in *Non-Cycle Plays*; *Mundus et Infans* and *Hickscorner*, in J. M. Manly (ed.), *Specimens of the Pre-Shakespearean Drama*, 2 vols (Boston, Mass., 1897), vol. I; *Everyman*, ed. A. C. Cawley (Manchester, 1961). – Ed.]
3. For this theory, see Jacob Bennett, 'A linguistic study of *The Castle of Perseverance*', unpublished Ph.D. dissertation (Boston University, 1960): *Dissertation Abstracts*, XXI (1961), p. 872.
4. For an analysis of the theology and structure of *Wisdom*, see Molloy, op.

cit. He refutes earlier speculation that *Wisdom* was written for a monastic audience, and stresses the play's application to mankind in general, pp. 198ff.

5. The change of costume to denote repentance is a well-established morality convention (cf. *Wisdom*, 1068ff.), which is probably borrowed from medieval customs of public penitence and endures on the stage well into Elizabethan times (thus Hal's appearance in armour in *Henry IV, Part I*). On this subject, see T. W. Craik, *The Tudor Interlude* (Leicester, 1958), pp. 73–92.

6. At line 851 above occurs a previous parallel ('O Jesu help! All hath forsaken me') with Christ's words on the cross. See Thomas F. Van Loon, '*Everyman*: A Structural Analysis', *PMLA*, LXXVIII (1963), pp. 465–75.

7. *Mankind* is dated 1464–68 on the basis of coins mentioned in the text, by Donald C. Baker, 'The date of *Mankind*', *Philological Quarterly*, XLII (1963), pp. 90–1. On the geography of the play, see W. K. Smart, 'Some Notes on *Mankind*', *Modern Philology*, XIV (1916), pp. 306–7.

8. A. W. Pollard, introduction to *The Macro Plays*, ed. F. J. Furnivall, EETS, e.s. 91 (London, 1904), pp. *xi–xii*: Smart, op. cit., p. 312.

9. *Mankind* (43, 227).

10. Coogan, p. 94.

11. On this subject see Gertrude Hort, *Piers Plowman and Contemporary Thought* (London, 1938), pp. 138–41.

12. For a brilliant reconstruction of one such celebration, see Southern passim.

Bernard Spivack   'The Vice as a Stage Metaphor'   (1958)

> What man so wise, what earthly wit so ware,
> As to descry the crafty cunning traine,
> By which deceipt doth maske in visour faire,
> And cast her colours dyed deepe in graine,
> To seem like Truth . . .
>
> *The Faerie Queene*

Having produced the figure of Vice, the Tudor stage submitted to his spell. As homiletic showman, intriguer extraordinary and master of dramatic ceremonies, he emerged, before the middle of the century, into acknowledged theatrical prominence – both in the moralities proper and in plays that do not participate, except for his presence in them, in the allegorical convention. His role, much older than his histrionic title, came into its key position as soon as the martial allegory of the Psychomachia was transformed by the stage into a plot of intrigue. From the first he is elevated above his companion vices by his homiletic distinction as *radix malorum*, and exploited into special dramatic magnitude to illustrate his primacy in a sequence of moral evils – a sequence the schematic exposition of which is an important part of the homiletic purpose of nearly every moral interlude. His development over a century (roughly 1425–1525), until he earns the title which expresses his popularity and unique theatrical status, consists largely of his growing individuality and in the expansion of his role through its accumulation of standard pieces of stage business. Into his stock performance the Psychomachia distills its essence, its theme the source of his aggressive energy, its method as homiletic allegory the source of his dramatic style. In the moralities proper he invariably functions in homiletic association with several subsidiary vices, who follow him through the breach he makes in the moral defenses of humanity. This association disappears only when he is transferred into plays which, save that they exploit his role for its great theatrical value, are but partially within the allegorical convention or not at all, and are not, therefore, concerned with the exposition of a sequence of moral evils. . . . For the present we need to examine, in his typical character and performance, the Vice of the moralities.

It cannot be stressed too much that his whole action as intriguer and seducer is a dramatised metaphor with a meaning beyond its literal enactment on the stage. The principles governing his role are inevitably homiletic in their origin, and his typical stage behavior is inevitably abstract in its ultimate significance. Just as his very existence resulted from the homiletic concept of a *root* evil, so are the whole scope and the parts of his behavior concrete images of similar generalisations. His aim is the moral and spiritual ruin of his victim in order that he may demonstrate thereby the destructive force and characteristic effect of the evil he personifies. His separate actions and stock characteristics are likewise allusive, metaphorical, and expository – at least in plays that are thoroughgoing moralities. His performance, in its whole range and in its details, is a stereotype because as often as he appears on the stage he is a metaphor for the homiletic stereotype that medieval Christianity formulated in respect to the origin of moral evil and the method of its operation on the human heart. To illustrate this fact is to reproduce, at the same time, the typical dramatic image of the Vice – an image that remained alive on the stage for a considerable time after its original significance and the morality drama itself had passed away.

The heart of his role is an act of seduction, and the characteristic stratagem whereby the Vice achieves his purpose is a vivid stage metaphor for the sly insinuation of moral evil into the human breast. For its consummation he displays himself as an artist in persuasion who deftly manipulates his victim out of his virtuous inclination and turns him about in the direction of his ruin. Translated into dramatic terms, his stratagem is twofold. In one part it is to create a divorce between the human hero and the personifications of virtue who support and counsel him. In *Mankind* . . . Titivillus, by his insinuations and slanders, is able to alienate the hero from Mercy, his guardian personification. Folly, in *Mundus et Infans*, having created a similar breach between Manhood and Conscience, assures the audience 'That Conscyence he shall awaye cast'.[1] In *Nature*, Pride achieves his initial success in depraving Man by prevailing on him to get rid of Reason, and is soon able to announce:

> Reason nay nay hardely
> He ys forsaken vtterly
> Syth I cam to hys [Man's] company
> He wold not onys appere.
>
> [*Nature*, 1090–3]

Likewise in *The Four Elements*, Sensuous Appetite persuades Humanity to free himself from the solicitous tutelage of Studious Desire. In *Magnificence* the success of the plot of the vices against the well-being of the hero is signalised when Measure, who has been his counsellor, is thrown out of favor and driven from court. In the Protestant morality of *Lusty Juventus* the young hero of that name, having been set on the right path of life and religion by Good Counsel and Knowledge, is induced by Hypocrisy, in a long scene of clever seduction, to forsake his guardian personifications and to devote his attention to Abominable Living. In each of these actions, and in others too numerous to mention, the homiletic purpose creates the dramatic image of the Vice as the artful breeder of strife and alienation between his victim and his victim's true spiritual friends, the attendant personifications of virtue. He is the cunning instigator of discord and debate, and his success in this part of his stratagem appears when the frail hero attaches himself to the company and guidance of the Vice, rebuffing and insulting Virtue, who is left on the stage to vent his grief and admonition upon the audience.

According to the same homiletic logic, expressing the human decline from moral good to moral evil, the Vice accomplishes the remaining part of his enterprise in seduction when he is able to unite himself to his victim in the bond of friendship, in the relationship of servant to master, or in that of preceptor to pupil.[2] 'Your seruaunt

wyll I be', says Folly to Manhood in *Mundus et Infans*, as the hero
abandons his allegiance to Conscience and goes off, Folly guiding
him, to dine in Eastcheap and to sample sweet wine at the Pope's
Head Tavern.[3] 'Putte yourselfe nowe wholye into my handes', is the
ruinous advice that Avarice, alias Policy, urges upon Respublica.[4] In
Impatient Poverty the Vice attaches himself to the hero as his 'cosin',
and, since doctrinly he is the pioneer beating a way for other moral
evils to follow, he advises his victim to expect more company:

> I come hyther wyth you to dwell
> Ye muste haue moo seruauntes I do you tell
> Soche as were necessarye for youre person.
>
> [*Imp. Poverty*, 584–6]

And Mary Magdalene, in Lewis Wager's play of that name, is so
taken by Infidelity's blandishments that she fairly leaps at his sly bid
to be her servant and counsellor:

> I perceiue right well that you owe me good will,
>   Tendryng my worshipfull state and dignitie:
> You see that I am yong and can little skill
>   To prouide for myne owne honor and vtilitie.
>
> Wherfore I pray you in all thyngs counsell to haue,
>   After what sort I may leade a pleasant life here;
> And looke what it pleaseth you of me to craue,
>   I will geue it you gladly, as it shall appere.
>
> [*Mary Magd.*, 138–45]

The Vice is only too willing:

> Say you so, mistresse Mary? Wil you put me in trust?
>   In faith I will tell you, you can not trust a wiser.
> You shall liue pleasantly, euen at your heart's lust,
>   If you make me your counseller and deuiser.
>
> [146–9]

So much then for the intention of the Vice's stratagem, which, while
he remains in the moralities proper, is always one and the same: to
manipulate the human hero out of the virtue which is the Vice's
homiletic opposite and to insinuate himself instead (that is, the evil he
personifies) into his victim's bosom, dominating him and enticing
him headlong down the road to damnation. The constant and
compact stage image created by the metaphor of the Psychomachia is
that of an artless and credulous dupe who is tempted, fooled and
ensnared by a master craftsman in the fine art of seduction. . . .

SOURCE: extract from ch. 6, 'Moral Metaphor and Dramatic Image', in *Shakespeare and the Allegory of Evil* (New York, 1958), pp. 151–4.

NOTES

1. *Mundus et Infans* (652). [For text-references to this play, see J. M. Manly, *Specimens of the Pre-Shakespearean Drama*, 2 vols (Boston, Mass., 1897). Other play-text references in Spivack's study derive from the following:

For *Nature*: A. Brandl (ed.), *Quellen des Weltlichen Dramas in England vor Shakespeare* (Strassburg, 1898).

For *Respublica*: ed. L. A. Magnus, EETS, e.s. 94 (London, 1905).

For *Impatient Poverty*: ed. R. B. McKerrow, in W. Bang (ed.), *Materielen zur Kunde des alteren Englischen Dramas*, vol. 33 (Louvain, 1911).

For Lewis Wager's *The Life and Repentance of Mary Magdalene*: ed. F. I. Carpenter (Chicago, 1902) – Ed.]

2. The compact pattern of the twofold stratagem appears in the words with which the Devil, himself impotent, commissions the Vice against the hero of *Lusty Juventus*, Dodsley, II, p. 67;

> I would have thee go incontinent,
> And work some crafty feat or policy,
> To set Knowledge and him at controversy;
> And his company thyself greatly use,
> That God's Word he may clean abuse.

3. *Mundus et Infans* (638).
4. *Respublica* (507).

Joanne Spencer Kantrowitz　Allegory
(1975)

... the critic who demands characterisation and verisimilitude from this particular kind of literature [allegory] is doomed to frustration and subsequent distaste. Episodes are not framed and placed to reflect probability, but to present the reader with parts of the ... argument in a particular order or for a particular rhetorical effect. Character is not divulged primarily by demonstrated action, but by direct narrative – usually, indeed, by self-description. Individuals appear and disappear at the need of the topic, while time and distance are simply signified in the eternal world of allegory.

Looking at Sir David Lindsay's *Ane Satyre of the Thrie Estaitis* from this point of view, we can see that the play incorporates many of the conventions we have observed in the narrative allegory. Earlier scholars have characterised it as episodic or 'formless', but this is a criticism based on the concept of dramatic form as sequential action moving with increasing complications through a climax to the dénouement. The *Thrie Estaitis*, however, works from a different concept of unity, the unity of argument, and, while the play does fall into two distinct parts which are marked by an intermission, these parts are integral. The apparent protagonist, Rex Humanitas, is not a protagonist in the modern sense. Rather, like the pilgrim of the allegory, he is a vehicle for the argument. The topic is not a king's biography, but a dramatisation of the subversion and subsequent reformation of a kingdom. The king is important, not as an individual soul falling to perdition, but as a political leader whose moral condition determines the state of the nation, and Rex Humanitas is treated as such from his first appearance. From this point of view, part 1 is a description of the progress of decadence, or the causes of the realm's decay, while part 2 demonstrates the means for the removal or reformation of that social and political decadence.

In the depiction of time and space, the first part of the *Thrie Estaitis* is more like *King Hart* than any of the other allegories discussed [in an earlier part of the chapter – Ed.]. The locale of the play is limited to the court and a vague expanse of countryside around it which may be taken to represent the nation. (Rex Humanitas is not a traveller or pilgrim in the literal sense, but like the pilgrims and like King Hart, he is the naïf, the inexperienced youth who acquires experience. This, however, is the experience of a king, not that of the individual represented as a pilgrim or a monarch.) Yet while the locale is comparatively static, time and space are represented in the same way they are in the allegories. From the text and from what we know of contemporary staging, the actors appear to be positioned at various intervals on the playing field.[1] A change of scene is then represented by a simple shift of the dialogue from one set of characters to another, while the time it takes to travel from one point to another is represented by the character's walking from one group to another. For example, this occurs when Wantoness is sent on his journey to bring Sensualitie to the King, and when Chastitie successively looks for lodging with the various members of the three estates. Such practice is dramatic representation of comparable elements in narrative allegory, as suggested [earlier] by our discussion of Rolland's treatment of time and space in the *Court of Venus*.

The characters are static, too. While the rapid character shift depicted in Rex Humanitas's fall from initial grace does occur in the first five hundred lines of the play, one should not regard this as a crude attempt at characterisation. So it may appear to those educated by expectations of 'proper' motivation and probability, but Lindsay is not attempting to delineate the psychological process of temptation. He has compressed the process into a series of short scenes which the audience takes as a sign of that process. He is interested, not in the internal process as it affects character, but in the fact of the king's shift to the sensual life which, he demonstrates, is produced by the influence of the courtiers and in turn provides the conditions for the subsequent action which stands for the fact of national decadence.

From this examination of allegory, we see that the apparent disorder of *Ane Satyre of the Thrie Estaitis* is disorder only in terms of modern expectations. In fact, the play reflects the practice of its non-dramatic predecessors in the presentation of topic, character, time and place. But, so far, we have looked at narrative allegory to see what implicit assumptions the play shares with them in terms of basic artistic practice. Another group of texts supplements comparison with contrast, generalisation with differentiation. Earlier, we said the allegories varied across a long range of topics, including the nature of sin, of virtue, of love, of knowledge itself. If we limit ourselves to allegories concerned with political life, we can see that the range of artistic device is wide, even in this limited topical area.

Allegories can be differentiated on the basis of their fictions. One kind of allegory uses a *metaphorical* construction. Here, people can be presented as animals and the resulting story is a beast fable, like that in *Vox Clamantis*.[2] Man is represented as a pilgrim (*Pilgrimage*), a king (*King Hart*), a knight (*Example of Virtue*), and the story is a succession of adventures which convey meaning or a special experience which appears as a specific place or series of places (*Reason and Sensuality, Court of Sapience*). Here, the writer takes the topic or situation which interests him and turns it into a fable which provides the terms for his invention of equivalences.

The metaphorical allegory differs from that based on generalisation. This we may call the *literal* allegory. When the writer chooses to discuss kingship, for example, he talks not about a lion or about Mount Olympus, but about a king and his court. It is not an individualised representation of a specific king and his court; it is a generalised representation of a nonspecific king and a nonspecific court – not Richard II or James V, but simply a 'Rex Humanitas' or 'King'. This is a distinction based on the general character of the fiction. It ignores the usual classification based on character types or topic, yet it recognises basic differences analogous to R. W. Frank's description of allegory as symbolic or personified.[3]

If we interpret allegory along this general metaphorical-literal line, the terms are neither inflexible nor all-inclusive. An individual work may be an allegory, but allegory can also be a rhetorical device subordinate to a different sort of organisation. *Piers Plowman* is an allegory: in the whole poem, the commentary is subordinate to, and grows out of, the series of fictions presented. *Vox Clamantis* is not an allegory. It is a complaint, a critical essay in verse, which uses allegory as a device, a means for introducing the reader to the situation and for producing an emotional effect. This is not a matter of essential difference but of proportion. Both Langland and Gower comment on the action they present, but Langland, in general, speaks through the fiction, implying his attitude with comparatively brief commentary while Gower presents his fable for emotional effect while reserving his detailed analysis for the essay which follows it and expands its meaning. Gower speaks directly; Langland, indirectly. Both, however, construct their fables to the requirements of their theme.

The division between fable and exposition in *Vox Clamantis* is not as sharp in *Mum and the Soothsayer*[4] which, nevertheless, employs allegory as a device subordinate to direct exposition. Both writers construct beast fables. Gower tells of the Peasant's Rebellion as an attack by animals whose ferocity, unleashed, infects the domesticated animals, attracts swarms of noxious insects, and turns the entire animal world into beasts of prey bent on the destruction of everything that does not share their viciousness. Playing on our disgust for swarming flies, ravenous oxen, maddened geese, Gower produces loathing for the behavior of the brutalised peasantry and anxiety for a society overturned in chaotic violence. The horror arises from the perversions of the beasts' natures and their parallel to the actions of men who pervert the social order. The author of *Mum and the Soothsayer* uses a different range of meaning for his beast fable. He, too, wishes to tell the events which led to social chaos and the deposition of Richard II. However, he begins with a direct statement of the national condition and introduces his beast fable (passus secundus), not to pose the problem or describe the emotional effect, but to narrate the events which caused Richard's downfall. He deals primarily, not in the connotative meanings of Gower's beasts, but in the denotative meanings of heraldry: Richard is the White Hart; Bolingbroke, the Eagle; Gloucester, the Swan. Both writers use the allegorical beast fable as a rhetorical device subordinate to the structure of the whole poem, but the fables are conceived in different terms – one is connotative, the other denotative – and are introduced at different points in the work and for different purposes.

Mum and the Soothsayer is useful to our analysis for another purpose, too, for the author also creates a literal allegory to account for the king's deposition. In the third passus, he tells in 164 lines [207–371] the story of a court lost in debauchery where Witt, a greybeard in modest dress, is mocked and barred from the court. This action is eventually punished by God, the absolute King who calls his heavenly warriors together and destroys the recreant king and his court. This, too, accounts for Richard's fall, the event which underlies the fable. It illustrates the same theme: the unjust king (the hart) has surrounded himself with unjust retainers (the white harts; the young, debauched courtiers), refused the counsel of the wise (the Swan, Witt), and has been conquered by the agent of a just destruction (Bolingbroke, the Eagle; God, the Heavenly King). Though smaller in scope and less detailed in its analysis, this second, literal allegory operates within the same terms used in the first two visions of *Piers Plowman*. Langland examines the nature of society in the King's court and in the half-acre by generalisation, *not* by a system of metaphor. His king, however, *is* ruled by Conscience, Wit and Reason, a difference in event but not in *kind*. Both the second allegory of *Mum and the Soothsayer* and the first two visions of *Piers Plowman* treat the topics of social order, and both cast their discussions, not in metaphorical terms such as the beast fable, but in generalised representations. The differences within those representations result from the uses of the fiction: the anonymous writer shows the causes of decay in Richard's monarchy; Langland presents us with a picture of the rule of justice which he subsequently elaborates in the half-acre sequence. Both, however, are *literal* allegories, different in their meaning, scope and function within the poems of which they are a part, but similar in the terms of their basic construction.

In its use of a generalised fiction, *Ane Satyre of the Thrie Estaitis* shows the same characteristics. Langland uses Mede as the major term; Lindsay centers his play around Sensuality. As Langland shifts to the problem of the practical reform of society and the problem of just 'mede' in the half-acre episode, so Lindsay shifts the second part of his play to the practical reform of society's sensuality. Like the second allegory in *Mum and the Soothsayer*, the first half of Lindsay's allegory uses the ridicule of Wisdom (Gude-Counsall) and his banishment as a generalisation for evil rule, and the literal descent of God's avenger as a generalisation for the punishment of irresponsible government. All these are examples of literal allegory. Lindsay's greater use of typical characters in the second half of the play implies, again, not a difference in kind but in degree of generalisation. Both Veritie and Johne the Common-Weill, Sensualitie and Spiritualite are cast, not in the Palace of Fame or the Garden of Love, but in a generalised kingdom which represents no state of mind nor view of human nature, but a political state, and, specifically, the political state which is Scotland in 1552. The first half of the play relies more heavily on abstract presentation in its use of such characters as Sensualitie, Veritie and Chastitie; the second half employs a more specific presentation through the use of characters such as Johne, the Pauper and the Doctour of Divinitie. But both parts function in terms of the same view of the state in a fiction constructed in the same terms as the reality it represents: the kingdom.

We can see this fusion of representation and meaning more clearly, perhaps, if we turn to another allegory, *King Hart*. There the terms are the terms of kingship, but the meaning has nothing to do with kingship at all. The subject is the individual and his course through life, the same subject framed as a pilgrimage in Deguileville's poem, as a quest in the *Example of Virtue*. Yet King Hart rises, falls and rises again, just as Rex Humanitas goes through the same cycle. To classify the play and the poem together on this basis scarcely enlightens either and enlarges an apparent similarity of fiction to a principle of classification.[5] Both use the same fable, the career of a king, but the relation between fable and meaning sets them in very different groups indeed. *King Hart* is a metaphorical allegory: it discusses human life through a representation of kingship. *Ane Satyre of the Thrie Estaitis* is a literal allegory: it discusses the Scottish polity through a representation of political life or, in contemporary terms, it discusses Scottish kingship through a representation of Scottish kingship.

Yet, although one must first isolate and define the meaning of a text before evaluating its character as allegory, artistic value extends beyond the relative importance of the theme or the acumen with which it is analysed. There is more to allegory than that: the fable itself must be artfully invented to best express the theme. *The Complaint of Scotland*, written in 1548, provides us with an analogue as close to the meaning of the *Thrie Estaitis* as one is likely to find in literary history. Responding to the same events, lashing out against the same excess in national and religious affairs that Lindsay found so repugnant, the anonymous author of the *Complaint* has nevertheless written a very different sort of allegory.[6] Like Lindsay, he too represents the three estates and discusses their social failings through dialogue. But his handling is much more facile, much less imaginative. He simply invents an entity named Dame Scotia, representative of the entire Scottish nation, and endows her with three sons, Clergy, Commons, Nobility. The result is hardly a dialogue, an interchange, but a debate, a long series of set speeches, with Dame Scotia acting as moderator and rebuking each speaker in turn. This debate may be compared with the second half of the *Thrie Estaitis* where the same criticisms form the basic material of the play.[7] Lindsay, too, invents a situation to detail the Scottish excesses, but this is a dialogue peopled with much more individualised characters: Johne, Pauper, the Doctour, Common Thift, and the exaggerated, acerbic Spiritualitie with his train of Parsone and Nune. And around these characters, the dramatist builds the attack of the rebellious upstart, Johne, who even as he complains in truth risks the charge of heresy as payment for his pains. Lindsay's is, of course, a more dramatic situation: it is a drama; it was meant to be played, not read. But for all the difference between the allegory as narrative and the allegory as drama, one may still say that *Ane Satyre of the Thrie Estaitis* is a more imaginative allegory, a better artwork than its companion in Scottish politics, the *Complaint of Scotland*.

This is not to say that set speeches, in and of themselves, are artistically bad. On the contrary, they are an integral practice in allegorical literature. Lindsay's Gude-Counsall speaks the substance of the play's theme in his long speeches; Holicherche enunciates the principles in *Piers Plowman*.[8] But, in both cases, theory is enlivened by action. The principles are enlarged by action which both demonstrates and makes more specific the themes it illustrates. In the *Complaint of Scotland*, however, the long speeches are both the sum and substance of the allegory; they lack the variations of character and action which Lindsay so happily provides in the *Thrie Estaitis*. . . .

SOURCE: extract from the chapter 'Allegory' in *Dramatic Allegory: Lindsay's 'Ane Satyre of the Thrie Estaitis'* (Lincoln, Neb., 1975), pp. 95–101.

NOTES

[Reorganised and renumbered from the original. For short-form references to works, see Abbreviation List, p. 8 – Ed.]

1. See Southern; and A. J. Mill, 'Representations of Lyndsay's *Satyre of the Thrie Estaitis*', *PMLA*, 47 (1932), pp. 636–49. [References to this play are from D. Hamer (ed.), *The Works of Sir David Lindsay*, 4 vols, Scottish Text Society (Edinburgh, 1931–36), vol. 3 – Ed.] Southern argues that the stream shown in the *Castle of Perseverance* drawing must have been a moat behind the audience. Johne the Common-Weill's entrance (2428–30) is accompanied by

a stage direction, 'Heir sall Johne loup the stank [ditch] or els fall in it'. Another scene, that between the sowtar's wife and the taylor's wife (1368–87) takes place 'be the watter syde'. Both scenes, then, imply the 'ditch' was part of the playing field, at least in Lindsay's experience, or that he specifically wrote the play for the field at Cupar, where a small stream still flows along the edge of the town to join the river Eden.

2. *The Complete Works of John Gower*, ed. George C. Macaulay, vol. 4 (Oxford, 1902). A useful translation is Eric W. Stockton, *The Major Latin Works of John Gower* (Seattle, 1962). Stockton believes that book 1 of *Vox* is an 'afterthought' and not an integral part of the poem (p. 12). In this he emphasises Macaulay's suggestion that it 'has certainly something of the character of an insertion' (p. *xxxii*): an opinion Macaulay cautiously advanced on the basis of the Laud MS, one of the five then known. I believe an analysis of Gower's rhetoric would reveal a close connection between his subsequent 'animalistic' imagery and the substance of book 1. Unfortunately, *Vox* remains virtually unexplored.

3. R. W. Frank Jnr, 'The Art of Reading Medieval Personification Allegory', *English Literary History*, 20 (1953), pp. 237–50.

4. *Mum and the Soothsayer*, ed. M. Day and R. Steele, EETS, o.s. 199 (London, 1936).

5. Cf. Willard Farnham's description of the early drama in *The Medieval Heritage of Elizabethan Tragedy* (Berkeley, Cal., 1936).

6. *The Complaynt of Scotlande*, ed. James A. H. Murray, EETS, e.s. 17 (London, 1872). My comments here are restricted to the dialogue between Dame Scotia and her sons, the central presentation. Bibliographical evidence in the form of a large number of cancels suggests extensive revision of the original text, and the insertion of the pastoral scene as a 'filler'. Until the character of the cancels is ascertained, complete discussion of the *Complaynt* is necessarily based on questionable evidence.

7. Lindsay emphasises the excesses of the clergy, pokes fun at the merchants, but scarcely tweaks the nobility. In contrast, the author of the *Complaynt* emphasises the excesses of the Assured Scots, the nobles whose sympathies lay with the English, while apparently dealing less harshly with the sins of the commons, and especially the sins of the clergy. On this last, however, one may reserve opinion, since many of the cancels seem to appear at places where the clergy is under discussion – the result of some sort of censorship?

8. See T. P. Dunning, *Piers Plowman: An Interpretation of the A-Text* (Dublin, 1937), especially pp. 26–7.

T. W. Craik   On *Enough is as good as a Feast* (1958)

The prologue is the least attractive part of this play. Wager is far better at writing plays than he is at writing about the playwright's art; and the latinate rhyme-royal stanzas, laboriously invoking the Muses and diffusely stating the virtues and difficulties of eloquence, are sluggish and heavy. When the Worldly Man replaces the Prologue, his speech is full of life and energy, stuffed with the proverbs of worldly wisdom:

> Because I am a man indewed with treasure,
> Therfore a worldly man men doo me call:
> In deed I haue riches and money at my pleasure,
> Yea, and I wil haue more in spight of them all.
>   A common saying better is enuy then rueth,
> I had rather they should spite then pitty me:
> For the olde saying now a dayes proueth trueth,
> Naught haue naught set by as dayly we see.
>   I wis I am not of the minde as some men are,
> Which look for no more then wil serue necessitie:
> No against a day to come I doo prepare,
> That when age commeth I may liue merily.
>   Oh saith one inough is as good as a feast,
> Yea, but who can tel what his end shal be?
> Therfore I count him wurse then a Beast,
> That wil not haue that in respect and see.
>   As by mine owne Father an example I may take,
> He was belooued of all men and kept a good house:
> Whilst riches lasted, but when that did slake,
> There was no man that did set by him a Louse.
>   And so at such time as he from the world went,
> I mene when he dyed he was not worth a grote:
> And they that all his substance had spent,
> For the value of xij. pence would haue cut his throte.
>   But I trowe I wil take heed of such,
> They shall go ere they drink when they come to me:
> It dooth me good to tel the chinks in my hutch,
> More then at the Tauern or ale house to be.[1]

It should be noted that the Worldly Man is not unprovided with arguments. Improvidence can be wicked, as he says. But the audience is invited to see that his logic is false. The possibility that others may treat us selfishly does not justify our selfishness as a precaution. Covetousness is not the only alternative to waste. There is also the suggestion, supported by the final mention of tavern and alehouse, that the Worldly Man's father did not practise true hospitality but 'kept a good house' for revellers who spent his substance. Attention is drawn to these false arguments by the obvious greed of the first quatrain, and by the implication in the third that the speaker is the Rich Fool, preparing for a prosperous and self-indulgent old age; the corollary, that before the end of the play his soul will be required of him, is also implied.

The speech is directed at the audience, a public speech like the prologue, though of course in a colloquial style. The Worldly Man is justifying himself, expounding what he presents as a natural and proper way of life. He blandly assumes that he is persuading the hearers to applaud his worldly wisdom – a good device on Wager's part for arousing their opposition, which is maintained by such ironies as 'Yea, but who can tel what his end shal be?' (the speaker's thoughts are limited to material welfare; his own spiritual end is far from his mind). These confidences of the self-assured Worldly Man continue during his ensuing debate with the Heavenly Man and Contentation ('Oh, I tel you these are godly walkers'; 'Good reasoning betwixt vs now hear you shall'), and the debate is carried on in full knowledge that it is a public one, so that the exhortations of the Heavenly Man are not addressed solely to his opponent but also to the listeners:

> O you ancient men whome God hath furnished with fame,
> Be ye alwaies mindeful to walke in the waies of the Just
> . . .
> Ye poor men and commons walke in your vocation
> . . .

The conversion of Worldly Man is not gradual, but suddenly occurs when the argument has run its course. It is to be taken as genuine, and his absolute statement

> For I regarde neither treasure, Children nor wife

is paralleled by the action of Bunyan's Christian who leaves his family behind him in the City of Destruction. Wager is not concerned with the psychology of conversion but with the dramatic expression of it. Being totally unexpected, it is effective. (It is usual – in *Youth* and *Hickscorner*, for instance, or in Wager's own *The longer thou livest the more Fool thou art* and *The Trial of Treasure* – for the evildoers to resist the prayers and warnings of the just, whether they are to be at last reclaimed or destroyed.) Worldly Man takes Heavenly Man by the hand in formal alliance and they go out.

Immediately the vices come in singing the praises of their leader Covetous, who enters next with a long nonsense-monologue –

> At Black heath feeld where great Golias was slain,
> The Moon lying in childebed of her last Sonne:
> The Tiborne at warwick was then King of Spain,
> By whome the land of *Canaan* then was wun
>   . . .

– and so on for eleven quatrains. It has absolutely no significance, and (like the song) it serves to relax the spectators' minds while at the same time bringing the vice and his fellows before them. Suddenly, after a few farcical salutations, vigorous action resumes when Covetous is told that he 'standeth now at the point of banishment' owing to Worldly Man's reformation. With urgent oaths he calls for his gown, cap, and chain. The suggestion that Worldly Man can be left to backslide without assistance is instantly repudiated, because a repentant sinner forthwith obtains divine forgiveness; and therefore Worldly Man must not be abandoned to his spiritual safety for a moment. The disguise is brought, and Covetous puts it on:

> COUETOUSE: First to help on my gown some paines doo you take
>   And then I wil see what curtsie you can make.
> INCONSIDERATION: It is trim indeed, by the masse in that Gown:
>   Me thinks you be worthy to be Mayor of a town.
> COUETOUSE: Say you so? then how like you this countenaunce?
> PRECIPITATION: Very comely and like a person of great gouernaunce.
> COUETOUSE: Then all is wel, come, come doo your dutye:
> ALL THREE: O worthy Prince Couetouse we humbly salute ye.
> COUETOUSE: Body of me, that same wil marre all:
>   When in company I come if Couetouse you doo me call.

There is a good surprise here, when the disguise has made Covetous look respectable and the genuine homage of his fellows gives the game away. Three voices at once shout the name Covetous, and with an oath the vice instantly recalls them to the need for taking false names. These names are comically devised by Covetous (the direction bids him 'study', or meditate), who complains that his thoughts are disturbed by his fellows' eagerness to know their false names, and by the presence of the spectators ('Nay, that maid looks on me'). The worldly vices – Temerity, Inconsideration, Precipitation – are to masquerade as virtues, Agility, Reason and Ready Wit. Covetous himself is to be Policy. Thus the Worldly Man, wise in his own conceit, will rush blindly and greedily to destruction.

Covetous sends Temerity and Inconsideration out to disguise themselves ('In all the haste go thou and be thou disguised'; 'Look you make you trim as fast as you can') and to acquaint themselves with Worldly Man. They never reappear. He and Precipitation (who seems to be respectably dressed enough to avoid suspicion) remain, Precipitation summing up the plot against Worldly Man until Covetous warns him that their victim approaches. 'This is the worldly man I suppose indeed', says Precipitation – a necessary statement, for Worldly Man is 'in a straunge attire', something sober and decent, and might not at once be recognisable. He stands 'afar of', with 'poorly arayed' Enough, and they expound between them a moral allegory in which covetousness is described as a chariot going on the four wheels of contempt-of-God, forgetfulness-of-death, faint-courage and ungentleness, drawn by the two horses Raveny (rapine) and Niggardship, and driven by the carter Desire-to-have with his two-corded whip of acquisitiveness and tenacity. This is addressed to the audience, and would be readily accepted (it is obviously in the same tradition as Batman's moral picture-books).[2] . . . The Worldly Man adds his own contentment with Enough, 'which bringeth me to quiet in body & minde'. On the other side of the 'place', Covetous (in his wealthy disguise) and Precipitation prepare for a struggle, cursing Enough ('that beggerly knaue') because he is likely to stand in their way.

The temptation begins. It is both comic and sinister. Covetous surprisingly addresses himself first to Enough, and asks leave to speak privately with Worldly Man. Enough at once agrees, and there follows the direction 'Let the Vice weep & houle & make great lamentation to the Worldly man'. With noisy tears he poses as a well-wisher and threatens him with the reputation of a miser who renounces hospitality:

> He was wunt (saith one) to keep a good house:
> But now (saith an other) there is no liuing for a mouse.

(The echoes of Worldly Man's first speech remind us that it was before, not after, his conversion that he renounced hospitality.) It seems that Covetous may fail, and tension is kept up when Worldly Man turns to Enough as though to end this conversation, and is feverishly plucked back by Covetous:

WORLDLY MAN: He had need to liue very sircumspectly:
That would take vpon him to please all men directly.
Beholde Inough. (*Go towards him.*)
COUETOUSE: Nay hear you, this greeueth me worst so God me saue: (*Pluck him back.*)

> They say you keep company with euery beggerly knaue.
> WORLDLY MAN: Wher I keep company they haue nought to doo:
> As neer as I can into none but honest company I go.
> See you, I pray you *Inough*.
> COUETOUSE: Nay but hear you, is *Inough* his name?
> WORLDLY MAN: Yea indeed, it is euen the very self same.
> COUETOUSE: *Saint Dunstone*, a man would not iudge it by his cote:
> Now truely I would not take him to be worth a grote.
> Hark you, hark you, in faith knowe you not me?

One can hear the stress on 'me' and see the gesture with which Covetous contrasts Enough's appearance with his own. Having thus disparaged Enough, Covetous introduces himself and Precipitation as Policy and Ready Wit, chopping logic and maintaining that

> Inough is not inough without vs two:
> For hauing not vs, what can inough doo?
> Inough is maintained by wisdome and policy
> . . .

Precipitation argues that 'enough' is relative:

> You haue no more now then dooth your self serue:
> So that your poor Breethern for all you may sterue.
> But inough that commeth by vs twain:
> Is able your self and many other to sustain:

and Worldly Man eagerly assents to the specious argument:

> Your words are euen as true as the Gospel:
> As one named Reason of late to me did tel.

Worldly reason has already, as we know, been identified as the disguise of Inconsideration. The falsity of the argument, and the sinfulness of Worldly Man's approving phrase, are brought out by Enough, who reminds us of what the Gospel actually says on this point:

> Was not the poor widdow for her offring praised more
> Then all they that offred of their superfluitie & store?

But by now Covetous's ascendancy is such that (in his gown, cap and chain) he can patronize Enough:

> He sayes wel by Lady, yea and like an honest man,
> But yet Sir, riches to be good, wel proue I can.
> For euery man is not called after one sorte:
> . . .
> Therefore euery man (as his vocation is) must walke:
> I am sure that against this you wil not talke.

In other words, if Worldly Man's vocation is to make money (which
he blandly assumes it is), to lose the chance of making money is to
subvert the divine scheme. The superb insolence of this, and the
attentiveness of Worldly Man, cause Enough to depart with the
indignant statement 'The worldly man wil needs be a worldly man
stil', while Covetous derides him as a deserter of his friend, and
Worldly Man rejoices over what he considers a lucky escape from
Enough and Contentation:

> A shame take them all, I haue spent on them xx. pound:
> That I had of money and of mine owne good ground.
> I am ashamed of my self so God me saue:
> Because I haue solde almoste all that euer I haue.

Again the hearers are invited to weigh these remarks, to note the
inconsistency between the first and the fourth lines, to remember
Christ's instruction to the young man of great possessions, and to
mark the irony of the oath. He embraces both Covetous and
Precipitation, and after a speech of self-praise by 'Policy' is led out by
them.

A short monologue by the Heavenly Man sums up the degenera-
tion of Worldly Man and provides an interval before the perfected
wickedness of the sinner is shown. The next person to address us is an
old countryman, complaining of his rent-racking landlord ('Oh
masters, is not this euen a lamentable thing?'). We guess that this
landlord is Worldly Man, and so it proves:

> Chad thought a while ago my Londlord would not haue doon thus
> For he said he would be a heauenly man I wus.
> But zoule, the Deuil is as Heauenly as he:
> Three times worse then he was beuore as var as I can zee.

A servant and a hired brickmaker, from whom Worldly Man
withholds board and wages respectively, add their complaints, with
vigorous country rhetoric ('The dropping of his nose he would not
loose'). They talk of their master's ambition, the old tenant comparing him to the Rich Fool:

> Thou foole (saith Christ) this night wil I fetch thy soule from thee:
> And then who shall haue the things that thine be?

Covetous, as steward, refuses their requests for their dues, and is
supported by Worldly Man, who enters 'all braue' and makes a
spectacular figure. He is unmoved by their warnings that divine
vengeance will fall upon him:

> Ha, ha, ha, I must laugh, so God me saue:
> To see what a sort of suters now a dayes we haue.

He is planning for the immediate, not the ultimate, future: like the Rich Fool once more, he resolves 'I must make my barnes more great'; and like Ahab, he has designs on his neighbour's property, 'the little tenament that by my house dooth stand'. But suddenly a voice is heard:

> PROPHET WITHOUT: O thou Earth, Earth, earth, hear the woord of the Lord:
> Knowe thy self to be no better then Clay or dust:
>
> *(Let the Worldly man looke sudenly about him.)*
>
> Se that thy life to Gods trueth doo alwaies accorde:
> For from earth thou cammest and to earth thou must.

The prophet Jeremiah comes in, and states that the wicked steward who misuses his master's goods will be cast into 'vtter darknes'. His speech is marked off from the surrounding couplets by being in two rhyme-royal stanzas. It is addressed to the hearers in general, not to Worldly Man, and its dramatic effect is that the Bible has taken human form and has walked in to denounce the evildoer. Covetous scoffs, but Worldly Man is disturbed and sends for his chaplain Devotion (really Ghostly Ignorance, mentioned by Covetous earlier in the play as a companion of his) to expound the warning.

As he awaits the return of Covetous with the chaplain, Worldly Man feels sickness coming upon him, and lies down to sleep. As he lies on the floor, *Enter Gods plague and stand behinde him a while before he speak.* God's Plague, probably wearing a devil's mask, blows upon him and strikes him with a sword; both these are symbolic acts, and like the spoken judgement on the sleeper (that he will die and receive no mercy, that his goods will perish or be dispersed, that his family will decay) they do not wake him.[3] When God's Plague goes, Covetous returns with the comic old drunkard Ghostly Ignorance. They find Worldly Man, still asleep, dreaming and calling out that he is in Hell. He wakes in agony, and Ghostly Ignorance (instead of being asked to expound the warning, for which purpose he was brought) is sent to fetch a physician. Left alone with Covetous, Worldly Man persists in thinking of his wealth, which is more real to him than his soul:

> Oh policy sick, neuer so sick, oh holde my head:
> Oh sira, what shal become of all my goods when I am dead?

Ghostly Ignorance returns with the Physician, who busily attends the dying man, propping him against a pillow and giving him aquavitae, while Covetous officiously fools about and calls him Flebishiten (flea-beshitten). He revives Worldly Man – who says, with terrible irony,

> You might haue let me go, I was wel out of my pain –

but warns him that he must prepare to die. Worldly Man's response is astonishing:

> Go thy waies I pray thee and trouble not my minde:
> For these newes, to giue thee any thing, in my hart I cannot finde.

And, the Physician indignantly gone, the dying man devises frauds against his creditors: his estate is to be kept intact, even though he has enough to pay every man his due. Next he prepares to make a will, with Ghostly Ignorance as scribe:

> IGNORANCE: Heer is Ink and Paper, what shall I write?
> WORLDLY MAN: In the name, first of all doo thou indite.
> IGNORANCE: In the name, in, in, in, in the name, what more?
> WORLDLY MAN: Of.
> IGNORANCE: Of, of, of, what more?[4] *(fall down.)*
> COUETOUSE: Body of me, down with the paper, away with the Ink:
> IGNORANCE: Passion of me Couetouse he is gone me think.
> Holde, holde him, let vs see if any life in him be:
> COUETOUSE: Nay holde him that will, the Deuil holde him for me.

The dramatic tension of this race against death is not incompatible with the sinister comedy. Along with the solemn satisfaction that God will not permit his name to be used in a wicked will, there goes a derisive satisfaction that Worldly Man's sins have recoiled upon him. The scribal fumblings of the priest, and the off-hand yet significant phrase with which the vice drops the corpse, play their part in producing this mixed response to the scene.

This is not the end of the play. The corpse (still 'all braue' in its dress) is abandoned, a grotesque and yet a pitiable object, to the spectators' reflections. The actor of Ghostly Ignorance is meanwhile changing his costume and will soon reappear. There breaks in upon these reflections the sound of roaring, and Satan comes in:

> Oh, oh, oh, oh, all is mine, all is mine . . .

He speaks the final judgement on Worldly Man:

> The worldly man (quoth he) nay the diuilish man than . . .

(since the play has been built round the antithesis of the worldly and the heavenly, this phrase is a dramatic surprise; for all the earlier talk of heaven and hell, a deeper gulf seems to open). Satan is confident, radiant with infernal hospitality. He pays tribute to the genius of

Covetous and to that of the Worldly Man himself. He offers a smiling invitation:

> All you worldly men, that in your riches doo trust,
> Be mery and iocond, builde Palaces and make lusty cheer:
> Put your money to Usury, let it not lye and rust,
> Occupye your selues in my lawes while ye be heer.
>   Spare not, nor care not, what mischeef you frequent,
> Use drunkennes, deceit, take other mens wiues:
> Passe of nothing, one houre is inough to repent,
> Of all the wickednes you haue doon in your liues.
>   Oh if you wil thus after my Lawes behaue,
> You shall haue all things as this worldly man had:
> Be bolde of me, what you wil to craue,
> And dout you not but with you I wil play the loouing lad.
>   Yea, and after death I wil prouide a place,
> For you in my kingdome for euer to reign:
> You shall fare no wurse then dooth mine owne grace,
> That is to lye burning for euer in pain.

As the spectators recoil, he turns back with a shrug to the corpse, addressing it as though it were still alive, and thus providing a terrible reminder that the soul lives still:

> Come on mine owne Boy, go thou with me,
> Thou hast serued me duely, and hatest me neuer:
> Therfore now for thy paines rewarded shalt thou be:
> In euer lasting fire that burneth for euer.
>   (*Bear him out vpon his back.*)

After another short pause, Contentation, Enough and the Heavenly Man enter together (the player of Satan reappearing as Contentation). In weighty stanzas of rhyme-royal they contrast the unquiet life and death of the Worldly Man with the tranquillity of the Heavenly Man. This tranquillity is personified as Rest; he now comes in to reward the Heavenly Man, who thanks God for the great gift (perhaps symbolised by a crown). With this the action ends, and there follow the customary prayers for the Queen and all her subjects:

> Inough is as good as a feast, heer let vs stay,
> We haue troubled our audience, that let vs remember:
> Let vs conclude therfore, but first let vs pray,
> That it wil please God in mercy our good mistres to tender,
> Our faith to stablish wherin we be slender.
> That at the last day when the trump shall blowe:
> For to be heauenly men the Lord may vs al knowe.

SOURCE: extract from chapter 'Action' in *The Tudor Interlude* (Leicester, 1958), pp. 100–10.

NOTES

[Reorganised and renumbered from the original – Ed.]

1. Play-text citations are from W. Wager, *Enough is as good as a Feast*, ed. S. de Ricci (New York, 1920).

2. See S. Batman, *A christall glasse of Christian reformation* (London, 1569), Sigs Biv, Civ^v, Hi; *The travayled Pylgrime* (London, 1569), sig. Bi^v; *The new arival of the three Gracis into Anglia* (London, 1573), Fi^v.

3. Worldly Man, when he awakens, tells Covetous

> And me thought before me the plague of God did stand:
> Redy to strike me with a Sworde in his hand.

Similarly, the denunciation of Lust by God's Visitation in *The Trial of Treasure* – 'Thou insipient foole that hast folowed thy luste' – is apostrophe, for Lust is unaware of his presence and continues to dally with Treasure and Pleasure: it is an effective scene. With the direction in *Enough* compare 'Dispayre enter in some ougly shape, and stand behind him' in *Tide Tarrieth no Man* (the temptation of Wastefulness to suicide). This formal positioning of the characters is meant to show that the happenings are taking place at a spiritual, not a physical, level.

4. The text has, in error,

WORLDLY MAN: Of, of, of, of, what more?

I have restored the prefix to Ignorance's speech.

4. ASPECTS OF PERFORMANCE

David M. Bevington   'The Popular Troupe'   (1962)

... The attempt [here] is to reconstruct a composite picture of a mid-century popular troupe, and to discern trends in its development culminating in the London companies of the 1580s and 1590s.

The first enquiry concerns the employment of boy actors for the women's parts. Were the female roles invariably assigned to a boy, and only to him? Was there one boy in every troupe of four, five or six players, and only one? Was this boy actor limited to portrayal of women and children, or could he fill other roles? Does the number of boy actors tend to increase in the 1560s and 1570s as troupe size increases? J. A. Symonds's summary of the acting tradition of these strolling players, based in part on the play within the play of *Sir Thomas More*, may serve as a convenient and perhaps too widely accepted generalisation which will be tested: 'The leading actor played the part of Vice and undertook stage management. There was a boy for the female characters; and the remaining two or three divided the other parts between them.'[1]

As it happens, investigation of the casting lists reveals no single instance to support this generalisation in its literal sense. That is, no play in the group distributes its roles so that one player handles all the female parts and only female parts. Some of these plays, in fact, have no identifiable female roles at all: *Impatient Poverty*, *Wealth and Health*, *Like Will to Like*, and *Enough is as good as a Feast*. In such cases, the boy member – if indeed he existed for the troupe in question – would have to play an equal assortment of demanding male roles with the other supporting players of his group. In *Like Will to Like*, for example, he might be assigned to play Lucifer, Ralph Roister, Good Fame and Severity, or perhaps Philip Fleming, Pierce Pickpurse and Honor. The remaining sets of roles are no less thoroughly male, and in every case the supposed boy would have to perform the burlesque routines of comic villainy. The more logical assumption is that the troupes which performed these plays employed no boy.

Still other plays offer only one, or perhaps two, feminine or juvenile roles, so distributed that the person playing these roles had also to play other parts of a dominantly adult and masculine character. In Bale's *Three Laws*, for example, Idolatry 'decked lyke an olde wytche' is the only female character, and doubles with Law of Moses and with Hypocrisy, apparelled 'lyke a graye fryre'. Idolatry appears in part of one scene only; the others appear throughout the play. Because of the scarcity of feminine roles in all of Bale's printed plays, it is probable that 'my Lord Cromwell's players' consisted of five men rather than four men and a boy.[2] In *Juventus*, lacking a casting list but convincingly offered for four players, Abominable Living is the only female, and any feasible scheme for doubling requires that she double with at least two male parts, perhaps Satan and God's Merciful Promises.

In *All for Money*'s list of thirty-two *dramatis personae*, the aged Mother Croote is the only woman. Thomas Lupton plainly wrote this play for four adult actors. In fact he altered his source (a sermon by Latimer) in order to eliminate female roles. He keeps off stage a woman infanticide who bribes a judge, permitting her only to communicate by letter, and he changes the sex of a petty thief who was a woman in Latimer's account. Lupton also makes humorous use of his professional players in juvenile roles. The birth of Satan as a full-grown adult allows the actor to make comic capital out of his maturity, thereby reversing the customary quip in the boys' theater arising from the immaturity of the young actor.[3]

New Custom describes Hypocrisy on the title page as 'an old Woman'. Hypocrisy is assigned to player two, along with Ignorance, an 'elder' Popish priest, and Edification, 'a Sage'. Hypocrisy is on stage for only seventy-four lines; the other parts are important supporting roles, appearing for the major portion of the play. In the later boys' companies, star performers like Salomon Pavy often imitated old men, utilising the treble voice as a stock characteristic of stage oldsters. Such assignments, however, were the product of the peculiar casting limitations in boys' theater. The popular troupes had no reason to anticipate this practice. Instead, they were evidently more inclined to assign incidental female parts to the men, especially if the women were disfigured and unfeminine like Idolatry, Mother Croote and Hypocrisy, or courtesans like Abominable Living.[4]

The Tide Tarrieth no Man offers perhaps the most striking example of this undertaking of female roles by a seemingly adult player. Its one female role, Wantonness 'the Woman', is assigned to player four along with five other parts, all of them male and some of them vividly comic: Feigned Furtherance, Greediness, the Sergeant, Authority and Despair. The rapid transition from Greediness to Wantonness and then to the Sergeant is a remarkable demonstration of the flexibility demanded of this player in shifting from one sex to the other and back again. Greediness exits at line 1198, and during the absence of player four the Vice and his companion Hurtful Help 'fighteth to prolong the time, while Wantonnesse maketh her ready' [1215]. Wantonness enters at line 1247, transformed not only in garment but in personality. She departs at line 1362, and thirty lines later the Sergeant appears to play his part. It would be unsafe to assume that this group of roles, and the others already mentioned, would of necessity require the talents of a boy.

In at least eight plays offered for acting and in *All for Money*, then, it is presumptuous to suppose that the boy had any function whatsoever. Many of these plays are pre-Elizabethan, four of them quite early: *Three Laws*, *Impatient Poverty*, *Wealth and Health* and *Juventus*. In fact, no pre-Elizabethan play offered for acting provides positive evidence of the existence of the boy.

Early plays without casting lists, even though lacking evidence as to doubling, seem to offer few feasible roles for a boy actor. The author of *Mankind* consciously avoids female roles, for the portrayal of Mercy as a male priest ('I, Mercy, hys father gostly,' [758]) is a departure from the traditional representation of this abstraction as a woman.[5] Apart from Mercy and the title figure, the *dramatis personae* are all rude, swearing, fighting vice figures. *Mundus et Infans* and *Hickscorner* have no discernible feminine roles. Infans, despite his juvenile name, grows into 'Manhood' and 'Age' and has the leading role in the play. In Bale's *King John* the only woman, the widow England, doubles with Clergy. Heywood's popular plays, *Four PP* and *The Pardoner and the Friar*, provide no opportunity for differentiation of acting talents between boys and grown men. If the boy participated in these productions, he did so on an equal footing with other members of the troupe. All told, fifteen plays of the popular canon reveal no need for a boy.

Remarkably few plays – in fact, only two – appear to call for the services of one and only one boy. *Trial of Treasure* gives both of its women's parts, Trust and Treasure, to 'the fourth' player, probably a boy. Even so, he is not limited to female roles. Player four must render the part of Elation, one of the boisterous companions of the Vice (pp. 271–5).

Horestes also seems to demand one boy, who performs both female and male roles. Yet additional female roles are distributed to other distinctly adult members of the troupe. The female leading role, Clytemnestra, and Menelaus's daughter Hermione, are assigned to player six. Even he, as in the case above, is burdened with some very difficult assignments: the profane and scurrilous Hempstring, who is directed to 'fyght at bofites with fystes' with his Newgate companion, Haltersick [389]; and also Provision [926f], who acts as marshal for the kings of Greece. Allowing player six to be the boy notwithstanding, we still find that Horestes himself, the male lead, plays 'a woman like a begger, rounning before they sodier' [625f]. Nature, who appears to be a motherly sort of woman [400f], is played by the Vice.

In *Cambises* the adult players undertake female roles, even though the troupe includes two boys. The casting list is fairly careful to segregate feminine and juvenile roles for the last two of the eight players, and even distinguishes in ability between the leading boy and the younger boy. Player seven portrays Meretrix, Shame, Otian (Sisamnes's son), Mother, the Lady (the Queen). Shame, although a neutral allegorical figure, may have been thought of as a male role; his brief appearance at line 340 comes at a time in the play when all the adult players are busily occupied in immediately adjoining scenes, and the part appears to have fallen to the leading boy by default. Player eight is limited to Young Child (seven speaking lines) and Cupid (six lines). Notwithstanding this careful distinction, the exigencies of doubling in such a sprawling and ambitious play require that the goddess of beauty, none other than Venus herself, be rendered by the player of Lord, Commons' Cry, Commons' Complaint, Lord Smirdis, and – *mirabile dictu* – the redoubtable desperado Ruf. Thus even the later and more professionally advanced plays of the popular theater, although tending to specialise the boy's role, were constantly required by expediency to provide numerous exceptions to the rule.[6]

The longer thou livest appears at first glance to come closer than any other play to fulfilling Symonds's definition of the boy's position in a popular troupe. Its sole feminine role, Lady Fortune, is the responsibility of the player whose only other part is that of Moros, the harebrained central figure. Moros is a child at heart, if not in years, and his character might suit a boy actor's age. Yet Moros is also the leading role, requiring the sort of adept comic acting later perfected by Tarleton and Kemp. The part is the acting plum of the play, and it is hard to imagine that the leading player would yield it to his boy. Besides, the casting lists of these popular plays offer no instance of a boy actor's having undertaken the broadly comic idiom of the fool.

Three late casting lists demand two boy actors. *Cambises*, already discussed, is one of these. *Marriage of Wit and Wisdom* offers a remarkably clear case: of its six actors, two play all the female parts and do nothing else. One plays Indulgence (Wit's mother), Wisdom (the heroine) and Mother Bee. The other plays Wantonness, Fancy and Doll. The third instance is the late romance *Mucedorus* (ca. 1590), helpful perhaps in suggesting a trend in the 1580s toward increased specialisation of boys' roles. The heroine, Amadine, whose important part requires the talents of the leading boy, doubles no other roles. The younger boy, player six, has four 'bit' parts: Comedy in the induction (who calls herself a 'woman'), a Boy with the boar's head, who speaks no lines, Ariena (one speaking line) and an old woman. The last three characters appear only briefly in single scenes. Here, as in *Cambises*, one sees the development toward a ranking of the boy actors into a leading boy and his considerably less experienced assistant.

It is erroneous, then, to speak of 'the boy' as a predictable and unchanging member of these popular troupes. His position during the sixteenth century was evidently subject to continual redefinition. Even though his function became more specialised with time, the progression was not steady. Some of the plays requiring no boy's talents at all occur quite late, such as *All for Money*, and it seems reasonable to suppose that some strolling troupes may have had one or even two boys when other troupes had none. Again, there seems little basis for thinking that boys were used from the very first solely for feminine or juvenile roles. Nearly all the early impressions of these boy actors suggest versatility and not specialisation.

Nevertheless, the adult players seem always to have been reluctant to portray female characters other than those absolutely necessary for the plot. The early plays, which apparently employed no boys, tend accordingly to present as few females as possible. Even in a later play, *Cambises*, the adult player who undertakes the role of Venus does so only in an especially difficult situation, when all his fellow actors are otherwise employed; there are actually eight players on stage [872f]. The limitation on the number of women's roles imposed on Shakespeare and his contemporary playwrights for the public theater is seen even more clearly in the predominantly male casts of early popular plays.

No evidence suggests that women ever acted in the troupe theater. They appeared occasionally in medieval plays on the Continent and in England. The Chester cycle assigned the play of the Assumption of the Virgin to 'ye wyfus of ye town', and women were paid for appearing in a London Lord Mayor's show in 1523. Even so, such occasions are late and infrequent, with no hint of that free association of men and women found in the jongleur bands of the Middle Ages.[7] Whether owing to the moral climate of opinion or to the weakness of feminine voices, women never entered the ranks of the professional players.

Perhaps the clearest summary that can be constructed is as follows.

In pre-Elizabethan times most, if not all, popular troupes appear to have performed without a boy. The adult actors avoided feminine and juvenile roles as much as they could, but when necessity demanded a woman for the plot, any member of the troupe could double such a part. Even the leading player might take a female role. When the troupes began belatedly to take on young apprentices, they evidently preferred to have two rather than one. Such boys were likely to receive female roles, but might also perform male parts. Female roles might still go to the adult players when no other arrangement was feasible. By and large, however, the tendency was toward specialisation of the boys for female roles, and toward a hierarchical distinction between fully trained and less experienced apprentices. On the other hand, all-adult troupes appear to have been in existence throughout the Elizabethan era prior to 1576.

Our next concern is with the leading player. Once again Symonds's generalisation, and the picture of an old morality production in *Sir Thomas More*, may serve as the basis of discussion: 'The leading actor played the part of Vice and undertook stage management.' To this may be added W. J. Lawrence's conclusion that the Vice enjoyed the privilege of not being doubled.[8] What evidence is there that every troupe had such a leading player? Does this leading player always take the part of the Vice? To what extent is the Vice the dominating role in the play, and does the extent of his dominance vary in different periods of the sixteenth century? How often is the leading man called upon to double other roles? How many and how demanding are these roles? These are some of the questions for which the plays offered for acting can provide documentary illustration. The inquiry presupposes that the popular plays being studied are in fact moralities containing Vice characters, a correspondence which was demonstrated in the previous chapters on canon.

In a majority of popular plays, the Vice has indisputable command of the stage. In *Three Laws* Infidelity is the recognised chieftain of 'the six vyces', and is actually on stage for 1561 of the play's 2081 lines, far ahead of the nearest contender. He doubles two roles, which at first glance seem as many as any of the supporting members of his troupe. But the roles are 'Prolocutor', or prologue (35 lines), and Christian Faith, who appears in the last ninety lines of the play in order to speak a sort of epilogue. Thus the leading player introduces and then apologises for his play, as the stage manager might be expected to do. In the meantime he appears almost continually in the role of Vice, occupying the center of attention and manipulating the action.

Several other plays confirm the dominance of the Vice. In *Impatient*

Poverty, Envy, although not named as such, appears to be the Vice. He is present on stage for 532 of 1100 lines, more than any other character, and doubles only with the 'Sommer' (Summoner) who appears briefly toward the end of the play for 99 lines. 'Idleness the vice' in *Marriage of Wit and Wisdom* doubles only with prologue and epilogue, like Infidelity in *Three Laws*. Idleness occupies the stage for 669 lines of 1290. In *Trial of Treasure*, 'Inclination the Vice' is the only one of five players not required to double. All the others have at least three parts. Inclination is on stage for 723 of 1148 lines; the nearest role, Lust, is considerably far behind with 487 lines. Again, 'Nichol Newfangle the Vice' in *Like Will to Like* is assigned to player five without doubling, whereas the other four players have at least three roles each – frequently four. Newfangle is an unusually dominant Vice, being on stage almost continually, for 1077 lines of a total 1277. Tom Tosspot is second with a mere 408 lines, Virtuous Living third with 265. The Vice of *New Custom*, 'Peruerse Doctrine, an olde Popishe priest', has an equally dominating role. He appears in all but 110 of the play's 1076 lines. Some part of his dominance stems from his being the mankind hero as well as the Vice, converted to true Christianity at the end of the play. He is the only player of four not required to double.

In *The Tide Tarrieth no Man*, 'Corage the Vice' doubles only with Debtor, a minor character appearing in one 47-line scene [1393–1439]. This instance affords an illustration of the conditions under which the Vice might take such a role. The other three actors are either on stage during this scene, or are off stage preparing to appear almost immediately. In other words, the Vice may be expected to double with minor parts in a difficult situation, when the rest of the troupe is already employed. Otherwise he is left to perform his specialised and demanding role without added burden other than prologue and epilogue. Courage's role by itself is taxing enough. He is on stage for all but 420 of the play's 1879 lines, and has no near rival.

The dominance of the Vice in the plays mentioned so far can be demonstrated neatly by the position of his name on the printed casting lists. In nearly every case so far mentioned, the Vice is named first or last among the list of characters, and the grouping on the page is often such that the Vice's name receives typographical prominence. His name is first in the casting lists of *Three Laws*, *New Custom* and *Marriage of Wit and Wisdom*. It is last in *Impatient Poverty*, *Trial of Treasure*, and *Like Will to Like*. Only in *The Tide Tarrieth no Man* is his name placed between those of other players.

In the remaining plays covered by this investigation, however, the dominance of the Vice is beginning to yield to other forces.

Correspondingly, one finds in this group that the Vice's name tends to disappear from its position of prominence in the casting list. In *The longer thou livest*, for example, Moros is given to player two of four players, and in *Cambises* Ambidexter is given to the sixth of eight players. In these plays, and in *Horestes* and *Enough is as good as a Feast*, the secularising tendencies at work in the mid-century morality are bringing to the fore new figures and personages, often from history, legend or romance, whose increasing importance in the hybrid plays inevitably comes to rival and even surpass the traditionally central function of the Vice. In *Enough*, for example, 'Couetousnes the Uice' occupies the important last position in the casting list, but his prominence is offset by Worldly Man, the human protagonist, in first position. Both parts are assigned without doubling, and Covetousness's 986 lines of a total 1541 are closely rivalled by Worldly Man's 870. In *The longer thou livest* the role assigned to the leading player may not accurately be described as 'Vice'. Moros, like Worldly Man, is the human protagonist, a secular figure who dominates this play instead of the Vice. *New Custom*, already mentioned, presents a leading figure in Perverse Doctrine who performs the function of Vice throughout most of the play only to be transformed into the virtuous hero at the end.

As secular figures grew in importance, the relationship between the Vice and the leading player must have grown more tenuous until at some point the leading player shifted his talents to a portrayal of the human hero. This tendency was already apparent in *Horestes* and *Cambises*. In *Horestes* both 'the Vice' and the title role are assigned to actors each of whom play two additional parts, but these demands are small when compared with the duties of the other players. The actor of 'the Vice' also portrays Nature (about forty-eight lines on stage) and Duty, a minor personage in the final scene whose real function is to speak the epilogue and the prayer for Elizabeth, her Nobles, the Lord Mayor, and so on. The actor of Horestes doubles as Prologue (whose part is not printed, but is assigned in the casting list) and with 'a woman like a begger' appearing for twenty-two lines. Thus the two leading players divide between them the labor of prologue and epilogue. The other four players have from four to seven roles each. Horestes and 'the Vice' are on stage for nearly the same length of time: Horestes for 521 lines of a total 1205, 'the Vice' for 557. Despite the Vice's slight edge in these statistics, however, it is evident from a reading of the play that Horestes has taken over the central position. The Vice is only an instrument; Horestes controls the action and speaks the important lines.

Cambises exhibits a notably similar troupe structure. The actor playing Ambidexter the Vice doubles only as Trial, a minor character who appears for forty lines and speaks once [405–6]. Even this brief appearance might have been avoided except for a critical moment in which all the other adult players are on stage and occupied at the time. King Cambises himself is played by an actor who doubles only as Epilogue, rising like Nell Gwyn of later years to 'speak the Epilogue' after having died on stage. The other adult players all take five to seven roles each. Ambidexter is on stage for 436 of the play's 1248 lines; Cambises, incontrovertibly the leading role, is on stage for 604 lines. The essential groundwork has been prepared for the later dominance of Tamburlaine, Hieronimo and Richard III, although the gradual nature of the change may be seen in Richard's blend of the traditions of Vice and leading human protagonist.

Such an important transition raises the interesting possibility of a second leading adult player in the make-up of the popular troupes. In several of these plays, especially the hybrids, we find two players standing above the rest in importance, and distinguished from the others by doubling only in unusual cases: Worldly Man and Covetousness, Horestes and 'the Vice', Cambises and Ambidexter. Significantly they are from plays performed by growing troupes: *Horestes*, six plus extras; *Enough*, seven; and *Cambises*, eight. Although it may be doubted whether a hierarchy of two leading players became fixed and standard during this period of the late 1560s and 1570s, it is reasonable to suppose that as the troupes expanded they discovered a capacity not previously feasible for distinguishing between first-rank supporting players and those who would specialise in minor parts. . . .

[Bevington's discussion goes on to enquire into the distribution of roles among supporting players, and other topics – Ed.]

SOURCE: extract from the chapter 'Four Men and a Boy' in *From 'Mankind' to Marlowe* (New Haven, Conn., 1962), pp. 73–83.

NOTES

[Reorganised and renumbered from the original. For short-form references to works, see Abbreviations List, p. 8 – Ed.]

1. J. A. Symonds, *Shakspere's Predecessors in the English Drama* (London, 1884), p. 177. See also C. F. Tucker Brooke, *The Tudor Drama* (Boston, Mass., 1911), p. 58: 'The later moralities were usually performed by companies of four or five men and a boy, – the boy, of course, taking the woman's parts.' [Play-text references in Bevington's study derive from the following:

For G. Wapull, *The Tide Tarrieth no Man*: ed. E. Ruhl, *Jahrbuch der Deutschen Shakespeare-Gesellschaft*, 43 (1907).

For *Mankind*: J. M. Manly, *Specimens of the Pre-Shakespearean Drama*, 2 vols (Boston, Mass., 1897), vol. 1.

For *The Trial of Treasure*: Dodsley, III.

For *Horestes*: A Brandl (ed.), *Quellen des weltlichen Dramas in England vor Shakespeare* (Strassburg, 1898).

For *Cambises*: ed. C. R. Baskervill et al., *Elizabethan and Stuart Plays* (New York, 1934) – Ed.]

2. Honor McCusker, *John Bale, Dramatist and Antiquary* (Bryn Mawr, 1942), p. 76.

3. T. W. Craik, *The Tudor Interlude* (Leicester, 1958), pp. 34–5.

4. Cf. W. J. Lawrence, *Pre-Restoration Stage Studies* (Cambridge, Mass., 1927) p. 73, who concludes (erroneously I believe) that doubling involving a mixing of the sexes was rare in Elizabethan drama, and was usually done only by adult actors taking on elderly female roles. In the plays here cited, Wantonness and Abhominable Living are obviously courtesans doubled by adult actors.

5. Coogan, p. 1, n. 4.

6. See W. W. Greg, review of *The Elizabethan Stage* by E. K. Chambers, in *Review of English Studies*, 1 (1925), pp. 101–2; and Lawrence, op. cit., pp. 73–4, concerning the unreliable casting list by 'Dramaticus' for *The Shoemakers' Holiday* which assigns four female parts to grown men.

7. Salter, p. 48; Wickham, I, pp. 271–2; and Allardyce Nicoll, *Masks, Mimes and Miracles* (London, 1931), p. 192. The assertion of Southern, p. 10, that a woman played Lechery in *Perseverance* has insufficient textual support.

8. Lawrence, op. cit., p. 54.

Meg Twycross & Sarah Carpenter
Purposes and Effects of Masking   (1981)

. . . We now come to the question of why masks were used in the cycle plays. Can we tell what the purpose of these masks was, and what were the assumptions behind their use? There are various kinds of evidence about attitudes to masks and masking in the late Middle Ages which may help to clarify the background, but they throw rather little light on the mysteries themselves since they are all concerned with different, and often rather more learned, use of masks. . . . What does seem to emerge is that there are several different masking traditions active during the period. While there must be a certain amount of overlap between them, both from the point of view of the maskers and of the audience, we cannot safely treat them as a unified tradition assuming that they had the same purposes and effects. Masks were used for very different reasons. They might be used simply to indicate a physical fact as in the Cornish saint's play *Meriasek*: when the Emperor Constantine is stricken with leprosy, a stage direction indicates *a vysour aredy apon Constantyn ys face*, and when the leprosy is cured, another stage direction reads *ye vysour away*.[1] In the morality plays, on the other hand, masks are used as moral emblems. A mask will provide a physical symbol for a spiritual state, usually a change of state, and must be read symbolically. So the King in *The Cradle of Security* has a pig's mask put on his face when he falls asleep in the arms of Pride, Covetousness and Luxury;[2] Wit in *Wit and Science* has his face painted with spots by Idleness;[3] and Natural Law in Bale's *Three Laws* is painted leprously to signify his corruption by Idolatry and Sodomy.[4]

In the tradition of masquing the masks seem to serve a different function again. There the masks are exotic, indicating the strange, mysterious and foreign. Possibly more important, the mask is also used as a disguise. In 'informal' masquing, forbidden by [Pope Gregory's decretals, 1227–41], the mask is specifically worn to conceal, and so protect, the wearer's identity. In more 'formal' court masquing, the audience are tacitly invited to penetrate the disguise. Although the convention is that the maskers are unknown strangers, they are usually in fact well-known to the audience, and the masque itself often leads up to the unmasking of the performers, as in Henry VIII's masque at Greenwich in 1527:

and when they had daunsed there fill, then the quene plucked of the kynges visar, & so did the Ladies the visars of the other Lordes, & then all were knowen.[5]

The tantalising relationship between the unknown mask and the concealed face behind it is clearly an important element in masquing.

These uses of masks are clearly quite different from each other, relying on different assumptions. When considering the masks in the mysteries we need to try to evaluate what particular kinds of attitudes were being activated. This is, of course, fairly difficult since there is very little external evidence which would give us an idea of the assumptions involved. We have to depend almost solely on the play texts themselves, perhaps taking into account any analogous theatrical traditions.

The one reference we do have to the actual use of masks in the mysteries, which is almost contemporary with the cycles themselves, is the well-known stanza of the 'post-Reformation' Chester *Banns* recorded by Rogers in 1609. This stanza discusses the use of the gold God-mask. It might appear to be a most seductive piece of evidence since it does, apparently for the first time, talk about the purpose and effect of putting God into a mask. What the *Banns* actually say is slightly confusing in detail, although the general drift is fairly clear. The audience are warned not to expect the sophisticated techniques of the contemporary theatre. For then, we are told

> . . . shoulde all those persones that as godes doe playe
> In Clowdes come downe with voyce and not be seene
> ffor noe man can proportion that godhead I saye
> To the shape of man face, nose and eyne
> But sethence the face gilte doth disfigure the man yat deme
> A Clowdy coueringe of the man, a Voyce onlye to heare
> And not god in shape or person to appeare [6]

The terms of this passage are, in themselves, not very easy to follow. The exact significance and stress of *proportion, shape of man, disfigure*, and so on, are difficult to determine. The last three lines of the extract are perhaps the most potentially ambiguous. One thing to point out is that *disfigure* at this period appears to mean no more than 'disguise'. It does not convey the later connotations of our *deform*, but seems to have a neutral sense nearer to our 'un-figure' or 'alter the shape of'. Difficulties with punctuation also make the last three lines hard to assess. What they seem to be saying is, 'since the golden face conceals the identity of the actor, think of that golden face as if it were a cloud machine concealing the whole man, so that we only hear the voice of God coming from this cloud cover (or mask), and do not see God himself supposedly appearing physically on stage'.

Even having sorted out the verbal difficulties of the passage, it is still fairly hard to follow its implications. It is wrong, it suggests, for any man to try to 'act' or imitate God, because no human being can *proportion* the Divinity. But, it tells us, we can get round this problem if we think of the mask or gilded face as an equivalent to the modern cloud-machine which completely hides the actor, allowing a 'voice of God' to speak. This comparison urges that the mask, like the cloud-machine, must be thought of as completely abolishing the man, the actor himself. We do not see him representing or pretending to *be* God, but only hear the voice speaking God's words. The argument then goes on a further stage. Even the mask itself is not representing God mimetically, as an actor might. It is an emblem or sign, like the cloud-machine, which stands for God without actually imitating

Him. That is why we do not see God 'in *shape* or person to appear'.

Interesting as this stanza is, though, it offers a view of the God-mask, and perhaps even of masked acting in general, which may be only partially helpful in illuminating the practice of the cycle plays. Firstly it shows an uneasiness about the appearance of God on the stage that seems foreign to the mysteries, and in fact to almost all medieval drama. The sense of impropriety in human actors playing God seems to be largely a post-Reformation, even a post-Renaissance, development. During the Middle Ages generally, there is hardly any argument against it (except from the Lollards[7]), and the portrayal of God on stage seems to have excited no more, if no less, controversy than the portrayal of God in pictures. This is true not only of the mystery cycles, but also of the early moralities like *The Castle of Perseverance* and *Everyman*. Nor does it seem specifically a Roman Catholic attitude, for it continues well into the sixteenth century, after the Reformation. John Bale's plays, though violently anti-Catholic, introduce *Pater Coelestis, Deus Pater* and Christ as characters without any apparent qualms, Christ also being ready to address the audience invoking their devotion to himself.[8] The fragments of the Protestant play *Christ's Resurrection* dramatise Christ, even inventing for him a non-biblical scene which is only alluded to in the Gospels, and thus going further than most of the cycles in the portrayal of God on stage.[9] And even as late as (probably) the 1580s, the 'part of God in a playe' known as the *Processus Satanae* was copied.[10] The play concerns an investigation into the Redemption prompted by Satan and carried out by the Four Daughters of God. So the copying of the actor's part seems to imply performance of a play, perhaps in the 1580s, which is not a cycle play, and therefore traditional, but nevertheless portrays God as a character without any noticeable hesitation. The Chester *Banns* therefore suggest a *religious* uncertainty behind the use of masks in this case which does not appear to have been operative in medieval performances.

This leads on to a more general aspect of the *Banns'* argument. The sense of unease over the propriety of a human actor impersonating God, and the way in which the mask is justified, suggests a self-consciousness about masking itself. This is seen in the clear distinction that is made between the man who is the actor and the mask that is to conceal him. The words of the *Banns*, explaining the 'proper' reaction to the mask, imply that the audience are in fact likely to be aware of looking behind the mask and what it represents to the face beneath, and are aware of a tension between the two.

Although this is an attitude which does exist in the Middle Ages in relation to masques and disguisings, it does not seem to have applied to the use of masks in the mystery plays. There is plenty of evidence for such a response to other forms of masking. The decretals condemning disguising, and the descriptions of court masquing, all reveal an interest in the concealing properties of masks. The audience are aware that the mask is a 'false' face hiding the 'true' face beneath. (In folk masking, however, the maskers seem to have used the mask as a cue to abandon their normal selves). The terms *disguise* and *disfigure* themselves suggest a recognition of the presence of the usual *guise* or *figure* beneath the mask. This interest in mask as concealment or disguise has persisted in the post-Renaissance European theatre, right through until the twentieth century. The interest seems to be most often in the relationship between the mask and the face behind it. This tends to encourage the audience to look behind the mask to try to discover the man beneath. Alternatively the interest may be in the sense of trapping stasis that the mask imposes on the character. By its very nature the use of a mask implies lack of character development. While this is quite natural to, for example, the allegorical personifications of the morality drama, or the traditionally fixed biblical or moral roles of the characters of the cycles, it is something that the twentieth century tends to find worrying, both dramatically and psychologically. The early twentieth century interest in masks and their use in plays by playwrights like Pirandello, Yeats and O'Neill concentrates on the fact of masking itself, as did the masques of the medieval and Tudor period.

But, as we said, the use of masks in the cycle plays does not really seem to belong to this tradition. Partly because of their popular, 'native' element, and partly because of their religious material, they come much closer to ancient traditions of masking such as we see in Greek, Roman, Oriental, Asian and African popular religious theatre.[11] These traditions do not seem to encourage their audiences to look behind the mask, or recognise a tension between it and the actor. The concentration is on the character, often a god, mythical hero, or evil spirit, who is represented by the mask, not on its relationship to the wearer. Once the mask is on, the actor as an individual man simply disappears behind or into it: only the character is left. This can be seen from the texts and performances of these dramas, as one who has seen the demonstrative masks of Kabuki theatre, Javanese dance drama, or perhaps even reconstructions of masked classical Greek plays will know. As John Jones has remarked of the ancient Greek theatre, the masks are used to reveal, and not to conceal the face: 'They did not owe their interest to the further realities lying behind them, because they declared the whole man. They stated: they did not hint or hide.'[12] This seems much closer to the mask tradition of the mystery cycles. The texts of the plays suggest no self-consciousness about the masks at all. They demonstrate a character, or an idea: they do not conceal or disguise anything.

All this seems to be congruent with the whole medieval interest in emblem, sign and figure. In the drama, as in painting, visual details are rarely simply decorative, but almost always semantically expressive, designed to explain ideas and reveal meanings. Obviously this is particularly clear in the moralities' use of 'emblem' masks, or the sometimes allegorical masks of court shows, both specifically designed to express moral ideas: so Discord may wear a head with snakes, or Dissimulation may wear a double-faced mask. But this use of visual symbols clearly carries over into such things as the use of attributes for saints and apostles, which express ideas more than naturalistic facts. The visual conventions associated with the biblical figures of the mystery cycles appear to have the same kind of explanatory function. When Pauper explains the significance of the image of the Virgin in *Dives and Pauper* he interprets all the conventional iconographic features as emblematically expressive:

> . . . þe ymage of oure lady is peynt wyt a child in here lefght arm in tokene þat she is modyr of God, and wyt a lylye or ellys a rose in here ryght hond in tokene þat she is maydyn wytouten ende and flour of alle wymmen [13]

Presumably this, too, is the function of the masks. They are used to express an idea rather than an actuality. And it is an idea about the character that is portrayed, not about the actor and his relationship to the mask. When the angels wear haloes, when God, Christ, and the exalted Apostles wear masks, these presumably have the same effect as the finery of the saints in church paintings. And *Dives and Pauper* makes it clear that this purpose is the symbolic expression of ideas. When Dives asks Pauper about the Apostles' haloes, 'Quhat betokennyn þe rounde thynggys þat been peyntyd on here hedes or abouten here hedys?', Pauper replies, 'þey betokenyn þe blisse þat þey han wytouten ende, for as þat rounde þyng is endeles, so is here blisse endeles'.[14]

Sometimes Pauper will offer different significations for the same visual conventions, as with the splendid robes of the saints. When Dives objects, 'þey weryn non so gay in clothyng as þey been peyntyd', he replies, 'þat is soth. þe ryche peynture betokenyȝt þe blysse þat þey been now inne, nought þe aray þat þey haddyn vpon erthe'.[15] Yet later he puts forward a different interpretation, one that makes particularly clear that the aim of this splendour is not naturalistic authenticity:

DIVES: I suppose þat þe seyntys in herthe weryn nought arayid so gay, wyt shoon of syluer and clothys of gold of baudekyn, of velwet, ful of brochis and rynggys and precious stonys . . . for þey shuldyn an had mechil cold on here feet and sone a been robbyd of here clothis.

PAUPER: Soth it is þat þey wentyn nought in sueche aray. Neuereles, al þis may be doon for deuocion þat meen han to þe seyntys and to shewyn mannys deuocioun.[16]

Perhaps all this goes some way towards suggesting the general purposes behind the use of masks in the mystery cycles. But how far is it possible to gauge the effects, both on the overall dramatic spectacle and on the meaning of particular plays? Again, lack of direct evidence is a problem. But there are some fairly obvious suggestions that we might make from working with masks on stage. When an actor wears a mask, his face is not available to convey expression. This is a banal but important factor, since nowadays, and especially since the development of films and television, we are all conditioned to acting with our faces. When the face is hidden all expression has to come from the body, the stance and movement of the actor, and the way he tilts the mask. This clearly will tend to slow actors down. All movements become significant, so it is hard to make trivial or unnecessary gestures. The actor's gestures therefore become more emphatic and larger. He uses the positioning of his whole body more deliberately. Another important consideration for the actor is that there is less sense of personal exposure. His own personality is less directly engaged with the audience, and indeed even with the character he plays. Even more than an unmasked actor he needs to concentrate on what the audience sees, rather than on what he himself feels, because his own feelings will not be transparently reflected in his face. Because of this the whole acting process seems to move slightly nearer towards being a dance that has been learned, or a demonstration. There is a formal quality to masked acting, and a certain necessary stylisation.

This is not to say that masks are inexpressive: while a mask can express stasis very powerfully, a good mask can also, if required, be astonishingly expressive and moving. Slight movements and tilts of the head alter the light on the mask, and consequently its expression, quite profoundly. Nor is it to suggest that masked actors are not emotionally involved in their acting. There are useful contemporary remarks on the masked actors of Ancient Greece and Rome that make this clear. In Plato's *Ion* an actor himself states, 'At the tale of pity my eyes are filled with tears, and when I speak of horrors, my hair stands on end, and my heart throbs'. He also shows how emotionally affecting such acting can be, for he goes on to describe the response of the audience: 'I look down on them from the stage and behold the various emotions of pity, wonder, sternness, stamped upon their countenances when I am speaking.'[17] Cicero also remarks on the actor's emotional commitment to the part he plays in the *De Oratore*: 'tamen in hoc genere saepe ipse vidi, ut ex persona mihi ardere oculi hominis histrionis viderentur spondalli dicentes' [On the stage I myself have often observed the eyes of the actor through his mask appear inflamed with fury when he was speaking these verses].[18] As this confirms, masked acting can be just as expressive, and just as emotional, as unmasked acting: but the emotion itself tends to be formalised, stylised and externalised. It becomes, as it were, a public and shared statement rather than a personal feeling of the actor.

The use of masks therefore appears to dictate a particular kind of stylisation. But what is especially interesting in the cycle plays is that the masked actors are moving among unmasked figures. While we know too little about medieval conventions of acting to know what difference this would make, it seems quite possible that the formality of masked acting combined and interacted with a more naturalistic mode. This probability is confirmed by various other evidence. We can tell from the Guild records that a good part of the visual effect of the mystery plays was non-naturalistic. The Virgin, even in the most ordinary activities, may appear in a crown.[19] The Tree of Paradise is hung with figs, almonds, dates, raisins and prunes as well as apples; Peter and Christ may wear gilded wigs; and Christ himself at the Resurrection may appear in a leather suit under his red cloak, a suit which signifies nakedness rather than simply using the actor's own body.[20] As with the masks, these visual details are expressive rather than gratuitously ornamental, signifying various spiritual ideas. Yet this overall stylisation contains details which can themselves be domestic, homely and familiar: the real baby paid for by the Coventry Weavers, the domestic gifts given by the Shepherds to the infant Christ, or the ropes, hammers and tools used by the soldiers at the Crucifixion. Stylisation ranges from the most formal and exotic to the most ordinary and familiar.

Similarly the texts of the plays themselves seem to call for varying styles of acting. We can move from the stately oratory of God to the virulent colloquial abuse of Cain, from the moving seriousness of the Annunciation to the earthy comedy of Joseph's Doubts, from the down-to-earth violence of the Soldiers to the highly formalised laments of the Maries, without any sense of discontinuity. Even within the same character the Shepherds can move from naturalistic grumbling to learned exposition, Mrs Noah from vulgar irresponsibility to docile humility, without any apparent unease. All this supports the evidence of the masks – that ornate stylisation deliberately coexists with naturalism to form a composite style. This appears to be a characteristic of most 'folk' theatre, and it may well be that the cycle plays with their popular, communal and seasonal elements, do in some ways come closer to the dramatic traditions of the folk theatre than to more learned forms. A recent essay on the folk theatre has pointed out: 'In the folk theatre the simultaneous use of the most diverse styles in the same play is a widespread phenomenon, a special theatrical device of form.'[21] This is clearly equally true of the mysteries, and the use of masks seems to be a significant element in this assured exploitation of diverse theatrical styles.

SOURCE: concluding section of 'Masks in the Medieval Theatre', *Medieval English Theatre*, 3, no. 1 (1981), pp. 29–36.

NOTES

[For short-form references to works, see Abbreviations List, p. 8 – Ed.]

1. Whitley Stokes, *Beunans Meriasek* (London, 1872), pp. 76, 104.
2. Ralph Willis, *Mount Tabor* (London, 1639), p. 113.
3. John Redford, *Wit and Science* [431–2, 763–821], in Peter Happé (ed.), *Tudor Interludes* (Harmondsworth, 1972).
4. John Bale, *The Three Laws*, in J. S. Farmer (ed.), *The Dramatic Works of John Bale* (London, 1907), p. 25ff.
5. Edward Hall, *Chronicle* (1809, repr. New York, 1965), p. 724.
6. L. M. Clopper (ed.) *REED: Chester* (Toronto, 1979), p. 247.
7. The implication of the argument in the *Tretise of miraclis pleyinge* constantly touches on the impropriety of impersonating Christ and God [see excerpt in Part One, above – Ed.]. Cf. the satirical lyric against the Friars and their plays, Thomas Wright (ed.), *Political Songs and Poems* (London, 1859), I, pp. 268–70.
8. John Bale, *The Chief Promises of God*, *The Three Laws*, and *The Temptation of Our Lord*: all in Farmer, op. cit. (note 4, above).
9. J. D. Wilson and B. Dobell (eds.), *The Resurrection of Our Lord*, Malone Society Reprint (Oxford, 1912).
10. *Processus Satanae*, in *Malone Society Collections*, vol. 2, part 3 (Oxford, 1931) pp. 239–50.
11. On the use of masks in various cultures, see Andreas Lommel, *Masks* (London, 1972).
12. J. Jones, *On Aristotle and Greek Tragedy* (London, 1962) p. 45.
13. P. Barnum (ed.), *Dives and Pauper* (Oxford, 1976), p. 91.
14. Ibid., p. 94.
15. Ibid.
16. Ibid., p. 100.

17. Plato, 'Ion', in *The Dialogues*, trans. B. Jowett (London, 1892), vol. 1, 494–504. The dialogue actually concerns the rhapsode, or public reciter, but the actor's skill is bracketed with and spoken of as equivalent to that of the rhapsode throughout the dialogue.

18. Cicero, *De Oratore*, ed. A. S. Wilkins (Oxford, 1881), Book 2, 46, 193.

19. 'For mendyng our ladys crowne'; 'for skowryng of maryes crowns': T. Sharp. *A Dissertation*, pp. 55–6; cf. Clopper (ed.), *REED: Chester*, op. cit. (note 6, above), pp. 67, 78.

20. *Non-Cycle Plays*, pp. *xxxii, xxxiv, xxxv*.

21. Petr Bogatyrev, 'Semiotics in the Folk Theater', in Ladislav Matejka and Irwin R. Titunik (eds), *Semiotics of Art* (Cambridge, Mass., 1976), p. 40.

William Tydeman 'Costumes and Actors' (1978)

. . . in several places it . . . appears to have been customary for the players, in addition to decorating their own scaffolds . . ., to supply their own costumes and the less expensive properties.[1] At Romans [in France] only certain of the more unusual characters such as Lucifer and Proserpine were provided with costumes, and at Lucerne only the dress and properties for Judas were supplied at the city's expense (Judas being an unpopular part), although occasional 'grants towards expenses' were made to less affluent actors. Various methods of obtaining costumes were devised: the organisers were fortunate in that contemporary clothing was usually worn by the majority of characters. The Coventry Smith's accounts for 1487 include a 'reward to Maisturres Grymesby for lendying off her geir for Pylatts wyfe'; in 1579 the Smiths hired or borrowed a gown of the Tailors and Shearmen's Guild, and the Mercers' accounts for 1584 record a payment of 32s. 'for hieringe apparell for the players'. For *Le Mystère de l'Incarnation et de la Nativité* at Rouen in 1474 the church authorities lent an archbishop's cross, ornaments, and tunics for the angels; at Lincoln in 1515 the city council announced

That wher divers garmentes & other heriormentes [*] is yerly Boroyd in the Cuntrey [†] for the Arryeyng of the pagentes of Scaynt Anne gyld, now the knyghtes & gentylmen be Freyd with [‡] the plage So that the graceman [§] Can Borowght none Sutch garmentes, wherfore every Alderman Schall prepare & Setfoorth in the Seid Arrey ij good gownes And every Scheryff

pere [‖] A gowne And every Chaumberlen pere A gowne & the persons with
Theym To weyre the Same

[*Ornaments   †district   ‡scared of   §chief guild officer   ‖ former sheriff]

which, although probably referring to a procession rather than a play,
indicates clearly the necessity for obtaining clothing of sufficient
quality to grace the shows of the late Middle Ages. In 1521 the same
problem arose, and the council agreed to borrow 'A gowne of my
Lady Powes for one of the Maryes & thother Mary To be Arayed in
the cremysyng [crimson] gowne of velvet that longith to the Same
gyld'.[2]

Some guilds may have been bequeathed clothes for their actors, if
the will of William Pisford of Coventry is typical, for in 1517 he left the
Tanners' Company a scarlet and a crimson gown 'to make use of at
the time of their plays',[3] and in this way organisations were able to
build up theatrical wardrobes for their own needs, and to hire out to
others. An inventory of church goods made by the churchwardens of
Chelmsford in 1563 includes such a collection of costumes mostly
made from old vestments, and over the next twelve years hiring fees
brought in about £29, this versatile collection being eventually sold off
in 1574 when it fetched almost £7.[4] When Worcester Cathedral sold
its 'players gere' in 1576 the inventory included 'A Ks [king's] cloke of
Tysshew', 'a lyttil cloke of tysshew', 'A gowne of silk', 'A Jerkyn of
greene, 2 cappes, and the devils apparell'. The Brotherhood of the
Crown of Thorns at Lucerne evidently had such a store of costumes
and properties, but as is so often the case, control was insufficient, and
garments and other items were loaned out and not returned, so that
stern rules had to be laid down for their safety.[5]

It would be impossible to cite every available detail of costumes
worn in the vernacular religious dramas. In many cases vestments
that had served the liturgical drama so well continued to form the
staple of a large number of costumes, but a greater freedom was
probably possible. We do not know, for example, how the diabolical
characters were clad in the few liturgical plays in which they feature,
but in the vernacular pieces we hear of 'the devill in his featheres all
ragged and rente' (Coventry 'Late Banns'), of 'ij pound of heare [hair]
for the demons cotts & hose' (Coventry Drapers 1572), or of the devil
Enguignart in *Le Jour de Jugement* dressed as a young dandy of the day
in a blue surcoat with long ermine-lined sleeves falling almost to the
floor, and a red hood; attendant devils on this occasion were painted
red or black, with wiggling tails, and gaudily coloured shields which
they beat with their pitchforks. Rabelais describes, probably from life,
a parade of devils in which the demons are 'decked out in the skins of

wolves, calves and rams, topped with the heads of sheep and the horns of bulls, and huge kitchen hooks, with strong leather belts round their waists from which great cow-bells and mule-bells hung, making a horrific din'.[6]

In many places masks were an important feature of devilish costume, and they also feature among the details of Herod's equipment; allusions to 'the fauchon and Herod's face' or 'peyntyng and mendyng of Herodes heed' are found several times in the Coventry list of expenses, and his other accoutrements from time to time include a 'crest' or helmet, which was probably embellished in some way to show his kingship. One ingenious use for a mask occurs in *The Life of St Meriasek* when the Emperor Constantine's leprosy is graphically indicated by means of 'a vysour'. Herod doubtless was provided with a sword, just as at Coventry Pilate was celebrated for wielding his 'malle' or 'cloobe' which features so often in the accounts of the Cappers' Company. Satan is often provided with a weapon of some kind too. Herod's costume at Lucerne was to be the 'most costly and splendid' that could be obtained, with a Jewish and heathen feeling about it; Pilate was to be dressed 'as a provincial bailiff or governor, rich, rough, with a draped pointed hat, heathen and imposing, in a burgher's coat with sleeves reaching below the knee, sabre and high boots. A sceptre or staff in his hand'. Colour was an important element: the N-Town text describes Annas as 'be-seyn after [arrayed like] a busshop [bishop] of the hoold lawe, in a skarlet gowne, and over that a blew tabbard furryd with whyte and a mytere on his hed after the hoold lawe'.

God at Lucerne wore the traditional alb and magnificent cope of earlier days with a diadem, long grey hair and a beard, but elsewhere there was less reliance on ecclesiastical vestments:[7] for the Coventry play of Doomsday and elsewhere a large number of skins were purchased for his 'coat'; at Coventry in 1565 three yards of 'redde sendall' were bought 'for God', and at New Romney the relatively large sum of 4s. 8d. was 'payd to Burton for skynes for the ij[d] godheddes Coote & for makyng'. At Norwich 'a face and heare for the Father' indicate that there at least God was masked and wore a wig. (Fake hair seems to have been a favourite method of disguise for many characters: in the Chelmsford inventory of 1563 we read that the church possessed twenty-three fake beards and as many wigs.) Christ, too, was often an expensive figure to clothe, even in a play such as the Coventry *Trial and Crucifixion* where we might expect only a simple white garment to suffice: in 1451 the Smiths paid 18d. for 'vj skynnys of whit leder to Godds garment', and in 1553 five 'schepskens' were needed, 3s. being spent on their purchase and having them made up, and it has been suggested that this was in fact a protective garment to resemble a naked torso in the flagellation scene . . . . The York Mercers made provision in 1433 for Christ's tunic to display the marks of his Passion, and we read of 'a sirke [shirt] wounded'. In 1490 the Coventry Christ seems to have worn a gilded wig (cheverel); in Jean Michel's *Passion* of roughly the same period, at the Transfiguration Christ reappears to the disciples in 'the whitest robe that can be obtained with his face and hands all burnished gold. And behind him a great sun with rays streaming from it'. The Mons accounts also place great stress on the garments to be furnished for Christ, and there are three separate references to the Transfiguration costume, where he wears 'a robe of white sackcloth and white hose' and his hands and face are burnished. This reflects the relative artistic integrity of the Mons production, in contrast to the Bourges presentation of *Les Actes des Apôtres* in 1536 where all the resources of a prosperous textile industry could be deployed; where the Mons apostles were dressed *en leur habis mecanicques* (as artisans), those at Bourges wore velvet, satin and damask robes, St Andrew's robes being of gold brocade and his cloak embroidered with pearls; those playing queens displayed a plethora of expensive jewellery, Herod's wife wearing a velvet dress of crimson-violet, its sleeves slashed to reveal their cloth-of-gold linings and a purple satin mantle lined with silver; her black-velvet headdress was set with pearls, and a sapphire was set into the point of each shoe. But even the poorer characters were costumed in rich silk.

By contrast with such excess, various accounts describe what characters intended to appear naked actually wore on stage: the total nudity of Adam and Eve before the Fall is not impossible, since we know that naked women sometimes posed in street pageants during the fifteenth and sixteenth centuries and appeared in Italian court entertainments;[8] . . . but given that Eve was usually played by a man, some kind of basic garment to conceal the fact was no doubt needed, even for audiences not preoccupied with strict verisimilitude. When in *Le Mystère de saint Vincent* the saint is told that he will be stripped completely naked (*Despouilles serez tres tout nu*) the stage direction tells us that 'they strip him down to a loin-cloth [*jusques aux petits draps*]', and one takes '*jusques aux*' to mean 'thus far and no farther'.[9] Probably the same basic garment was worn in many productions by Adam and Eve, by Marcellus, the young man divested of his cloak in the Garden of Gethsemane in the Donaueschingen Passion play, and by the adult souls released from Hell later in the same play, who are said to be '*nackent*' in contrast to the many small children '*Gantz nackent*'.[10] Presumably Christ crucified on the cross was similarly dressed in a loin-cloth.

In several instances Adam and Eve were clad in the medieval equivalent of the modern body-stocking or leotard and tights.[11] The 1565 inventory of the Norwich Grocers' Guild who presented the Creation includes '2 costes and a payre hosen for Eve, stayned [dyed]' and 'A cote and hosen for Adam, steyned', although these may be post-lapsarian garments only, as in the Mons play of 1501 where two *plichons* (fur-cloaks) are given the characters to hide their nakedness. However, some confirmation that the Norwich costumes were worn throughout is found in the Lucerne accounts, where in 1538 Adam and Eve are simply listed as '*nackend*', but in a later list we are informed that they are '*in lybkleider alls nacket*' [in body-clothing, as if naked], and a 1583 entry confirms that they wore '*Lybkleidern über den blossen lyb*' [body-clothing over the bare skin]. Adam should have long hair (not grey or black) and a short beard. Eve's 'beautiful long feminine hair' was, one assumes, a wig. The English stage-directions to the Cornish *Creation of the World* also confirm the idea; Âdam and Eve are to be 'aparlet in whytt lether', but they act as if naked, for there are to be 'fig leaves redy to cover ther members', and (as at Mons) there are 'garmentis of skynnes to be geven to Adam and Eva by the angell'.

Of the quality of the acting performances themselves very little can now be gleaned; hardly any direct accounts of late medieval acting have come down to us. Again one must assume that convention and tradition governed much of what was seen on the medieval stage, although there were no doubt individuals who stood out for their willingness to play a part to tear a cat in, or for their incompetence (a young girl Dijon in 1511 who mocked a feeble actor was beaten by his wife as a result!);[12] but there is no valid reason to assume that medieval Europe suffered from a dearth of creditable amateur actors: the sheer actability of many of the rôles in medieval drama does not suggest players unable to take advantage of the histrionic opportunities offered them. Of course, there are attacks on performers' acting abilities, the most savage that mounted by a procurator-general against the Confrérie de la Passion in 1542 where he described the players thus:

Both the organisers and the players are ignorant fellows, labourers and mechanics, not knowing A from B, who have never been taught or trained to perform such plays in theatres and public places, and, moreover, they lack fluency of speech, propriety of diction, correctly accented pronunciation, and any notion of what they are saying, so much so that . . . derision and public clamour often arise in the theatre itself, to such an extent that instead of producing enlightenment, their performance results in uproar and mockery.[13]

Against this we may set the compliment paid to the actors who presented *Les Actes des Apôtres* at Bourges in 1536,[14] by an eye-witness who described the plays as 'well and excellently performed by earnest men who knew so well how to depict the characters which they represented by signs and gestures, that the majority of the onlookers considered the business to be the truth and not pretence'.

That the actors needed to be dedicated men in many cases is made clear by a variety of anecdotes – for example, those narrow escapes from death by characters such as Christ and Judas, or an unfortunate Satan in the *mystère* of St Martin at Seurre in 1496, whose costume caught alight as he was about to emerge from the trapdoor of Hell, and who was badly burnt on the buttocks; 'but he was so speedily rescued, undressed, and re-costumed, that without betraying any sign that something was wrong, he went out and played his part'.[15] Such stoical indifference may be felt to be within the very best traditions of the amateur theatre! Familiar also are the strictures expressed here and there about unauthorised additions being made to the official text. A French manuscript of a play staged in 1456 includes the acid comment: 'Rejected and not included in this manuscript are any unusual additions which some of the players of this *mystère* thought fit to add at will [*cuidèrent adjouster à leur plaisance*], in that they were irrelevant to the subject and were censured by masters of theology.'[16]

From several accounts and pictures of medieval productions it is clear that the *maître du jeu* actually appeared on the stage himself during the play to prevent mishaps and to give the players what aid he could; his likeness appears in the famous illustrations by Hubert Cailleau for the Valenciennes play of 1547, a script in one hand and a short staff in the other, but portrayed off-stage, as a lone figure. In Jean Fouquet's illustration of the staging of *The Martyrdom of St Apollonia*, . . . however, he is a much more forceful presence, standing boldly forth among his actors, vigorously gesturing with his stick, and with the prompt-copy open in his other hand. Richard Carew in his account of the Cornish cycle supports this pictorial evidence when he writes that 'the players conne not their parts without booke, but are prompted by one called the Ordinary, who followeth at their back with the book in his hand, and telleth them softly what they must pronounce aloud',[17] which presumably means that the Ordinary cued the players and generally supervised the performance from on stage. As we have seen [in an earlier part of the discussion – Ed.] actors were in fact supposed to know their lines, or most of them.

As to the acting style employed, we may again assume that psychological realism was neither expected nor sought after; it is unlikely that the technique of acting differed greatly from those employed in the Latin church-drama, except that perhaps greater scope was offered for uninhibited and expansive performances in some of the more virtuoso rôles such as Lucifer, Herod and Pilate, while the comic vignettes of Cain, Mrs Noah, Joseph and the individual devils could be more fully developed outside a liturgical framework. But there is little to suggest that the more devotional rôles such as God, Christ, the Virgin Mary, angels and apostles, were played in a more naturalistic style as a result of being featured in public vernacular dramas. Indeed, in such parts, striving for the realism encountered in everyday life would have been considered indecorous; these characters were still deemed to represent the Creator of the Universe, the Son of God, the Mother of Christ, and any attempt to stress their humanity by making their impersonation on stage conform too closely to actual beings of the mundane world would have been deplored. Iconographical tradition, too, would have controlled the conventions here, as in so many other aspects of the pre-Renaissance stage, and spectators would not expect to witness an 'individual interpretation' of figures already familiar to them from stained-glass window or sculpted façade. In processional performance, where several actors would be required to present God or Christ or Mary, a certain agreed convention of playing would perforce prevail.

Before we leave the amateur theatre, mention must be made of the countless 'dramatic societies' recruited from the inhabitants of English towns and villages who staged plays in their own community and visited other towns to perform there.[18] In towns these groups, like the professionals, seem to have attended on the mayor of the community or the lord of the manor, and then, having performed to official satisfaction, were allowed to play for the benefit of the populace; at court and in monastic institutions, one command performance might be all that could be hoped for. What seems to be an early reference to such a troupe occurs in the records of Winchester College for 1400 when a gift was made to *'lusoribus civitatis Wynton'* (players of the city of Winchester), and a similar troupe were paid 2s. at Epiphany 1466 for presenting four interludes. Between 1422 and 1461 Maxstoke Priory paid various sums to players from 'Eton', Coventry, Daventry and nearby Coleshill, and Henry VI was generous to some *'jeweis* [Jews or, more probably, *joueurs*] *de Abyndon'* who played interludes before him at Christmas 1427. Obviously such amateur companies could not afford to play far from their place of origin: the household accounts of the Howard family of Stoke-by-Nayland in Suffolk cite payments to players from Stoke itself in

January 1466, from Thorington Street, Coggeshall and Hadleigh in
1481, from 'Esterforde' (now identified by John H. Harvey as
Kelvedon in Essex) in 1482, from Sudbury (1483), Chelmsford
(1490), and 'Lanam' (1472) which Chambers identifies with
Lavenham, but which might be read as 'Langham', a village a few
miles from Stoke. At all events, all these places (even Lavenham) lie
within a thirty-kilometre (twenty-mile) radius of the Howard home.
It was performances by such groups that the king enjoyed or endured
as he travelled the country on his royal progresses; when players came
to the court in London to appear before royalty and the nobility, it
does not appear that they were recruited from much farther away
than East Anglia, although 'Frenche Pleyers' were received in 1494
and again in 1495.

Amateur players appear to have visited each other's towns fairly
often during the second half of the fifteenth century, if the Kentish
records are typical of the country as a whole. Such exchanges are well
documented for Kentish east coast towns: thus, between August 1450
and July 1452 Lydd gave hospitality at the home of Richard Glover to
the '*lusoribus de Romene*' [the players of New Romney] and the wording
of the entry suggests their play was also presented in the house; at
Christmas 1452 'the men of Herne' played before the mayor of Dover;
on 7 July 1454 the people of Lydd entertained players from Ham
Street some ten miles off, the play presented possibly having some
connection with the Translation of St Thomas of Canterbury
celebrated that day. On 1 November of the same year the players of
New Romney staged a play at Lydd to commemorate the dedication
of the church there, and they did the same in November 1462; they
appeared at Lydd again on Whit Monday 1466, and again in
1476–77. New Romney entertained the Lydd troupe in 1456–57, and
again in 1467–68; actors from Hythe appeared there in 1465–67. In
1462–63 the citizens of Sandwich enjoyed something of a festival of
amateur drama, for during this period they entertained players from
Herne, nearby Ash, Deal and Canterbury, and even found 8d. to
reward two performers from their own town. By 1489–90 the mayor
was witnessing a play brought from as far away as Reading. But it was
perhaps Dover which witnessed the widest range of amateur drama-
tics: in addition to local companies like those from Herne, Thanet,
Hythe, Boughton, Sandwich and Canterbury, as well as many
anonymous '*homines ludentes*', the town also entertained as early as
1475–76 'a pleyar of Pykardy' and 'iiij Playeres of london' in 1484–85
(who may be identified with those receiving 10s. at court in July
1498); in 1486–87 a company from Calais performed in Dover,
receiving 5s. and helping to consume 18d. worth of wine, 2d. more

than the Canterbury players drank earlier in the same year. Besides local and visiting presentations collaborative productions between towns and villages were not unknown: on 20 July 1511 twenty-seven East Anglian villages combined to stage a play on St George at Bassingbourn, near Cambridge.[19]

SOURCE: extract (with minor revisions by the author) from the chapter 'The Performers', in *The Theatre in the Middle Ages* (Cambridge, 1978), pp. 209–17.

NOTES

[Reorganised and renumbered from the original. For short-form references to works, see Abbreviations List, p. 8 – Ed.]

1. M. B. Evans, *The Passion Play of Lucerne* (New York, 1943), p. 176, n. 1; *Corpus Christi Plays*, pp. 87, 90, 103; G. Cohen, *Histoire de la mise en scène dans le théâtre religieux français du Moyen Age* (Paris, 1906; 2nd edn, 1925), p. 226.

2. S. J. Kahrl (ed.), *Records of Plays and Players in Lincolnshire, 1300–1585*, in *Malone Society Collections*, VIII (Oxford, 1974), pp. 43, 49.

3. *Corpus Christi Plays*, p. 105.

4. Chambers, II, pp. 346–8.

5. For Worcester, see Chambers, II, p. 398, and G. Wickham, *The Medieval Theatre* (London, 1974), p. 87; for Lucerne, see Evans, op. cit., p. 190.

6. See Cohen, op. cit., pp. 221, 227–8.

7. Evans, op. cit., p. 191; *Corpus Christi Plays*, pp. 100, 85–6; G. E. Dawson, *Records of Plays and Players in Kent, 1450–1642*, in *Malone Society Collections*, VII, (Oxford, 1965), p. 208; Cohen, op. cit., pp. 223, 227; R. Lebègue, *Le Mystère des Actes des Apôtres* (Paris, 1929), p. 93.

8. J. Huizinga, *The Waning of the Middle Ages* (1924; pb edn, Harmondsworth, 1955), pp. 314–15; A. M. Nagler, *Theatre Festivals of the Medici, 1539–1637* (London, 1964), pp. 10, 18.

9. Cohen, op. cit., pp. 231–2.

10. M. B. Evans, 'The staging of the Donaueschingen Passion play', *Modern Language Review*, 15 (1920), pp. 285–6.

11. Chambers, II, p. 388; Evans, *Lucerne*, op. cit., pp. 177, 181, 191; Whitley Stokes (ed.), *Gwreans an Bys* (London, 1864), pp. 28, 70, 78.

12. Lebègue, op. cit., p. 198.

13. Cohen, op. cit., p. 237.

14. Lebègue, op. cit., p. 197, suggests that lapses in the text of *Les Actes des Apôtres* resulting in ludicrous nonsense bear the Procurator out! For the Bourges compliment, see p. 100; Cohen, op. cit., p. 235; Frank, p. 193.

15. Cohen, op. cit., p. 240.

16. Ibid., pp. 239–8.

17. Wickham, *The Medieval Theatre*, op. cit., p. 83.

18. See Chambers, II, pp. 240–8, 329–406 for examples; Dawson, op. cit., pp. 1–155.

19. See Chambers, II, p. 338.

Paula Neuss The Staging of *The Creacion* *of the World* (1979)

The Creacion of the World is the least known of the surviving Cornish plays, none of which is exactly familiar, having been so long out of print.[1] In fact, the *Creacion* may well be the least known of all cycle plays[2] extant in England. This is unfortunate, for it is of great interest, not least because of its stage directions, which are unusually full – much fuller than those of the other Cornish plays or anything in the English cycles except perhaps the *Ludus Coventriae* Passion plays. Like the title (Stokes's Cornish title was an invention), the stage directions are all in English, and seem to fall into two main types: either authorial instructions to the actors, e.g.

Lett eva looke stranglye on the Serpent when she speakethe   [551 sd. (not in Stokes)]

Let not Cayme looke in the father is face but look down and quake   [1164 sd.]

Lett Tuball fall a laughing   [2299 sd.]

and on the design of the sets, e.g.

Let paradice be finelye made with ij fayre trees in yt
And an appell vpon the Tree and som other frute one the other   [359 sd.]

ij pyllars made, the on of brick and thother of marbell   [2186 sd. (not Stokes)]

or what seem to be prompt-copy instructions to the stage-manager:

ffig leaves Redy to cover ther members   [871 sd.]

A lamb redy with fyre and insence   [1079 sd.]

A chawbone Readye   [1109 sd.]

tooles and tymber redy, with planckys to make the Arcke, a beam a mallet a Calk yn yre
Ropes mastes [masses MS] *pyche and tarr*   [2254 sd.]

The manuscript of the *Creacion* (Bodleian MS 219) contains no diagram or staging plan, unlike those of the other Cornish plays[3] (see diagram). Nevertheless, it has usually been assumed that its method

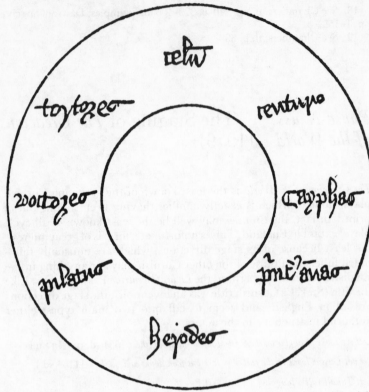

A diagram showing the arrangements of the stations for the Cornish play *Ordinalia*, 2nd day. [The words, clockwise, are: Celum, Centurio, Cayphas, Princeps, Annas, Herodes, Pilatus, Doctores, Tortores – Ed.]

of staging would have been similar to theirs, that is, playing in the round, in an open amphitheatre, in the manner Richard Carew described:

> The Guary miracle, in English, a miracle-play, is a kinde of Enterlude, compiled in *Cornish* out of some scripture history. . . . For representing it, they raise an earthen Amphitheatre, in some open field, having the Diameter of his enclosed playne some 40. or 50. foot.[4]

Two amphitheatres exist in Cornwall today, at St Just-in-Penwith and Perranzabuloe. These are the only remaining examples of the *plen-an-guary* or 'playing place'[5] which Carew seems to be describing. That the Cornish *Ordinalia* was intended for performance in such a

round seems proven not only by the three diagrams in the manuscript, but also by the success of the production of it in Perran Round
by Bristol University Drama Department in 1969. There has been no
similar production of the *Creacion* and I rather doubt that there could
be.

Southern suggests that the word *playne* which occurs twice in the
Creacion stage directions is used in the same sense as *place* or *platea* in
the other Cornish plays and in *The Castle of Perseverance*, and that this
implies use of the same kind of staging, that the play was performed in
the round.[6] The two examples are from early in the play:

devylls of lether and Sprytys on Cordys Runing into ye playne   [326 sd.]

Let the Serpent walke in the playne   [488 sd.]   [7]

However, although the word is the same as that used by Carew, there
is no evidence that I can find in the *Creacion* that this *playne* was
'enclosed' in the manner Carew described and which is indicated in
the diagrams of the other Cornish plays. The surviving diagrams for
'theatre-in-the-round' all show a number of stations or mansions
grouped round the *place*; eight in each of the three days of the *Ordinalia*,
thirteen in both days of *Meriasek*, and five in the *Castle*. The *Creacion*,
however, seems to have had only three stations: Heaven, Hell and
Paradise.

The structures of Heaven and Hell were clearly extremely elaborate. It appears from the scene in which the angels are created that
Heaven may have had three tiers or levels. The first level contained
God's throne, and that this was higher than the other parts of Heaven
can be seen from the directions *Let hem* [Lucifer] *offer to assend to ye trone*
[202 sd.], and *Let Lucyfer offer to go vpe to the trone* [314 sd.] – both of
which occur while Lucifer is still in Heaven. There are three degrees
of angels: the first three 'next [or nearest] to my throne' [37]; the
'second degree' [51], which is probably lower; 'the third degree below'
[59]. The ordering of the angels is one of status, and may not have
been represented physically, but Heaven must have had at least two
levels including that containing the throne. There are three concen-
tric circles in Heaven in the Cailleau miniature of the Valenciennes
Passion Play . . . ; and in the Fouquet miniature of the martyrdom of
St Apollonia, the angels in Heaven appear to be arranged in tiers . . . .
In the *Creacion* these levels were possibly also divided into sections or
special places for each kind of angel. The direction for the War in
Heaven reads: *All Angels must . . . com to ye Rome wher Lucyfer ys* [299 sd.],
and although *rome* here may mean simply 'space, area' (*OED*: room,
sb.[1] 5), its meaning may be closer to the modern sense. The expression
rowmys [2258] clearly means 'rooms' (or cabins), for it refers there to

the living quarters of the Ark, the *mansiunculae* of the Vulgate. Each angel may have had his own special *rome*, space or position (cf. *OED*: room, *sb.*[1] 5e, 'square on a chessboard'). One is reminded of Archdeacon Rogers's description (written in 1609) of the Chester pageant-houses: 'a highe place made like a howse with ij rowmes'.[8] An interesting point is that if Heaven were so constructed, with three levels divided into sections, it would closely resemble the Ark with its 'thre chese chambers', as the Towneley play describes it,[9] its three rows of living quarters. This would make an excellent visual association, for Augustine had laid down that the Ark signified the Church.[10]

The station for Hell also appears to have had two levels: the *pytt* [330, 422, 1721, 2035], which is 'on [the] lowest side' [2034], and the *clowster*, 'cloisters' [2027], or *Lymbo*, which is 'on the upper side' [2026]. The direction

Lett hell gape when ye father nameth yt   [244 sd.]

shows that the *pytt* was a Hell-mouth, and Hell was commonly so represented on the medieval stage. The structure used in the *Creacion* must have resembled that of the Digby Mary Magdalene play, where Lucifer enters *In a stage, and Helle ondyr-neth þat stage*,[11] and also those in the Valenciennes and Fouquet miniatures, both of which have two levels, the lower being a Hell-mouth . . . .

Hell is also referred to as 'the kitchen' [2013] and probably a large cooking-pot was part of its design, as it was in the illustration of the Last Judgement in *The Holkham Bible Picture Book* . . . . There seems to be a cooking-pot containing souls insides the Valenciennes Hell-mouth, too . . . . Cauldrons symbolise Hell in *The Croxton Play of the Sacrament* and *The Jew of Malta*; the Chester Harrowing of Hell is presented appropriately by the Cooks and Innkeepers, while in the *Jeu d'Adam* devils are instructed to 'dash together their pots and kettles'.[12] The devils in *Resurrectio Domini* (the third play of the *Ordinalia* Trilogy) announce:

> We will die making a fire
> Under the kettle.
> Drink, there are with me
> More than a million souls
> In a very fair broth.[13]

'The kitchen' seems sometimes to be a euphuism for Hell in Cornish expletives,[14] and this may have arisen through its stage presentation.

Paradise was perhaps less elaborate than Heaven and Hell, though it was *fynelye made*, as the direction at 359, already quoted, shows, and it contained, besides the two trees, *a fowntayne . . . and fyne floures in yt paynted* [359 sd.]. It must have been quite large, for in the Fall scene it contained both Eve and the Serpent, and Adam some distance away.

No other *loca* are mentioned in the stage directions, but it might be thought that the speech-heading *Lamec in tent* [1429] points to the existence of at least one other station, for these are sometimes called *tenti* (otherwise *pulpita*) in the stage directions of the *Ordinalia*. In *Passio Domini* (the second play of the Trilogy) for instance, there are references in the directions to the *tenti* of Pilate, Herod, and Cayphas [454 sd., 1573 sd., 1616 sd., 1687 sd., 1882 sd., 1934 sd., 2066 sd.]. These are all names that appear on the perimeter of the circular diagram for that day, or round the edge, apparently, of the amphitheatre (see diagram). A similar position might therefore be deduced for Lamech's *tent* in the *Creacion*, and if he had one, other characters may have done too, although no other actors' stations are mentioned. Lamech's first words are similar to those of Enoch and Noah in that they all declare their names, somewhat in the manner of the characters in the *Ordinalia* who parade on their scaffolds. As Lamech speaks first *in tent*, possibly Enoch and Noah had *tenti* too.

However, these figures are not major characters like those who have their own *tenti* in the *Ordinalia*. Noah does not have one in *Origo Mundi*, and he is no more important a character in the *Creacion*. I believe that Lamech is the only character in the *Creacion* who had a *tent*, and that it was not a curtained booth on a raised platform like the *tenti* of the *Ordinalia*, but a literal tent with an iconographic significance. Lamech was thought to be the inventor of tents:

> hit is kynde of man,
> Sith Lamek was, that is so longe agoon,
> To ben in love as fals as evere he can;
> He was the firste fader that began
> To loven two, and was in bigamye;
> And *he found tentes first, but yf men lye.*

> [*Anelida and Arcite*, 149–54][15]

Robinson comments: 'It is really Jabal, Lamech's son, who is called "the father of such as dwell in tents" ', referring to Genesis iv.19–20.[16] Lamech's tent in the *Creacion* draws attention to what was thought to be an aspect of his character. I believe it to have been a movable property like the Ark, and not a fixed station. If it had been present throughout the entire action, like the *tenti* in the *Ordinalia*, it could not have had any iconographic significance.

So there seems to have been only three fixed stations, hardly enough to constitute a 'round'. Moreover, the stations in the other

Cornish plays and the *Castle* were raised, for actors had to go up to them and down from them. But the only references in the *Creacion* to ascending or descending are made in connection with Heaven. God descends to the earth [74–5]; *Lucyfer . . . goeth downe to hell* [from Heaven] [326 sd.]; *Let the father assend to heaven* [953 sd.]; *desend angell* [971 sd.]. Heaven, then, was a raised station of some kind. There is nothing, however, to suggest that Hell and Paradise were not on the same level as the rest of the action, nor, supposing Lamech's *tent were* a fixed station, does he make any mention of ascending or descending, unlike the characters with *tenti* in the *Passio Domini*. If Lamech's *tent* were on the edge of an amphitheatre, one would expect him to *go down* into the *place*. If the stations were not raised it is most unlikely that they would have been arranged in the round, since it would have been very difficult for the audience to see the action.

The stations could, of course, all have been in the *place*, like the Castle in the *Castle*, and Meriasek's chapel. But in the diagrams for these plays only the one *locus* is shown in the *place*, and sight lines would have been obscured if there had been more. The person who drew the *Castle* diagram was concerned about *lettyng of syt* as it was, with the Castle in the middle of the place.[17] The *Creacion* stations were obviously quite substantial, and also there are a number of other items of scenery besides Heaven, Hell and Paradise that would have to be in the *place* for part of the action: Mount Tabor, the bush in which Cain hides, the 'forest' [1491 sd.], Adam's bed and his tomb, the Ark, as well as Lamech's tent. Admittedly some of these might have been natural features of the *place*,[18] such as the bush and the 'forest' (if it was not too large). Mount Tabor (which might be specially built from a heap of earth, leaving a ditch in which Cain could throw Abel's body: *Cast abell into a dyche* [1136 sd.])[19] may have been quite small. But still the *place* would have been extremely cluttered if the stations were in it. And this in any case would not conform to the usual conception of 'theatre-in-the-round', which has the stations surrounding the *place*.

The *Creacion* was not staged then, in quite the same way as the other Cornish plays seem to have been, for Heaven is the only raised station, and there are not many other *loca* mentioned. Most of the action apparently took place in the *playne*. This may not have been circular, but possibly semi-circular or even oblong, with the stations arranged in a line or semi-circle behind it, and the audience in front: the kind of arrangement that is shown in the miniature of the manuscript of the Valenciennes Passion play, where several stations ranging from Paradise to Hell seem to be grouped together in a line . . . . Compare also the Fouquet miniature . . . (though Southern says this shows part of an amphitheatre).[20]

The relative position of the stations is not indicated in the *Creacion*. Normally in England, Heaven seems to have been placed in the east (the position of the altar in a church), and Hell in the north, with the good characters in the south and the worldly ones in the west; this is the positioning in the *Ordinalia*. Such an arrangement could still be retained in a semi-circle, with Heaven at centre back, Hell to the extreme left, and Paradise and the good characters to the right of Heaven. The World in the west would then be represented by the audience. On the other hand, the arrangement might have been more like that usual in the French plays, where Paradise and Heaven are placed on the left, and Hell on the extreme right,[21] as in both the Valenciennes and Fouquet miniatures. (This of course *is* Heaven's left.)

One scene in the play seems to defy either of these arrangements of the *loca*, but there seems no possible organisation that would suit it. In Seth's account of his vision of Paradise, he describes the tree whose branches reach up into Heaven, while its roots run down in to Hell [1825–38, 1897–1910]. If this vision were to be represented on stage, Paradise would need to be on a level between Heaven and Hell. This would involve an impossibly cumbersome structure, since both Heaven and Hell have more than one level. Probably the production did not attempt to stage this part of Seth's vision: he gives two detailed descriptions of Paradise; possibly because the audience was not shown all of the vision. The arrangement of the tree's roots and branches is not mentioned in the stage directions, although other elements of his vision, the Virgin and Child in the Tree, and Cain in Hell, are detailed in the directions at 1772 and 1804.

There are other factors to take into account besides the evidence relating to the stations. In the directions to the actors, great emphasis is laid on the expression of emotion. While this can be done by the kind of physical movement that an audience could see from some distance, e.g.

Eva is sorowfull tereth her heare and falleth downe vpon Adam he conforteth her   [1245 sd.]

and the direction to Cain to *look down and quake* already quoted, in the *Creacion* scenes are frequently directed to convey feelings by facial expression:

then eva wondreth of the Serpent when she speakyth   [548 sd.]

Let eva looke Angerly on the Serpent and profer to departe   [625 sd.]

Eva loketh vpon Adam very stranglye   [865 sd.]

Such emphasis on facial expression would tend to suggest a rather smaller type of theatre than at least the surviving Cornish rounds (St Just is 126 ft in diameter). The expressions and gestures the actors are directed to make in the *Creacion* are rather intimate, not of the grand kind essential to displaying oneself on a raised station:

hic pompabit Abraham   [*Origo Mundi*, 1258 sd.]

filling a large area of the *place*:

Et verberabit eos super terram   [*Castle*, 1777 sd.]

or making the most of both station and place, as in the famous direction in the Coventry pageant:

Here•Erode ragis in the pagond and in the street also[22]

The speeches, too, are generally shorter, suggesting that the actors did not have a large area of *place* to cross while they were speaking.

I imagine, then, a much more intimate kind of setting for the production of the *Creacion* than that evidently used by the other Cornish plays. There was perhaps not as great an opportunity for spectacle as in the rounds, though the war in Heaven was obviously very exciting:

Let them fight with swordys and in the end Lucyfer voydeth and goeth downe to hell apariled fowle: with fyre abowt hem turning to hell and every degre of devylls of Lether and Sprytys on Cordys Runing into ye playne and so remayne ther nine angells after Lucyfer goeth to hell   [326 sd.]

This was obviously the kind of effect Carew was referring to in his description of 'devils and devices, to delight as well the eye as the eare',[23] as was also the mechanical cloud with hinged sections in which God was lowered from Heaven:[24]

The father must be in a clowde and when he Speakythe of heaven let ye Levys open   [1 sd.]

After the father hath spoken lett hem departe to heaven in a clowde   [420 sd.]

The production was clearly extremely elaborate, and evidently needed an experienced stage-manager. This person is mentioned twice in the stage directions:

Adam and Eva aparlet in whytt Lether in a place apoynted by the Conveyour and not to be sene tyll they be called and then knell and ryse   [343 sd.]

Lett Adam laye downe and slepe wher Eva ys and she by the conveyour must be taken from Adam is syde   [392 sd.]

The word has been interpreted in various ways, none of which seems satisfactory. It has been taken to mean a kind of prompter similar to the ordinary of Carew's account:

> . . . the players conne not their parts without booke, but are prompted by one called the Ordinary, who followeth at their back with the booke in his hand, and telleth them softly what they must pronounce aloud.[25]

Chambers suggested the ordinary and the *conveyor* were identical,[26] but the direction at 343 indicates a more important role for the *conveyor* than just prompting, while that at 392 denotes a physical action. M. D. Anderson implies that she thinks of the *conveyor* as a 'stage creator'[27] but this tells us little more than the *Creacion* direction. Nance thought that the *conveyor* was a kind of secret passageway that allowed actors to enter unseen (compare *OED*: convey, *v.* 6, 'to manage secretly'), and he believed that the 'Devil's Spoon', a hollowed-out area in Perran Round, was used for this purpose;[28] but the suggestion has since been made that the 'Devil's Spoon' was a cooking trench.[29] Nance's suggestion seems invalid anyway, for the second mention of the *conveyor* indicates an agent or instrument: *by* [392 sd.] cannot mean 'beside', or even 'via'.

It is helpful to compare an entry in the York Civic Records for 1486 which states that one Henry Hudson was appointed to have the '*conueance* of the making and running of the shew' (a reception for Henry VII).[30] This means in effect the 'running' of the show (*OED*: conveyance, *sb*. 10, 'management'). Running a production of a miracle play, being a Pageant Master, meant, among other things, looking after the book of the play, possibly writing or redacting it.[31] A *conveyor* may very well mean a redactor as well as a director/stage-manager (*OED*: convey, *v.* 9b, 'to transmit to posterity, to hand down'; 9d, 'to communicate, to express in words'; 12, 'to conduct [an affair], to carry on, manage'). In the direction at 343, *a place apoynted by the Conveyour* obviously means 'a place decided by the director/stage-manager'. However, at 392 the *conveyor* seems (as Anderson implies) to mean God, for he says 'I will make for thee a spouse' just as the direction occurs. He has just taken a bone from *Adam is syde* [389 sd.], and in many medieval illustrations of this episode (including that in the Creation window at St Neots church in Cornwall) God is shown lifting Eve from Adam. . . . I have shown elsewhere that the 'author' of the *Creacion* almost certainly played the part of God the Father.[32] So in 392 *by the conveyour* means 'by the redactor [who is playing God]', i.e., 'by God'. So in the *Creacion* the *conveyor* means in effect 'William Jordan' who not only 'wrote' (i.e. redacted) the *Creacion*[33] but also almost certainly stage-managed it (this would explain why the manuscript contains both authorial instruction to the actors and entries we might expect from a prompt-book), and played the part of God the Father in it. We may compare him with Robert Croo of Coventry who

> not only redacted the surviving *Shearman and Taylors'* Pageant and *Weaver's* Pageant and provided the Drapers with 'the boke' for their pageant, but wrote a play called *The Golden Fleece* for the Cappers. In addition he played the part of God in the Drapers Pageant of Doomsday in 1560, the book of which he provided three years earlier. That same year he was also paid 'for mendyng the devills cottes'. Four years earlier he had been paid 'for makyng iij worldys' and two years later 'for a hat for the pharysye'. There was thus hardly any aspect of the production with which he and his like were not familiar.[34]

It appeares that 'William Jordan' is another example of the English Pageant master Wickham describes, and it turns out to be most appropriate that the play is commonly known as 'Jordan's Creation'.

SOURCE: article in *Theatre Notebook*, 33 (1979), pp. 116–25 (with revisions by the author).

NOTES

[For short-form references to works, see Abbreviations List, p. 8 – Ed.]

1. The *Creacion* was edited by Whitley Stokes, *Gwreans an Bys: The Creation of the World, a Cornish Mystery* (London, 1863; Berlin, 1864). Line references, revised for this Casebook, are to my edition (New York, 1983), though quotations, stage directions and punctuation follow the manuscript (with abbreviations expanded).

2. The title states that the *Creacion* is *the first daie of playe*, but the remaining days of the cycle are no longer extant.

3. The plans are reproduced in Edwin Norris (ed.), *The Ancient Cornish Drama* (Oxford, 1859), I, pp. 219, 479; II, p. 200; and (in diagram form) Whitley Stokes (ed.), *Beunans Meriasek* (London, 1872), pp. 144, 266.

4. Richard Carew, *Survey of Cornwall* (London, 1602), p. 71.

5. See R. Morton Nance, 'The Plen an Gwary or Cornish Playing-Place', *Journal of the Royal Institution of Cornwall*, XXIV (1934), pp. 191–211, for a description of these rounds and a list of places in Cornwall where others may have existed.

6. Southern, p. 225.

7. Stokes's reading 'wait in the plain', printed by Southern, is incorrect.

8. Quoted *Digby*, p. *xix*. Rogers thought that the lower *rowme* was a kind of tiring-house. Chambers, II, p. 135 said that *rome* in the *Creacion* meant one of the stations. This is impossible, for the fight in Lucifer's *rome* takes place in Heaven.

9. *Wakefield Pageants*, pp. 17, 129.

10. Kolve, p. 69.

11. *Digby*, p. 67 (357 s.d.).

12. Quoted, e.g., in A. M. Nagler, *A Source Book in Theatrical History* (New York, 1959), p. 47.

13. Norris, op. cit., ıı, p. 13. Cf. also Thurstan Peter, *The Old Cornish Drama* (London, 1906): 'During the quarrel between Beelzebub and Lucifer a demon named Tulfric makes some remarks that I do not fully understand, but they clearly intimate he is concerned in some way in the *cooking of souls*' (p. 30).

14. Henry Jenner, *A Handbook of the Cornish Language* (London, 1904) p. 55, remarks however, 'Another serio-comic but rather cryptic expletive, peculiar to Camborne, or at any rate to the Drama of St Meriasek, is *Mollath Dew en gegin!* God's curse in the kitchen! It does not seem to mean anything in particular, except perhaps that one's food may not agree with one.'

15. F. N. Robinson (ed.), *The Works of Geoffrey Chaucer*, 2nd edn (Cambridge, Mass., and London, 1957), p. 306.

16. Ibid., p. 790.

17. See Southern, p. 72ff.

18. The production of Lyndsay's *Ane Satyre of the Thrie Estaitis* at Cupar, for instance, took advantage of natural features of the area. See Glynne Wickham, 'The Staging of Saints Plays in England', in Sandro Sticca (ed.), *The Medieval Drama* (Albany, N.Y., 1972), pp. 114–15. [See also J. S. Kantrowitz's discussion of the play in section 3 of Part Two above – Ed.]

19. Cf. Southern's view that a mound was thrown up when the ditch in the *Castle* was dug (pp. 50–6). However, Natalie C. Schmitt – 'Was there a Medieval Theatre in the Round? A Re-examination of the evidence', *Theatre Notebook*, xxııı (1968–69), pp. 130–42; xxıv (1969–70), pp. 18–25 – believes that the ditch is 'merely the moat round the castle'.

20. Southern, p. 91ff.; Schmitt (op. cit.) disagrees, pp. 312–13.

21. See Frank, p. 164.

22. *Corpus Christi Plays*, p. 27 (783 s.d.).

23. Carew, op. cit., p. 71.

24. Cf. the 'duble clowde' listed in the records of St Swithin's, Lincoln, mentioned by Craig, p. 279. 'In all the cycle plays there is much mechanical to-and-froing between earth and heaven. When the York Jesus is about to ascend into heaven he says, 'Sende doune a clowde, fadir', and a cloud comes down; he gets into it and is hoisted aloft out of sight': Kolve, p. 26.

25. Carew op. cit., p. 71. William L. Tribby – 'The Medieval Prompter: A Reinterpretation', *Theatre Survey*, v (1964), pp. 71–6 – doubts the accuracy of this account, as do I.

26. Chambers, ıı, p. 140.

27. Anderson, pp. 142–3.

28. Nance, op. cit. (note 5, above), pp. 203–5.

29. See Treve Holman, 'Cornish Plays and Playing Places', *Theatre Notebook*, ıv, 3 (April–June 1950), pp. 52–4.

30. Sydney Anglo, *Spectacle, Pageantry and Early Tudor Policy* (Oxford, 1969), p. 23 (my italics).

31. See Wickham, I, pp. 297–300.

32. Paula Neuss, 'Memorial Reconstruction in a Cornish Miracle Play', *Comparative Drama*, v (1971), pp. 129–37.

33. The colophon states that the *Creacion* was *wryten by William Jordan: the xii^th of August 1611*.

34. Wickham, I, p. 299.

Sheila Lindenbaum   The York Cycle at Toronto: Staging and Performance Style (1978)

Because the York Corpus Christi cycle drew so much of its dramatic power from the life of the medieval community, it presents formidable problems to modern producers. One obvious difficulty stems from the anachronistic dramatisation of scripture history. How can one convey to a twentieth-century audience the contemporaneity of a play in which Pilate holds a Parliament with his 'bishops' and Christ enters Jerusalem like a king passing in royal procession through the gates of a medieval walled city? The forty-seven separate pageants in which the York cycle treats the story of man from the Creation to the Last Judgement were mounted by the craft guilds of the city under the supervision of the municipal authorities. By what process are these pageants to be produced today without the social and economic structure of the towns that gave to cycle plays the character of a truly civic drama? Finally, what performing style is to be used by modern actors? Even if the modern productions were to employ a historically accurate style (supposing that one could be reconstructed from surviving evidence), this style would only very partially convey to a modern audience the devotional, didactic and ceremonial purposes of the medieval cycle.

These problems have been avoided rather than solved in the best-known modern revival of the cycle, the triennial productions that have been taking place since 1951 at the York Festival. While using medieval costumes and the ruins of St Mary's Abbey church as a setting, the York Festival productions have taken the easy course of translating the cycle into an essentially modern theatrical idiom. The forty-seven pageants have typically been compressed into a continuous drama with a single 'story line' and performed in a style one reviewer has described as a mélange of Oberammergau Passion Play, pre-Raphaelite tableaux and twentieth-century church drama.[1]

The [1977] revival of the cycle at the University of Toronto, produced as it was by the Poculi Ludique Societas and the University's Records of Early English Drama project, was a far more scholarly affair, with the aim of presenting the play in a manner 'as historically accurate as possible'.[2] The surviving text of the cycle, the Register of pageants compiled in the late fifteenth century, was presented intact for the first time in modern stage history, and a date of 1485 was set as the 'original' of the performance. Since the 1951 York Festival, a growing enthusiasm for producing medieval drama has resulted in revivals, though often in abbreviated versions, of almost all of the extant medieval English plays. The Toronto revival, however, like the nearly complete York cycle presented at Leeds University in 1975, was unusual in its attempt to embody the results of recent scholarly research. Inevitably, a production that aims at historical accuracy will lack the immediacy the cycle had for its original audience. Still, the Toronto production had much to suggest about the continuing sources of the cycle's appeal, at the same time as it offered a special opportunity to review scholarly thinking about its medieval staging and style of performance.

For the scholarly audience, the production was particularly interesting because it contributed to a fierce debate concerning the manner in which the cycle was staged by the medieval guilds. Until a few years ago, most authorities accepted the idea that the cycle was mounted on a series of pageant wagons that moved through the city, stopping at a number of stations where each pageant was performed in its proper order. Alexandra Johnston and Margaret Dorrell have recently defended this view in the course of preparing a new edition of the York dramatic records; but others have argued that the cycle was too long to stage processionally during the single day given to a medieval performance.[3] The Toronto production, whose Planning Committee was chaired by Professor Johnston, was in part intended to give the processional (or 'station-to-station') theory a practical test. University and community groups, mainly from Toronto, took responsibility for the individual pageants much as the craft guilds did in medieval York. The plan was to perform the pageants at each of three stations set up in King's College Circle, using nine wagons and allowing a day and a half for the entire cycle.

As it happened, pageants eleven through thirty-three (*Exodus* through *The Condemnation of Christ*) were driven indoors by a heavy rain, and the performance overran its original fourteen-hour schedule by about five hours. But even the initial plan was a considerable modification of the staging conditions in medieval York, where each pageant had its own wagon and stopped at as many as seventeen stations in a single day. As a result, although it showed that an enormous cast could be organised with remarkable efficiency, the Toronto production could not really test whether impossible delays would occur at later stations when short pageants had to wait for longer ones to finish, as opponents of the processional theory have argued. Even if some pageants had been cut, as they probably were in 1535 when only thirty-two were scheduled,[4] a performance at three stations could only test the general effect of staging the pageants on wagons in a processional manner.

The effect created, at least at Toronto, was a rich and fluid theatrical environment. As the brilliantly colored wagons made their way around the stations, and the actors appeared in a seemingly endless display of medieval costumes ranging from royal regalia to shepherds' weeds, one could sense much of the visual excitement of a medieval spectacle. Part of the audience crowded into stands and a few perched in the windows of surrounding buildings, as records indicate they did in medieval York. They could also walk from station to station to see a pageant a second time, and many did this for the popular *Harrowing of Hell*. The line that separated the actors from the audience was therefore constantly shifting. The audience was pushed back by soldiers in the Passion sequence and raided by the devils in *The Day of Judgement*; the actors' space was invaded in turn by curious spectators, photographers, and the many children and stray animals who failed to distinguish the dramatic performance from the larger festival event.

The fluid quality of the performance was instructive, in view of the point scholars often make that staging a series of pageants on wagons places each pageant in sharp focus, as if it were a single compartment in a narrative series of manuscript illustrations or stained glass windows.[5] The pageants at Toronto did function as independent elements within the whole, and some emphasised their separateness by using framing structures from the visual arts – a tryptich in *The Purification*, twin arches in *The Condemnation*. But at least in the outdoor performances the pageants differed from the compartmentalised scenes in art as a result of the shifting line between actors and audience and the movement of the wagons within the ebb and flow of the procession.

A medieval performance would, of course, have lacked this processional flow if it had taken place in the chamber at Common Hall gates, as Alan Nelson has argued,[6] or on wagons gathered at the last station, the Pavement, as Martin Stevens has proposed.[7] Both

Nelson and Stevens believe that the procession of wagons and the dramatic cycle were separate events, with the cycle being performed in a single place at the conclusion of the procession. Given Nelson's theory, in particular, it was interesting to see the changes that occurred when some of the pageants at Toronto were forced indoors. These pageants were acted on a wagon brought from outdoors, not the platform or open space one might expect in a hall; yet one could see that the lines between actors and audience and between groups within the audience were more firmly drawn in the indoor auditorium, as they may have been if the cycle were mounted for a few powerful officials in a hall rather than a large popular audience in the streets. Lacking the natural effects that redeemed some clumsy performances in the open air, where a magnificent flock of Canadian geese flew over *The Creation* and a rainbow appeared during *The Day of Judgement*, a greater professionalism also seemed required indoors.

Although the weather made it difficult to draw any further conclusions about a station-to-station presentation, much could be learned about the technique of staging the individual pageants. In deference to the narrow streets and low house overhangs in medieval York, the wagons used at Toronto measured only twelve by six feet, with the flat roofs topping some of them rising about eight feet above the wagon stage. They were thus much smaller than scholars have imagined, and much simpler in line than the lavishly decorated and sometimes gabled Brussels wagons, known from a seventeenth-century illustration, that are often cited as analogues.[8] True, pageants that demand large groups of characters did seem rather cramped on these stages; in *Pentecost*, the Holy Spirit had to descend upon a combination of live Apostles and two-dimensional Apostle figures painted on a backdrop. Moreover, some of the wagons equipped with superstructures and backdrops looked incongruously like tiny proscenium-arch stages with an invisible fourth wall. It was perhaps because the setting of *The Annunciation* so closely resembled an actual room, in imitation of the subject in art, that the audience was amused when Mary walked through the fourth wall in order to pay her visit to Elizabeth.

Nevertheless, the problem of staging pageants that often specified several levels, multiple locations and movement between locations on these wagons was often solved effectively, without resorting to the extra wagons or supplementary platforms sometimes proposed in scholarly reconstructions.[9] The solution in most cases was simply to use the ground in front of the wagon to extend the acting space, a procedure justified by the famous stage direction from the Coventry play in which 'Erode ragis in the pagond and in the strete also'. The ground became a *platea* in which space and time were generally more flexible than on the more localised wagon stage. In *The Creation and Fall of Lucifer*, with which the University of Toronto Centre for Medieval Studies began the cycle, God emerged on the pageant roof, up to which Lucifer reached boldly before falling from the angels' 'heaven' on the wagon itself, through a hellmouth constructed as a chute, down to the *platea* which designated his timeless hell. In *Noah and the Flood* (University of Toronto Drama Centre), the bright yellow wagon representing the ark bore a raised lookout post, whence Noah sent a paper dove via a wire to investigate conditions on the flooded 'mid-earth' in the *platea* below. 'Mid-earth' at the beginning of the pageant had contained a *locus* of its own, a stool indicating the 'home' where Noah's wife sits and frets. The only questionable aspect of this procedure was the use of the off-stage *loca*. It seemed appropriate to play the scourging of Christ on the ground, since that suggested Christ's humility in relation to Pilate's court on the wagon; but it made less sense to have Christ rise from his tomb in the same place, especially after the parallel raising of Lazarus had been played on the wagon itself.

Some of the stage devices used at Toronto, like the windlass raising God to his rooftop 'heavens' in *The Day of Judgement*, have been documented from medieval records;[10] others, like the architectural properties and the many tableaux of Apostles, Doctors, angels and saints, derived from the visual arts; still others – some of the most striking ones, like Noah's wired dove – were apparently modern inventions. Whatever the degree of authenticity, the staging was most effective when it established a telling relationship between the audience and the play. The art of the cycle playwrights depends heavily on the rhetoric they use to sermonise, threaten, reassure, call to devotion, condemn and bless their audience. The staging, we may assume, was intended to work together with this rhetoric, most simply to give the audience an image to contemplate (the descent of the Holy Spirit), provide a bridge to the main action (Noah's wife on her stool), or set up an equation between the audience's level and a level of action in the play (Satan's hell). At its most complex, the staging could also suggest parallels between the devices of stagecraft and the divine manipulations evident in scriptural history. When the artistic director of the production, David Parry, took the role of God in *The Day of Judgement*, the analogy (and distinction) between the human and divine artificer was made by the smooth stage machinery carrying God to his heavens and the script that the overworked human actor consulted for some of his lines.

The relationship between the audience and the play established in a pageant will also depend on the style in which it is performed. On this subject, too, one finds considerable disagreement among scholars. V. A. Kolve has argued that the Corpus Christi cycles present us with a 'special game world' whose rules require that the actors self-consciously perform their roles rather than identify with them and the audience remain aware that it is witnessing a play.[11] Anne Righter, on the other hand, describes the cycles as a kind of ritual, a 'communion with sacred history', demanding that both actors and audience passionately identify with their parts.[12] As different as these views may seem, both may have some validity for a play like the York cycle which seems to involve wide variations in performing style. In the Register of pageants one finds not only a wide range of verse forms indicating affinities with numerous other literary genres, but also signs of revision and expansion by several authors at different points in the cycle's development. It was not surprising, then, to see a variety of styles attempted in the course of the Toronto production, even though the Planning Committee had fixed the date of 1485 to ensure continuity within the performance.

Cornell University's *Christ Led Up to Calvary* was self-consciously theatrical, along the lines suggested by Kolve. A narrow strip of straw matting rolled down the wagon steps to the green indicated the road to Calvary, and the wagon was backed with a painted curtain showing a stylised city of Jerusalem. To the sound of trumpets, Christ entered like an actor through a part in this curtain and stood as a spectacle of fallen majesty, a Marlovian figure in his heavy iron crown, lavender robe and rough furs. His tormentors were rowdy young soldiers, consciously grand in their Roman helmets and military tunics. For them transporting Christ to Calvary was a game that challenged their ingenuity; it was with the air of a neatly struck upon solution that they recruited Simon of Cyrene, cleverly interpreted as the richly dressed 'gallant' of the *Everyman* woodcuts, to carry the cross of the exhausted Christ. The staging illustrated Christ's humility symbolically – in the outsize chain the soldiers used to drag Christ along, the get-down-to-the-dirt violence when Simon was impressed into service, and the ironic 'freeze' punctuated by trumpets when the soldiers raised the fallen Christ, at the line 'heave him up on high'. This pageant was hardly authentic in its effects – the stage emblems reminded one more than anything of Peter Hall's *Tamburlaine* at the National Theatre; but it conveyed the essence of the medieval play to the modern audience, and showed that a style based on theatricality and game-playing would have been a natural one for medieval actors to assume in this case.

As Christ passed out of the playing area at the end of this pageant, he paused for a few beats, fixing the audience with a piercing look of accusation. Christ himself, it became clear, was playing a deadly game which made each individual in the crowd a potential loser, one who like Simon stubbornly resisted the Christian's role. In the following pageant of *The Crucifixion*, played by Erindale College, Christ's reproaches had the very different effect of organising the audience into a willing community of believers. The lyrical 'reproaches' (*improperia*) in this pageant are actually words of forgiveness, and Christ accordingly appeared as the Image of Pity associated with the *improperia* in late medieval popular art.[13] Although he lacked the usual gory signs of the flagellation, Christ's white loincloth, crimson mantle and crown of thorns unmistakably recalled the ascetic figure portrayed in these Images, along with their appeal to contemplate both the pity Christ feels for sinful man and the pitifulness of his own sufferings. As in the previous pageant, the soldiers remain preoccupied with their grisly work, but here they have a harder time of it, straining to stretch the victim's limbs to fit the Cross on the green and laboriously hoisting the Cross into a mortise on the pageant wagon. These soldiers also differ from the others in declining to demand aid from the crowd, and the audience is therefore left freer to take the victim's part. At Toronto the crowd responded by forming a circle around the playing area as if to give the sacrifice a sacramental quality. The actors did not actually identify with their parts, and obviously no modern audience could identify with its role in this pageant in the same way as medieval Christians, but the response did suggest Righter's idea that members of the audience would think of themselves as participants in a ritual event, one more real than the commonplace happenings of their everyday lives.

Although Righter and Kolve differ sharply on the audience's relationship to the play, they agree that the Corpus Christi cycles must not be considered an 'illusionistic' form of drama which encourages the audience to suspend its disbelief in a dramatic fiction. In this they attempt to counteract the prejudices of early critics of medieval drama who found the cycles crude and naive because they judged them according to the criteria of illusionistic plays. Recently, however, critics have discovered a way in which some of the pageants in the York cycle may prove to be illusionistic after all. Both J. W. Robinson and Clifford Davidson have shown that the pageants written by the so-called York 'Realist' are related to fifteenth-century popular devotion in the way they encourage the outpouring of feeling through the use of naturalistic particulars.[14] The Toronto performance of the Realist's *Death and Burial of Christ* by Glendon College was evidently based on this conception of his work. A tableau of

Christ between the two thieves was spread out on a bare wagon and the final agonies of the three were enacted with sensational detail. The actor playing Christ pretended to be a real man being crucified; the Virgin Mary imitated the behavior of a real mother overcome with grief and swooning at her son's final cry. The intent was apparently to realise Davidson's idea that the 'York Realist invites his audience to suspend its disbelief and thereby to discover experientially what it would have been like to look upon the historical event'.[15] But Davidson also makes the point, unfortunately ignored in this performance that the characters' sufferings must be played with tact and control. The Realist's aim is not to show the audience uncontrollable emotion but to stimulate a fresh emotional response to the familiar iconography of the Crucifixion scene.

Like the *Death and Burial of Christ*, many of the pageants at Toronto illustrated the difficulty of reproducing an authentic fifteenth-century acting style. Moving warily in this undocumented area, most authorities do agree, primarily on the basis of stage directions, that medieval acting was 'highly stylised and demonstrative',[16] at least in plays that lack the Realist's concern for naturalistic detail. This conclusion makes sense in view of the medieval treatises that deal with drama as if it were a speaking picture closely allied to the visual arts, and the growing tendency to find the origins of the Corpus Christi cycles in processions of *tableaux vivants*. Some scholars, however, take 'highly stylised and demonstrative' to mean that the actors merely declaimed their lines from fixed positions, like the figures in medieval paintings who stand with ribbons of text emerging from their mouths. Rosemary Woolf seems to assume this method when she envisions 'considerable stillness' in the medieval productions: 'it may be assumed that characters stood still unless the plot demanded that they should move'.[17] At Toronto considerable stillness was employed to excellent effect in the simple, dignified *Last Supper* performed by the Estonian Arts Centre Players; but the same manner of acting had its drawbacks in other pageants, like *Exodus*, where the performers merely moved woodenly from stage picture to stage picture as 'the plot demanded'. Few of the diabolical or comic characters attempted to use this style. In Syracuse University's *Temptation of Christ*, for instance, a most successful Satan owed more to the masked challenger of folk drama, with his pugnacious and funny attack on the hero, than to any portrait of the devil in the visual arts. It is worth remembering, too, when relating medieval acting style to the visual arts, that medieval artists did not always convey a static image of Biblical scenes. The popular illustrations of the Passion that Grace Frank has related to the French drama, to cite just one example, include a great deal of movement, notably in the portrayal of Christ's tormentors. Like these illustrations, which Frank contrasts with 'the more static, stereotyped, and learned art of the churches',[18] the Corpus Christi plays often set the serenity of God's people against the bustle of his worldly enemies, and the actors must have been capable of conveying both kinds of behavior.

A more flexible interpretation of medieval acting than the one based on still tableaux derives from the rhetorical gestures medieval artists used in their portrayal of Biblical characters. One could see an example of this style in *The Harrowing of Hell* performed by the University of Toronto Drama Centre. The staging of this pageant bore a strong resemblance to the Doom painting in the Guild chapel at Stratford-on-Avon, which shows a two-part hell: a Limbo topped by battlements above and a Hell Pit below.[19] The Limbo on the wagon and the Pit below it were framed by the fiery dragon mouths also seen in medieval art. Like his counterpart in pictures, the actor playing Christ showed both his disdain for Satan and the stately majesty he takes on when he liberates his people from Limbo in stylised gestures. But translated into an acting style, the gestures became a fluid sequence of movements, far more expressive than a mere striking of attitudes. Also capable of conveying Satan's pretensions and eventual dismay, this style was not only effective for the modern audience but probably closer to a genuinely medieval style than any of the other acting at Toronto.

Not the least of the questions that emerged from the production as a whole centered on the stylistic unity that a medieval performance of the cycle may have had. A processional performance would have required much multiple casting: Christ, for example, would have been played, as at Toronto, by over twenty different actors in pageants requiring different conceptions of the role. Whatever the manner of performance, to what extent would an inherited set of acting conventions have imposed an overall unity? To what extent would the cycle's complex affinities with the visual arts, the folk drama and literary genres like the lyric have demanded a variety of performing styles? To what extent would the piecemeal rewriting of the cycle – the York Realist's contributions, most of all – have determined shifts in performing style from pageant to pageant? The Toronto production might have gone farther towards answering these questions had it not imposed a perverse kind of stylistic unity by using a monotonous and often incomprehensible modern English translation, oddly the one made by J. S. Purvis for the very differently conceived York Festival revivals.

Besides raising questions about staging and performance style, the production demonstrated what happens when the civic and ceremonial character of the cycle drama is too much subordinated to its religious side. Although the procession of wagons around King's College Circle helped generate an air of civic spectacle, the production as a whole catered to a view that holds the cycles to be exclusively didactic and devotional. One missed the ceremonial aspect especially in *The Entry into Jerusalem*, in which Christ receives the honors formally accorded an English monarch making a royal entry. The church group who acted this pageant simply recited the lines in a conventionally pious manner. Nothing, except perhaps the arch through which Christ passed, reminded the audience that this would have been a civic triumph, much like the one the citizens of York witnessed in 1487 when Henry the Seventh entered the formerly hostile city along the same route followed by the Corpus Christi pageants and remained to see the cycle performed in his honor. The *Entry* highlights the simultaneously religious and secular purposes of the medieval civic drama. It represents a familiar ceremony in which all present are joined in celebration, as the Burgesses, the Blind and Lame Men, and even the rich publican Zacheus acclaim Christ's power to unite the community under the law of charity. Just as the citizens of Jerusalem join together in honoring Christ as their king, the citizens of York joined in the production of the Corpus Christi cycle itself – a co-operative venture symbolising the common purpose and collective strength of the medieval city.

Although the *Entry* is a special case, being modelled on an actual civic ceremony, one of the purposes of all the pageants, individually and collectively, was to idealise the community pride and spirit of the city and its influential guilds. Now that the dramatic records of medieval York are about to appear in a new edition, scholars and producers might well turn their attention to the social dimensions of the cycle. Although the records have been consulted chiefly for information about staging, they also illuminate the involvement of the municipal authorities, the social composition of the audience, and the place of the cycle in the city's economic life. They document the history of the cycle well into the sixteenth century, through times of war, pestilence, economic decline and Reformation. A study of the cycle in the light of these records is likely to find that the play had as much to do with York's sense of its own identity and continuity as a community as with the desire to ensure the spiritual salvation of its individual citizens.

SOURCE: article in *Theatre Research International*, 4 (1978), pp. 31–41.

NOTES

[For short-form references to works, see Abbreviations List, p. 8 – Ed.]

1. John R. Elliott Jnr, in *Research Opportunities in Renaissance Drama*, 15–16 (1972–73), pp. 125–8. E. Martin Browne discusses his productions at the York Festival in *Drama Survey*, 3 (1963–64), pp. 5–15.

2. David Parry in the souvenir programme. See also the REED *Newsletter*, no. 1 (1977), pp. 18–19. The performance took place on 1 and 2 October 1977.

3. For processional staging, see Margaret Dorrell, 'Two Studies of the York Corpus Christi Play', *Leeds Studies in English*, n.s. 6 (1972), pp. 63–111; and Alexandra F. Johnston's review of Alan H. Nelson, *The Medieval English Stage* (Chicago, 1974) in *University of Toronto Quarterly*, 44 (1974–45), pp. 238–48.

4. Dorrell gave this information in a paper presented at the Annual Meeting of the Modern Language Association in 1973.

5. In *Traditions of Medieval Drama* (London, 1974), pp. 53–8, Stanley J. Kahrl discusses the restrictions imposed by the staging of pageants on waggons.

6. Nelson, op. cit. (note 3, above), pp. 65–81.

7. Martin Stevens, 'The York Cycle: From Procession to Play', *Leeds Studies in English*, n.s. 6 (1972).

8. M. James Young argues for a waggon measuring about ten by twenty feet in *Speech Monographs*, 34 (1967–68), pp. 1–20. Wickham (I, pp. 169–74) proposes a waggon measuring fifteen feet by twenty feet, supplemented by a scaffold cart of similar dimensions. For the Brussels waggons as analogues, see Wickham, pp. 173 and 396, and A. H. Nelson, 'Some Configurations of Staging in Medieval English Drama', in Jerome Taylor and Alan H. Nelson (eds), *Medieval English Drama* (Chicago and London, 1972), pp. 120–1.

9. See, for example, Wickham I, pp. 169–73. M. James Young, op. cit., pp. 10–12, argues against Wickham's suggestion, as does Nelson in 'Some Configurations of Staging', pp. 121–2. Nelson concludes that 'we must imagine that the ordinary *platea* was the humble earth'.

10. Johnston and Dorrell give a detailed reconstruction of the York Mercers' Doomsday pageant waggon of 1433 in *Leeds Studies in English*, n.s. 6 (1972), pp. 10–35. [See also Clifford Davidson's article in Part Two, section 2, above – Ed.].

11. Kolve, ch. 2.

12. Anne Righter, *Shakespeare and the Idea of the Play* (London, 1962), ch. 1.

13. See J. W. Robinson, 'The Late Medieval Cult of Jesus and the Mystery Plays', *PMLA*, 80 (1965), pp. 508–14.

14. J. W. Robinson, 'The Art of the York Realist', *Modern Philology*, 60 (1962–63), pp. 241–51; and Clifford Davidson [article reproduced in this Casebook – Ed.].

15. Davidson, op. cit., p. 281.

16. J. W. Robinson, 'Medieval English Acting', *Theatre Notebook*, 13 (1958–59), p. 83, and his qualification in 'The Art of the York Realist', p. 249.

17. Woolf, pp. 100–1.

18. Grace Frank, 'Popular Iconography of the Passion', *PMLA*, 46 (1931), p. 340.

19. The fresco is discussed by D. C. Stuart, 'The Stage Setting of Hell and the Iconography of the Middle Ages', *Romanic Review*, 4 (1913), pp. 338–9, and Anderson, pp. 128–9.

SELECT BIBLIOGRAPHY

For both texts and criticism, the works in the list of abbreviations are recommended, together with the post-1900 titles in the Introduction and the works excerpted. The following are also suggested:

PLAYS

R. Beadle (ed.), *The York Plays* (London, 1982).
D. M. Bevington (ed.), *Medieval Drama* (Boston, Mass., 1975).
K. S. Block (ed.), *Ludus Coventriae*, EETS, e.s. 120 (London, 1922).
P. Happé (ed.), *Tudor Interludes* (Harmonsworth, 1972); *English Mystery Plays* (Harmondsworth, 1975); *Four Morality Plays* (Harmondsworth, 1979).
Markham Harris (ed. and trans.), *The Cornish Ordinalia* (Washington, D.C., 1969).
M. Rose (ed.), *The Wakefield Mystery Plays* (London, 1961).
J. A. B. Somerset (ed.), *Four Tudor Interludes* (London, 1974).
G. Wickham (ed.), *English Moral Interludes* (London, 1976).

CRITICISM

R. P. Axton, *European Drama of the Early Middle Ages* (London, 1974).
W. A. Davenport, *Fifteenth-Century English Drama* (Cambridge, 1982).
C. Davidson et al. (eds), *The Drama of the Middle Ages* (New York, 1982).
N. Denny (ed.), *Medieval Drama*, Stratford-upon-Avon Studies, 16, (London, 1973).
A. Harbage (rev. S. Schoenbaum), *Annals of English Drama 975–1700* (rev. edn, Philadelphia, 1964).
M. R. Kelley, *Flamboyant Drama* (Carbondale and Edwardsville, Ill., 1979).
A. H. Nelson, *The Medieval English Stage* (Chicago, 1974).
G. R. Owst, *Literature and Pulpit in Medieval England* (2nd edn, Oxford, 1961).
N. Sanders et al. (eds), *The Revels History of Drama in English*: vol. 2, *1500–1576*, (London, 1980).
R. Southern, *The Staging of Plays before Shakespeare* (London, 1973).
S. Sticca (ed.), *The Medieval Drama* (Albany, N.Y., 1972).
J. Taylor and A. H. Nelson (eds), *Medieval English Drama* (Chicago, 1972).
A. Williams, *The Drama of Medieval England* (Berkeley and Los Angeles, 1961).

PERIODICALS

Comparative Drama (Kalamazoo, Western Michigan University).
EDAM Newsletter (Early Drama, Art and Music Project: Kalamazoo, Western Michigan University).
Medieval English Theatre (University of Lancaster).
REED Newsletter (Records of Early English Drama: University of Toronto).
Research Opportunities in Renaissance Drama (University of Kansas).

NOTES ON CONTRIBUTORS TO PART TWO

DAVID BEVINGTON is Professor of English in the University of Chicago, and President of the Medieval and Renaissance Drama Society. His publications include *Tudor Drama and Tudor Politics* (1968) and (as editor) *Medieval Drama* (1975) and *The Complete Works of Shakespeare* (1980).

SARAH CARPENTER lectures in the Department of English, University of Edinburgh. Her doctoral thesis on Morality drama was supervised by Rosemary Woolf at Oxford. Her interests include characterisation and theatrical techniques, and she has published in *Notes and Queries*.

T. W. CRAIK is Professor of English in the University of Durham, and General Editor (with Clifford Leech) of the Revels History of Drama in English. His publications include *Comic Tales of Chaucer* (1964) and (as reviser and editor) *Minor Elizabethan Tragedies* (1980).

CLIFFORD DAVIDSON is Professor of English, Western Michigan University, where he is also Executive Editor of the Early Drama, Art and Music Project of the Medieval Institute. His publications include *Drama and Art* (1977), *York Art* (1978) and an edition of *A Middle English Treatise on the Playing of Miracles* (1981).

STANLEY J. KAHRL is Professor of English, Ohio State University. He has edited the Dramatic Records of Lincolnshire, in *Malone Society Collections*, VIII (1974), and co-edited *N-Town Plays* (1977), and has produced medieval plays on television.

J. S. KANTROWITZ took her doctorate at Chicago University and has taught at Vassar College and Kent State University. Her research interests are medieval and Renaissance literature, allegory and critical theory.

V. A. KOLVE is Professor of English in the University of Virginia, Charlotteville. In addition to his influential *The Play Called Corpus Christi* (1966), his publications include '*Everyman* and the Parable of the Talents', in S. Sticca (ed.), *The Medieval Drama* (1972).

SHEILA LINDENBAUM teaches in the English Department of Indiana University, and is editor of the Medieval Supplement of *Research Opportunities in Renaissance Drama*.

DAVID MILLS teaches in the Department of Language, University of

Liverpool. With R. M. Lumiansky he has published two versions of the Chester Mystery Cycle: *A Facsimile of MS Bodley 175* (1973) and a critical edition for the Early English Text Society (1974).

PAULA NEUSS lectures in the Department of English at Birkbeck College, London. She has edited Skelton's *Magnyfycence* (1980) and the *Cornish Creacion of the World*, with a translation (1983).

ROBERT A. POTTER is Professor of Dramatic Art, University of California. As a Fullbright Scholar at Bristol University, he produced the only modern performance of Bale's *King John* (in 1964), and he has since directed many plays, some written by himself.

ELEANOR PROSSER is Margery Bailey Professor of Drama in Stanford University, California. Her publications include *Hamlet and Revenge* (1967) and *Shakespeare's Anonymous Editors* (1982).

BERNARD SPIVACK, Professor of English, University of Massachusetts (1964–81), is Professor Emeritus there. His research interests are in Shakespeare and Elizabethan literature, and his publications include *Shakespeare and the Allegory of Evil: The History of a Metaphor in Relation to His Major Villains* (1958).

MEG TWYCROSS lectures in the Department of English Language and Medieval Literature, University of Lancaster. She is co-editor (with Peter Meredith) of *Medieval English Theatre*, and has worked on productions of medieval plays, including the York *Resurrection* (1977) and the Chester *Purification* (1983).

WILLIAM TYDEMAN lectures in English at the University College of North Wales, Bangor. His publications include *The Theatre in the Middle Ages* and the Casebooks on Wilde's Comedies and (co-edited with Alun R. Jones) on *The Ancient Mariner and Other Poems* and on *Lyrical Ballads*. Forthcoming is his volume on *Dr Faustus* in the 'Text and Performance' series.

DONNA A. VINTER wrote her doctoral thesis at Harvard on 'The Uses of Narrative Drama: The English Mystery Plays', from which the excerpt in this volume is adapted. She teaches at the London centres of several American universities.

ROSEMARY WOOLF taught in the University of Hull, and later became Fellow and Tutor in English at Somerville College, Oxford. Her publications include *The English Religious Lyric in the Middle Ages* (1968).

ACKNOWLEDGEMENTS

The editor and publishers wish to thank the following who have given permission for the use of copyright material: David M. Bevington, extract from *From 'Mankind' to Marlowe* (1962) by permission Harvard University Press. Copyright © 1962 by the President and Fellows of Harvard College; T. W. Craik, extract from *The Tudor Interlude* (1958) by permission of Leicester University Press; C. Davidson, article 'The Realism of the York Realist and the York Passion' in *Speculum*, 50 (1975) by permission of The Medieval Academy of America; S. J. Kahrl, extract from *Traditions in Medieval English Drama* (1974) by permission of Hutchinson Publishing Group Ltd; Joanne Spencer Kantrowitz, extracts from *Dramatic Allegory: Lindsay's 'Ane Satyre of the Thrie Estaitis'* (1975) by permission of University of Nebraska Press; V. A. Kolve, extracts from *The Play Called Corpus Christi* (1966) by permission of Stanford University Press. Copyright © 1966 by the Board of Trustees of the Leland Stanford Junior University; Sheila Lindenbaum, essay 'The York Cycle at Toronto: Staging Performance Style' from *Theatre Research International*, IV (1978) by permission of Oxford University Press; David Mills, essay 'Approaches to Medieval Drama' in *Leeds Studies in English*, by permission of the editor; Paula V. Neuss, essay 'The Staging of the Creacion of the World' in *Theatre Notebook*, 33 (1979) by permission of the author; Robert A. Potter, extract from *The English Morality Play* (1975) by permission of Routledge & Kegan Paul Ltd; Eleanor Prosser, chapter from *Drama and Religion in English Mystery Plays* (1961) with the permission of the publishers, Stanford University Press. Copyright © 1961 by the Board of Trustees of the Leland Stanford Junior University; Bernard Spivack, extract from *Shakespeare and the Allegory of Evil* (1958) by permission of Columbia University Press; Meg Twycross and Sarah Carpenter, extract from *Medieval English Theatre* (1981) by permission of the authors; William Tydeman, extract from *The Theatre in the Middle Ages* (1978) by permission of Cambridge University Press; Donna Vinter, article 'Didactic Characterization: The Towneley Abraham' in *Comparative Drama* (1980) by permission of the editors; Rosemary Woolf, extracts from *The English Mystery Plays* (1972) by permission of Routledge & Kegan Paul Ltd.

INDEX

Numerals in **bold** type denote essays and excerpts in the selection. Primary entries in SMALL CAPS denote titles of Miracle, Morality and Interlude works, English play cycles (or collections), and major episodes from play cycles. Other literary works, and secondary entries for Miracle plays etc., are denoted by *italic* type. References to works by certain major writers (e.g., Jonson, Shakespeare) are confined to secondary entries under the authors' names

Abingdon 186
ABRAHAM & ISAAC plays,
  episodes: Northampton 85;
  Brome 85; see also CHESTER, LUD.
  COVENTRIAE, WAKEFIELD, YORK
ACTES DES APÔTRES: see Bourges
actors 50–1, 64–5, 70(n.48), 162–70,
  171(n.4), 184–6, 210(n.16)
acts, parliamentary: *For the Advancement
  of True Religion . . .* (1542) 124–5;
  1559 Act 125
Advent Lyrics 42
ALL FOR MONEY: see Lupton
Anderson, M. D. 17, 18, 197
Anglo-Saxon Chronicle 43
Aquinas, St Thomas 106
Aristotle 76–7, 127
Ash (Kent) 187
Ashton, Thomas (Shrewsbury) 126
Assembly of Gods: see Lydgate
ASSUMPTION OF THE VIRGIN: see CHESTER
Auerbach, E. 119
Augustine, St 75, 86, 192; *The City of
  God* 121
Axton, Richard 72

Bale, John 128(n.26), 174; *King
  John* 123–5, 164; *The Chief Promises of
  God* 179(n.8); *The Temptation of Our
  Lord* 179(n.8); *The Three Laws* 163,
  164, 167, 168, 172
Batman, S. (pictorialist) 155, 161(n.2)
Battle poems: *Brunanburh* 43; *Maldon*
  43
Beauvais 54
Beckett, Samuel 64
Bede 43, 122
Belles Heures du duc de Berry, Les 110

Ben Gorion, Joseph (historian) 126
Beowulf 41
Bevington, David M. 21, 125,
  128(nn.23, 25), **162–71**
Bonaventure, St 106
Bonner, Edmund (bishop) 57
Boughton (Kent) 187
Bourges plays: *Les Actes des
  Apôtres* 183, 185, 188(n.14)
Brecht, Bertolt 19, 64, 76–8, 84, 85, 87,
  138
Bristol (univ. prod.) 190
Brome 81
Brussels 203
Brut: see Layamon
Bungay (Suffolk) 57, 61
Bunyan, John 153
Burlin, R. B. 42
Burton, Roger (York) 114(n.2)

CAIN & ABEL: see CHESTER, WAKEFIELD,
  YORK
Cailleau, Hubert (artist) 185, 191
Calais 187
CAMBISES: see Preston
Cambridge 188
Campbell, Lily B. 117, 118, 126
Canterbury 187, 188
Carew, Richard 185, 190, 191, 196, 197
Carmina Burana 54
Carpenter, Sarah: see Twycross
Carré, M. H. 103
CASTLE OF PERSEVERANCE, THE 17, 21,
  57, 76, 130, 131–2, 135, 138, 139(n.3),
  150(n.1), 171(n.7), 174, 191, 194, 196,
  199(n.19)
Cawley, A. C. 120

Chambérs, E. K.   15, 16, 22(n.24), 36–7, 51, 55, 118, 125, 197

Chaucer   51, 93; *Anelida & Arcite*   193

Chelmsford   181, 182, 187, 192

CHESTER Cycle   11, 14, 17, 30–1, 44, 48, 49, 50, 52(n.10), 55, 65, 67–8, 115(n.19), 192; *Banns*   56, 62, 173–4; *Abraham & Isaac*   45–6, 120; *Assumption of the Virgin*   166; *Cain & Abel* [with *Creation & Fall*]   39–40, 49; *Harrowing of Hell*   192; *Herod*   47; *Noah*   50, 65; *Pentecost*   66; *Prophets*   56; *Shepherds*   50, 89, 91, 93; *Temptation*   96, 97

Christ: III (O.E. poem)   41

CHRIST'S RESURRECTION   174

Cicero (*De Oratore*)   178

City of God: see Augustine

Cleanness (or *Purity*, M.E. poem)   47

Codex Purpureus Rossanensis   105

Coffman, G. R.   60, 68(n.11)

Coggeshall   187

Coleridge, S. T.   114

Collier, J. P.   13–14

Collingwood, R. G.   120–1

Comestor, Peter (*Historia scholastica*)   43, 44

Complaint of Scotland, The   149–50, 151(n.6)

Confrérie de la Passion, La   184

CONVERSION OF ST PAUL: see DIGBY

'conveyor' (producer, redactor)   196–8

Coogan, Sister M. P.   137

CORNISH Cycle, plays   21, 189ff., 198(n.3); *The Creacion of the World* ('Gwreans an Bys')   184, 189–200; *The Life of St Meriasek*   172, 182, 191, 194, 199(n.14); *Ordinalia* trilogy   190–1, 195 [*Origo Mundi*   193: *Passio Domini*   193, 194: *Resurrectio Domini*   192]

Corpus Christi: Feast of   14, 40, 43, 44, 48, 51, 55, 57, 60–1, 64, 111, 113, 118–19, 205, 206, 207; in Trinitarian imagery   110, 116(n.35)

costume   98, 155, 171–80, 180–4

Court of Sapience   146; *Court of Venus* (Rolland)   145

COVENTRY plays   126, 180ff., 186, 198, 203; *The Destruction of Jerusalem* (1584)   126; *Doomsday* (Croo, 1557)   182, 198; *The Golden Fleece* (Croo)   198; (NB: these plays are wholly distinct from the LUD. COVENTRIAE cycle)

CRADLE OF SECURITY, THE   172

Craig, H.   16, 35, 114(n.1), 118, 199(n.24)

Craik, T. W.   21, **152–61**

CREACION OF THE WORLD (Jordan):   see CORNISH

CREATION plays, episodes: see CHESTER, CORNISH, YORK

CRISTEMASSE GAME . . .:   see Howe

Croo, Robert   64, 198; for plays, see COVENTRY

Croxton   192

Cursor Mundi   43, 44–5, 58, 74, 75, 78–9

DANIELIS LUDUS (Beauvais)   54; see also PLAY OF DANIEL

Dante (*Divine Comedy*)   42

Daventry   186

Davidson, Clifford   20, **101–17**, 206, 207

DAY OF JUDGEMENT, DOOMSDAY plays, episodes: see COVENTRY, *Holkham Bible*, JOUR DE JUGEMENT, YORK

DE PEREGRINO   54

Deal (Kent)   187

Deguileville, Guillaume (*Pilgrimage* poet)   146, 149

DESTRUCTION OF JERUSALEM: see COVENTRY

DIGBY MS plays: *The Conversion of St Paul*   55; *Mary Magdalene*   192

Dijon   184

Dives & Pauper (treatise)   73–4, 176–7

Dodsley, Robert   12–13

Donaueschingen (Passion play)   183

Donnington (Yorks.)   65

Dorrell, Margery   201

Dover   187

drama societies   186–8

Dryden, John   63–4

Duns Scotus   138

ENOUGH IS AS GOOD AS A FEAST: see Wager (w.)

EVERYMAN   131, 135–6, 138, 174, 205

Example of Virtue (allegory)   146, 149

Exodus (O.E. poem)   41, 42–3

FALL plays, episodes: see CHESTER, LUD. COVENTRIAE, JEU D'ADAM, YORK

FAMOUS VICTORIES OF KING HENRY V, THE (1586) 127
Festial (homilies): see Mirk
Fouquet, Jean (artist) 68, 71(n.65), 185, 191, 192, 195
FOUR ELEMENTS: see Rastell
FOUR PP: see Heywood
Franciscans 106–7, 112, 113, 115(n.16)
Frank, Grace 53(n.31), 207–8, 211(n.18)
Frank, R. W. 147
French plays, players 50, 54, 90, 93, 94(n.5), 180, 184, 185, 187, 191, 192, 195, 207–8
Fulwell, U.: *Like Will to Like* 162, 168

Gardiner, Fr H. C. 125
Gardner, John 78, 84
Garter, Thomas: *The Most Virtuous & Godly Susanna* 126
Gayley, C. M. 101
Genesis (O.E. poem) 41, 42; *Genesis & Exodus* (M.E. poems) 44, 45
GODLY QUEEN HESTER 123, 128(n.23)
GOLDEN FLEECE (Croo): see COVENTRY
GORBODUC: see Norton & Sackville
Gospel of Nicodemus 106
Gower, John (*Vox Clamantis*) 146, 147, 151(n.2)
Great Yarmouth 57
Greban, Arnoul: *Le Mystère de la Passion* 66
Greek drama 175, 177–8, 180(n.17)
Greenfield, S. B. 42
Grünewald, Matthias (artist) 108

Hadleigh (Suffolk) 187
Hales, Alexander of 138
Hall, Edward (chronicler) 118
Hall, Peter 205
Ham Street (Kent) 187
Harbage, A. (*Annals*) 127
Hardison, O. B. 16, 17, 35, 117
Harling (Norfolk) 57
HARROWING OF HELL plays, episodes: see CHESTER, YORK
HEGGE Cycle: *The Woman Taken in Adultery* 97–101; see also LUD. COVENTRIAE
Henry VIII 123–4
Herne (Kent) 187

HEROD: at Coventry 203; see also CHESTER, YORK
Heywood, John: *The Four PP* (? 1543), *The Pardoner & the Friar* (1533) 164
HICKSCORNER 134–5, 138, 153, 164
Higden, Ranulph (*Polychronicon*) 122
Hilarius: *Ludus super iconia Sancti Nicolai* 54
Holinshed, Raphael (chronicler) 118, 122
Holkham Bible Picture Book 115(n.18), 192
Hone, William 13
HORESTES: see Pykeryng
Hours of Catherine of Cleves, The 103, 108, 112–13; *Hours of the Cross* (York) 110
Howe, Benet: *A Cristemass Game* . . . 57
Hudson, Henry (York) 197
Huizinga, Johan 61, 70(n.43), 188(n.8)
Hundred Mery Talys, A 62, 90
Huppé, B. F. 42
Hurstfield, Joel 129(n.35)
Hythe (Kent) 187

Ibsen, Henrik 18–19
IMPATIENT POVERTY 143, 162, 164, 167–8
Inns of Court 139(n.2)
Ionesco, Eugene 64
Irving, E. B. 42
Isenheim altar 108

JACOB & ESAU 125
Jacob's Well (homilies) 137
James V of Scotland 146
Javanese drama 175
JEU D'ADAM, LE 192
JOB (1587) 127
Johnston, Alexandra 201
Jones, John 175
Jonson, Ben: *The Divell is an Asse* 21(n.2); *The Staple of News* 62; *Volpone* 58
Jordan, William (*Creacion*) 197–8; see also CORNISH
JOUR DE JUGEMENT, LE 181
JUDAS plays, episodes: see Montecassino, WAKEFIELD, YORK
JUDGEMENT: see DAY OF JUDGEMENT
JULIAN THE APOSTATE (1566) 126
JUVENTUS: see LUSTY JUVENTUS

Kabuki theatre 175
Kahrl, Stanley J. 20, **117–29**
Kantrowitz, Joanne S. 20, **144–51**
Kemp, William (actor) 165
Kempe, Margery (mystic) 116(n.43)
King Hart (allegory) 145, 146, 149
KING JOHN: see Bale
KING OF LIFE: see PRIDE OF LIFE
Kolve, V. A. 17, 20, 35, 40, 43, 44, 46,
  48, **54–71**, 118, 205, 206
Kyd, Thomas: *The Spanish
  Tragedy* 170

Langham (Suffolk) 187
Langland, William (*Piers Plowman*) 42,
  94, 147, 148, 150
Langton, Stephen (archbp) 124
Latimer, Hugh (bishop) 163
Lavenham (Suffolk) 187
Lawrence, W. J. 167
Layamon (*Brut*) 43
Leeds (univ. prod.) 201
Leland, John (antiquary) 124
LIKE WILL TO LIKE: see Fulwell
Lincoln 126, 180–1, 199(n.24)
Lindenbaum, Sheila 21, **200–11**
Lindsay, Sir David: *Ane Satyre of the
  Thrie Estaitis* 145–51, 199(n.18)
liturgical plays 36–40, 54, 60, 105
London 65, 125, 139(n.2), 187
LONGER THOU LIVEST. . .: see Wager
  (W.)
Love, Nicholas (*Mirrour of the Blessed Lyf
  of Jesu Christ*) 106, 112
LOVE OF KING DAVID . . .: see Peele
Lucerne 180, 181, 182, 184
LUDUS BREVITER DE PASSIONE (*Carm.
  Burana*) 54
LUDUS COVENTRIAE 13, 50, 52(n.10), 55,
  64–5, 66, 67–8, 71(n.63), 180ff.; *Late
  Banns* 181; *Proclamations* 55, 56, 57,
  62; *Abraham & Isaac* 81–2, 84, 86;
  Fall 57; '*Passion*' sequence 56, 65,
  178, 180, 182, 183, 189, 196, 203;
  Shepherds 91, 178, 196; *Trial of Joseph
  & Mary* 122; *The Woman Taken in
  Adultery* 97–101; see also HEGGE; (NB:
  these cycle plays are wholly distinct
  from COVENTRY plays)
LUDUS DANIELIS: see DANIELIS
LUDUS . . . DOMINICAE RESURRECTIONIS
  (*Carm. Burana*) 54

LUDUS . . . SANCTI NICOLAI: see Hilarius
Lupton, Thomas: *All for Money* 163,
  164, 166
LUSTY JUVENTUS 142, 144(n.2), 163, 164
Lydd (Kent) 187
Lydgate, John: *Assembly of Gods* 59;
  The Pilgrimage of Man
  (trans) 146; *Troy Book* 59

Mâle, Émile 107
MAGNYFYCENCE: see Skelton
MAÎTRE PATHELIN 90, 93, 94(n.5)
Malone, Edmund 13
MANKIND 13–14, 22(n.21), 130, 136–8,
  140(n.7), 142, 164
Mannynge, Robert 11, **28**
Marlowe 205; *Doctor Faustus* 130; *The
  Jew of Malta* 192; *Tamburlaine* 170,
  205
MARRIAGE OF WIT & WISDOM: see
  Merbury
MARTYRE DE SAINTE APPOLLINE, LE
  (*Martyrdom of St Appollonia*) 71(n.65),
  185, 191
MARY MAGDALENE plays, episodes: see
  DIGBY, Wager (L.), YORK
masks, masking 171ff., 182; see also
  costume, staging
Meditaciones vitae Christi 106, 108, 112,
  120; see also Love, *Mirrour . . .*
Medwall, Henry.: *Nature* (c. 1495) 42
Melber, Johannes (*Variloquus*) 60
Melton, William (at York) 113–14,
  116(n.43)
Merbury, F.: *The Marriage of Wit &
  Wisdom* 165, 168
Mercers' Pageant Waggon (York) 11,
  29–30, 210(n.10)
Michel, Jean: *Passion* 183
Michelangelo 113
Mills, David 17, 20, **35–54**
Mirk, John (*Festial*) 84
Mirror for Magistrates, A
  (miscellany) 117
Mirrour of the Blessed Lyf . . .: see Love
Modena 105
Mons plays 183, 184
Montecassino (Passion play) 105
Morwyng, Peter (translator) 126
MUCEDORUS 165–6
Mum & the Soothsayer (allegory) 147–8

MUNDUS ET INFANS 131, 133–4, 138, 142, 143, 164
MYSTÈRE DE LA PASSION: see Greban
MYSTÈRE DE L'INCARNATION: see Rouen
MYSTÈRE DE SAINT MARTIN, LE (at Seurre) 185
MYSTÈRE DE SAINT VINCENT, LE 183

N-TOWN texts 122, 182
Nance, R. M. 197
NATURE: see Medwall
Nelson, Alan 202–3, 210(nn.8, 9)
Neuss, Paula 21, **189–200**
NEW CUSTOM 163, 168, 169
New Romney (Kent) 182, 187
NOAH plays, episodes: see CHESTER, WAKEFIELD, YORK
Northampton 81, 85–6
Norton, Thomas & Thomas Sackville: *Gorboduc, or Ferrex & Porrex* (1561) 117, 126–7
Norwich 182, 184

Oberammergau (Passion play) 201
Ockham, William of 105, 138
O'Neill, Eugene 175
ORDINALIA trilogy: see CORNISH
ORIGO MUNDI (*Ordinalia*): see CORNISH
Orosius 43
Owst, G. R. 116(n.39)

Panofsky, Erwin 102, 113
Papal decretals (1227–41) 172
PARDONER & THE FRIAR: see Heywood
PASSIO DOMINI (*Ordinalia*): see CORNISH
PASSION, LA: see Michel
PASSION plays, episodes: see CHESTER; Confrérie; CORNISH; LUD. BREVITER; LUD. COVENTRIAE; Greban; Michel; Montecassino; Valenciennes; WAKEFIELD; YORK
Pavy, S. (actor) 163
Peele, George: *The Love of King David & Fair Bethsabe* (1587) 127
PENTECOST plays, episodes: see CHESTER, YORK
PERSEVERANCE: see CASTLE OF P.
Perranzabuloe (Perran Round) 197, 198(n.5)
Piers Plowman: see Langland
Pilgrimage (allegory): see Deguileville, Lydgate

Pirandello, Luigi 175
Pisford, William (Coventry) 181
Plato (*Ion*) 177–8, 180(n.17)
'play' 36, 39, 54–5, 58, 59, 69(nn.20, 24)
PLAY OF DANIEL, THE 120; see also DANIELIS LUDUS
PLAY OF THE SACRAMENT, THE CROXTON 192
Pollard, A. W. 137
Potter, Robert A. 21, **130–40**
Preston, Thomas: *A Lamentable Tragedy . . . Containing the Life of Cambises King of Persia* (1569) 127, 165, 166, 169–70
PRIDE OF LIFE, THE (c. 1350: also titled *The King of Life*) 10, 57, 132–3 (*K*), 138 (*K*), 139(n.2)
PROCESSUS SATANAE 74
PROPHETS: see CHESTER
Prosser, Eleanor 21, 70(n.52), **95–101**, 115(n.19)
Purvis, J. S. 208
Pykeryng, John: HORESTES 127, 164, 168, 170

QUEM QUAERITIS 43, 54
Quintilian 119

Rabanus Maurus 86
Rabelais, François 181–2
Rastell, John: *The Nature of the Four Elements* 142
Reading 187
Reason & Sensuality (allegory) 146
Redford, John: *Wit & Science* 172
Regularis concordia 54, 109
RESURRECTIO DOMINI (*Ordinalia*): see CORNISH
RESURRECTION plays, episodes: see above, and CHESTER, CORNISH, CHRIST'S R., LUD. DOMINICAE R., QUEM QUAERITIS, VISITATIO SEPULCHRI, YORK
Ribner, Irving 117
Richard II 123, 146, 147–8
Righter, Anne 205, 206
Robbins, Rossell H. 58
Robinson, J. W. 102, 206, 210(nn.13,14,16)
Rogers, Robert & David (Chester) 11, **30–1**, 173, 192, 198(n.8)
Romans (France) 180
Rose, Martial 53(n.36)

Rouen plays: *Le Mystère de l'Incarnation et de la Nativité* 93, 180

St Albans Psalter 110
St George, play of 188
St Just-in-Penwith 190, 196, 198(n.5)
ST MERIASEK: see CORNISH
SAMSON (1567) 126
Sandwich (Kent) 187
SATYRE OF THE THRIE ESTAITIS: see Lindsay
Seurre 185
Shakespeare 15, 16, 18, 20, 117, 166; *A Midsummer Night's Dream* 92; *Henry IV, Pt I* 140(n.5); *Richard III* 170; *Twelfth Night* 10–11
Sharp, Thomas 13, 14
SHEPHERD plays: see CHESTER, LUD. COVENTRIAE, Rouen, Vicente, WAKEFIELD, YORK (*Fergus*)
Shrewsbury 126
Sir Gawain & the Green Knight 44, 51, 58–9
SIR THOMAS MORE 162, 167
Skelton, John: *Magnyfycence* 57, 58, 59, 70(n.38), 142
Smart, W. K. 137
Smith (Coventry playwright) 126
SOUL & BODY, THE (Welsh) 132–3
Southern, Richard 17–18, 19, 64, 191, 195, 199(n.19)
Speculum Sacerdotale 76, 88(n.9)
Spenser (*The Faerie Queene*) 140
Spivack, Bernard 19, 20, **140–4**
staging 19, 49, 67, 98–9, 104, 150(n.1), 155–8, 162–71, 171–80, 189–200, 200–11
Stanislavsky, Konstantin 65
Stevens, Martin 125, 202–3
Stoke-by-Nayland (Suffolk) 186–7
Stokes, Whitley 189
Stratford-on-Avon 208
Sudbury (Suffolk) 187
SUSANNA: see Garter
Symonds, J. A. 15, 162, 165, 167, 170(n.1)

Tarleton, Richard (actor) 165
Tertullian 119
Thanet (Kent) 187
Thoresby, John (archbp) 111–12
THREE LAWS: see Bale

TIDE TARRIETH NO MAN: see Wapull
Tillyard, E. M. W. 117
TOBIT (1564) 126
Toronto (York Cycle at) 201ff.
TOWER OF BABYLON, THE 125
TOWNELEY plays: see WAKEFIELD
Très-Belles Heures de Notre Dame, Les 109–10
Tretise of Miraclis Pleyinge, A 11, 14, 19, **27**, 50, 59–60, 62–3, 174, 179(n.7)
TRIAL OF TREASURE: see Wager (W.)
Troy Book: see Lydgate
Twycross, Meg, & Sarah Carpenter 19, **171–80**
Tydeman, William 21, **180–9**

Valenciennes plays 185, 191; Passion play 191, 194–5
Van der Weyden, Roger (artist) 110
'Vice, The' 10, 19, 20, 140–4, 154ff., 162ff., 167ff.
Vicente, Gil: Nativity play 90
Vinter, Donna S. 19, **71–89**
Virgil 91
VISITATIO SEPULCHRI 38
Vox Clamantis: see Gower

Wager, Lewis: *The Life & Repentance of Mary Magdalene* 143
Wager, William: *Enough is as good as a Feast* 152–61, 162, 169, 170; *The longer thou livest the more Fool thou art* 153, 165, 169; *The Trial of Treasure* 153, 161(n.3), 164, 168
WAKEFIELD Cycle (TOWNELEY plays) 44, 49, 50, 52(n.10), 53(n.36), 65, 94, 95, 125, 192; *Abraham & Isaac* 19, 78–89; *Cain & Abel* 122; *Noah* 47, 192; *Shepherds* plays: First 14, 89–95, 119–20 Second 13, 14, 47–8, 89–95; '*Passion*' sequence: Crucifixion 109 Judas 74–5
'Wakefield Master, the' 49, 89, 90, 92, 122
Wapull, G.: *The Tide Tarrieth no Man* 161(n.3), 163, 168
Ward, A. W. 14–15
Warton, Thomas 11–12
WEALTH & HEALTH 162, 164
Welsh play: see SOUL & BODY
Wickham, Glynne 17, 69(nn.20,30), 116(n.45), 125, 199(n.18), 210(nn.8,9)

William of Ockham   105, 138
Wilson, F. P.   125
Winchester   54, 186
WISDOM, WHO IS CHRIST   130, 131, 133,
   135, 138, 139(nn.2,4)
WIT & SCIENCE: see Redford
WOMAN TAKEN IN ADULTERY plays: see
   HEGGE, LUD. COVENTRIAE, YORK
Woolf, Rosemary   17, 78, 79, **89–95**,
   102, 109, 207
Worcester   181, 188(n.5)
Wright, Thomas   14
Wycliffite doctrines   11, 27, 55, 59–60,
   62–3

Yeats, W. B.   175
York churches   107, 109, 110, 111, 200
YORK Cycle   11, 29–30, 48, 49, 50,
   52(n.10), 65, 101–17, 197, 200–11
      Old Testament: *Creation*   49, 203,
   204; *Fall of Lucifer*   204; *Cain &
   Abel*   49; *Noah & the Flood*   204;
   Abraham & Isaac   81; *Exodus*   65–6,
   201, 207
      Birth & Ministry of
   Christ: *Annunciation*   203;

Fergus   49; *Herod*   49, 56;
Purification   202; *Temptation*   207;
Mary Magdalene   49; *Woman Taken in
Adultery*   96–7
      Passion: 101ff., 183, 201, 202,
204–7; *Entry into Jerusalem*   200, 209;
Last Supper   207; *Judas*   103–5;
Condemnation   49, 102, 103, 201, 202;
Dream of Pilate's Wife   50, 105;
Flagellation   204; *Christ Led up to
Calvary*   106, 205; *Crucifixion*   49,
115(n.18), 106, 206, 207; *Death &
Burial (Mortificacio)*   106–7, 108–9,
111, 206–7 [*Deposition*   109–11]
      Resurrection & Last Things:
Resurrection   204; *Harrowing of Hell*
202, 208; *Pentecost*   203, 204; *Ascen-
sion*   67, 199(n.24); *Judgement Day*
29–30, 202, 203, 204
York Festivals   200, 201, 208, 210(n.1);
   see also Toronto
'York Realist, the'   101ff., 116(n.45),
   206–7, 208
Young, Karl   16, 35, 54, 55, 118
Young, M. James   210(n.8)
YOUTH   134, 138, 153